# JESUS, THE "ONE AND ONLY"

## Confronting 21st-Century Culture With the Gospel of John

### By Frank G. Tunstall

# DEDICATION

To my wife, Lu, who has been my faithful companion with a heart full of love for 49 years; and to Rosa Baker, my sister, who has never tired as a faithful supporter and professional critic of my work.

# ACKNOWLEDGEMENTS

I express my appreciation to Pastor Chris Maxwell, Bishop Chris Thompson, Dr. Chuck Chitwood, Dr. Dan Bellar and Dr. Danny Penny for their helpful insights and suggestions.

Great Command Ministries Inc.
8330 Willow Creek Blvd.
Oklahoma City, OK 73162

ISBN Number 978-0-615-81825-2

Printed in the United States of America

# TABLE OF CONTENTS

Introduction ..................................................................................................... 7

**John Chapter 1 – JESUS: THE SON OF GOD**
The Prologue, the Forerunner, and Calling the
First Disciples............................................................................................... 13

**John Chapter 2 – JESUS: THE SON OF MAN**
The First Christian Wedding
and the Temple Switch ............................................................................... 69

**John Chapter 3 – JESUS: THE MASTER TEACHER**
Nicodemus' Nighttime Visit....................................................................... 93

**John Chapter 4 – JESUS: THE SOUL WINNER**
The New Birth Illustrated........................................................................ 137

**John Chapter 5 – JESUS: THE GREAT PHYSICIAN**
Unveiling the Heart of God..................................................................... 171

To order additional copies of this book, go to www.amazon.com.

# INTRODUCTION

The belief that Jesus Christ is the Son of God is now navigating a season of ever-increasing pressure. This reality calls for a fresh look at the Gospel of John, the New Testament book that establishes Jesus as God's Son.

One of these points of tension comes from the arena of pluralism. *Political pluralism* opens many doors to mutual understanding in the sphere of politics and government. It is certainly wisdom to respect the rights and views of all citizens and let a ballot box instead of a gun settle differences.

## Religious Pluralism

This same kind of thinking is now being dangerously advanced under the banner of *religious pluralism*. This form of pluralism asserts no religion holds the singular answer to man's salvation; instead, each world religion is a valid path to God for its sincere adherents. This is considered to be true even if people are following such diverse approaches as the many forms of nature worship (pantheism), or the worship of many gods (polytheism), or the worship of one God (monotheism).

Religious pluralists maintain for people in the world community to get along, all beliefs must come together in mutual tolerance and find a new unity under the banner of pluralism. This reasoning has set up religious pluralism as a new shrine to which all religions are invited to come and find their common ground.

Pluralism draws significantly on the tools of sociology to analyze what all religions have in common. For example, each world religion has a god idea, a path to salvation, an explanation for the afterlife, etc.

Religious pluralism makes its claim that all religions are valid paths to God because, to pluralists, 21st-century popular culture is the proper lens for interpreting the Bible. But make no mistake: the crucifixion and resurrection of Jesus, as recorded in the Bible, is the gavel that will trumpet the final word of judgment on the values and ideologies of the 21st century.

## Christian Universalism

An additional sphere of increasing pressure is coming from *Christian universalism*. The core idea of this belief is characterized by the term *universal reconciliation*. Its advocates maintain people who reject Jesus in this life will ultimately be reconciled to God in the life to come and will live for eternity with God in Heaven. Use of the term "Christian" indicates proponents of this school of universalism may hold certain doctrines of Christianity, but reject the orthodox Biblical teaching of rewards and punishments, including such attributes of God as justice and judgment.

Pressure points like these and others, such as Jehovah's Witnesses, mandate that the body of Christ re-think the Gospel of John. The hope is the reader will pick up the additional themes and make his own applications. The modern church must rediscover, and in some cases encounter for the first time, the despised and rejected Messiah who proved Himself to be God's Son (Isa. 53:3).

## The Apostle John

Two millennia ago, John the son of Zebedee was an apostle in the inner circle of Jesus Christ. He wrote the Gospel of John in the second half of the first century, just a few decades removed from Jesus' death and resurrection about 30 A.D. The great apostle penned it in the very dominating and enslaving era of the Roman Empire. His book gives the evidence for Jesus of Nazareth as the Son of God. It became one of the four Gospels in the New Testament.

John expressed his thesis at the end of his book: "These are written that you may believe Jesus is the Christ, the Son of God, and that by believing you may have life in his name" (John 20:31).

To make Jesus' case, John offers an introduction to show the Son of God has existed from eternity (John 1:1-18). The eternal Word proceeded from His heavenly Father in an incarnation and was truly without sin in His humanity. It was at Nazareth that He was conceived by the Holy Spirit in the womb of the Virgin Mary, and He became Mary's Baby in the silent night of Bethlehem. "The word became flesh and dwelt among us" (John 1:14 KJV; Luke 2:15-19).

As John developed His narrative, he drew from Jesus' ministry seven miracles, seven discourses, and seven "I AM" declarations to frame Jesus' identity. John's assumption was that open-minded readers would be compelled to conclude only God could:

Do such miracles,
    Teach so masterfully,
        Die so nobly, and
            Rise from the grave so victoriously, all the while
                Loving people—all people worldwide—so totally.

A subtheme of John's work is to catalog the record of people who confessed Jesus of Nazareth as Messiah. The term *Messiah* is to be equated with such additional names as Son of God, Son of Man, Anointed One, the Christ, and the God-man. Another subtheme is John's faithfulness to record accounts of people who did not take this step of faith. A third portrays how Jesus kept His focus and did some of His greatest teaching and miracles amid the greatest opposition.

John sealed his case, giving the second half of his book to the last week of the Lord's ministry, including Jesus' brutal crucifixion and gloriously triumphant resurrection (12:12–21:25).

In the contemporary era of mass communication and marvelous medical technology, these seven miracles continue to prove only God can do such things. Modernity, with all of its genius, must stand back in awe of them.

## The Plan

Jesus' commitment to accomplish His Father's assignment to take away the sin of the world was a job description big enough to befit the Son of God (John 1:29, 34; Isa. 49:1-6). But predictably, it would also stir up resistance. Since his method for dealing with opposition must also be ours, the question is appropriate: How did He bear up under the load so that He successfully completed the work His Father gave Him to do?

The writer of the New Testament letter to the Hebrews framed Jesus' motivation, and it must also be ours:

> Let us fix our eyes on Jesus, the author and perfecter of our faith, who for the joy set before him endured the cross, scorning its shame, and sat down at the right hand of the throne of God (Heb. 12:2).

**Said another way: "The joy set before him" made it worth the price for Jesus Christ.**

The religious system in Israel rejected Jesus before the strong arm of Rome did. Anger in the priestly system began to raise its ugly head in Jesus' first visit to the temple in Jerusalem after His baptism. It intensified even more as His ministry progressed. By the time Jesus raised Lazarus from the dead, the fury had become a murderous hatred that despised Jesus (John 11; Isa. 49:7; 53:3). It must not be missed that "religion" became the first enemy of the Messiah, and then religion allied with the state to kill Him. [This same alliance of religion and the state is at work in the world today and will ultimately usher in the reign of Antichrist.]

## The Sanhedrin's Strategy; the Savior's Blueprint

Caiaphas, Israel's high priest, called the Sanhedrin into session almost immediately after Jesus' stunning miracle in which Lazarus walked out of the tomb that had held him for four days. Caiaphas led the Sanhedrin in forming a brutal plan to kill Jesus. The high priest then issued an all points bulletin for the Lord's arrest.

Jesus' sovereign blueprint called for Him to become the perfect sacrifice as "the Lamb of God," the "Passover lamb," who would "take away the sin of the world" (John 1:29; 1 Cor. 5:7).

Amazingly, the two plans of action were complimentary. The strategy of the Sanhedrin to kill Jesus meant Jesus' blueprint would succeed (Luke 23:34; Acts 3:17).

The struggle was colossal; it was an all-out war for the eternal destiny of the souls of men. For their part, these religious leaders did not voluntarily give up an inch of territory. Jesus had to "take it" every step of the way (John 1:29). As the struggle went forward, Jesus never used their methods, not even one time. For example, in His sovereignty Jesus did not coerce a single participant in the drama of Calvary. This meant these leaders and their followers acted in their own free will to arrest and crucify Jesus.

Amid all of the intrigue and drama to eliminate Jesus, the Lord controlled the timing. Jesus was determined His crucifixion would occur on the very morning of the Passover celebration at the same time the Passover lamb was slain in the temple.

Jesus needed no sword or spear to achieve His goal; His only instrument for the struggle was the love of God. A millennium earlier, young David could not wear Saul's armor. He needed only his sling and one of his five smooth stones to end Goliath's boastings permanently (1 Sam. 17:50). Time would prove the love of God, and not the sword, was the one force King David's messianic Son needed to compel Rome to bow at Jesus' Cross.

The love of God does indeed "*take away* the sin of the world" (John 1:29, 36).

Death itself was the ultimate instrument of control in the hands of these religious rulers. It was their willingness to kill that so effectively silenced the Jewish population. The dead always lose their voices; the solemn quietness in any cemetery is deafening.

Propelled by the love of God, Jesus had a surprise weapon His enemies did not see coming—the power of resurrection. As Jesus watched their anger turn into hatred, and then into a plot to murder Him, He continued to witness how well His Father's plan was working. Jesus taught His disciples: "Fear not them which kill the body, but are not able to kill the soul: but rather fear him which is able to destroy both soul and body in hell" (Matt. 10:28 KJV).

The Sanhedrin leaders thought the cross would silence Jesus forever; He would be permanently destroyed. In their fondest imagination they could not foresee Jesus walking out of His tomb, immortal and incorruptible!

**What a colossal underestimate! In fact, Jesus' enemies underestimated Him at every bend in the road. Even today, people who reject Jesus as the Son of God continue to misjudge Him.**

Jesus, on the other hand, understood fully what His resurrection would achieve. His triumph would …

... mortally humiliate death itself,

... wipe out its sting forever, and

... give eternal life to untold millions worldwide.

In the battle for Japan in World War II, the atomic bomb was the Allies' top-secret weapon, and it forced the Japanese warlords to surrender. With Jesus Christ, the surprise was His power of resurrection, accomplished and demonstrated in the love of the Triune Godhead.

Peter preached on the Day of Pentecost:

"Men of Israel, listen to this: Jesus of Nazareth was a man accredited by God to you by miracles, wonders and signs, which God did among you through him, as you yourselves know. This man was handed over to you by God's set purpose and foreknowledge; and you, with the help of wicked men, put him to death by nailing him to the cross. But God raised him from the dead, freeing him from the agony of death, because it was impossible for death to keep its hold on him. David said about him:

"'I saw the Lord always before me.
Because he is at my right hand,
I will not be shaken.
Therefore my heart is glad and my tongue rejoices;
my body also will live in hope,
because you will not abandon me to the grave,
nor will you let your Holy One see decay.
You have made known to me the paths of life;
you will fill me with joy in your presence'"
(Acts 2:22-28; see Ps. 16:8-11).

The plan Jesus came to fulfill worked perfectly!

When the Apostle John laid down His ancient quill, he had recorded the ageless story that has convinced readers in every generation, among all ethnicities everywhere that Jesus is God's Son. He is the Redeemer of all who repent and believe the gospel.

John's book makes the same powerful case in the 21st century. It remains God's answer that establishes the modern gods of this age, too, are but idols of the mind. Jesus alone holds the status of the Son of God.

**Son of God indeed! Moses was right when he prophesied 3,500 years ago—we "must listen to him" (Deut. 18:15; Matt. 17:5).**

This volume is written in a commentary style with applicational inserts and illustrations added throughout.

Book One covers John 1:1–5:47. John 1 lays the foundation of the book. For this reason, it receives the largest amount of attention in this volume. Book Two will begin at John 6:1 and continue through John 12:11. It will conclude John's account of Jesus' ministry leading up to Passion Week.

The story of the last week of the Lord's earthly ministry that climaxes with His horrible crucifixion and triumphant resurrection is yet to be written.

# CHAPTER 1

## JESUS: THE SON OF GOD
### The Word Became Flesh

*The Apostle John begins with a theological introduction (1:1-18) written to introduce Jesus as the Son of God. John asserts this Son, from eternity, has always held equality in the Godhead as the Word of God who created all things. This Word entered time and space in an incarnation as Jesus of Nazareth and was introduced to the world by His messenger, John the Baptist. The Baptizer announced in a bold prophecy Jesus was the Lamb of God who would take away the sin of the world. Chapter 1 ends on a very practical note, cataloging John's record of the first four people in Jesus' ministry who confessed Him as the Son of God (1:35-51).*

## JOHN'S PROLOGUE
### John 1:1-18
#### The Deity of the Eternal Word

**1 In the beginning was the Word, and the Word was with God, and the Word was God. 2 He was with God in the beginning.**

The flow of the Apostle John's pen in this introduction begins by asserting the Son of God has existed from eternity (v. 1). It concludes, unveiling "the Word [who] became human and made his home among us." He is "the unique One, who is himself God," [and] "is near to the Father's heart; He has revealed God to us" (John 1:14, 18 NLT). What follows the Prologue is how John actually presents the evidence that demonstrates Jesus of Nazareth is the Son of God.

The eternal Word (the *logos*, v. 1) that became a flesh-and-blood man in Jesus of Nazareth (v. 14) was not created by His Father. Instead, the son has existed from eternity. Jesus spoke of this relationship in His High Priestly prayer: "Father, bring me into the glory we shared before the foundation of the world" (John 17:5 NLT). The Greek term for "world" in this verse is *kosmon*, transliterated into English as *the cosmos*. The word embraces the glory Jesus enjoyed with His Father before anything came into being in the entire created order of God.

The name used in the Greek for God in v. 1 is *theos*. The sense of the phrase "the Word was God" is "the *logos* was *theos*." It is a strong assertion that the Son of God has always, from eternity, possessed the essence of God.

The phrase "in the beginning with God" also illustrates the limitation of language. How can God have a beginning? "In the beginning with God" is a figure of speech using very human language to communicate *eternality*.

As this river of revelation surges forward in the Gospel of John, its life-giving water blossoms the true identity of Jesus of Nazareth. The mission of John's Prologue is clear. The Apostle identifies the man, Jesus, this humble servant who did not act kingly, as this divine Word (*logos*) come to earth (John 1:14; Matt. 2:23; 11:29). In doing so, John challenges his readers to look past Jesus' disguise of flesh and blood and see Him also as God's intimate companion, who "was with God in the beginning."

## KING JESUS, THE DISGUISED

I suspect most of us do not honor and obey Jesus appropriately because he often comes to us much like King Edward the Disguised. Mark Twain's *The Prince and the Pauper* introduces Prince Edward and a poor boy named Tom Canty. In the opening pages, they meet each other and discover they look identical.

Since each one is dissatisfied with his social situation, they decide to swap places and see what life's like from the other side. Tom takes on the life of Prince Edward, and Prince Edward adopts the life of pauper Tom.

During the course of the novel, King Henry dies, at which point Prince Edward becomes King of England. For the rest of the story, Edward has to convince others that he is the legitimate king. All they see, of course, is a poor boy in rags.

Many people—not just the wise men—had trouble spotting the Son of God and King Jesus in his day, because they were looking for the trappings of royalty instead of an infant in a manger, or a young man in a carpenter's shop.

*Mark Galli, "King Jesus the Disguised," Christianity Today magazine (December 2006). Cited in PreachingToday.com.*

As the Son of God, Jesus was in the position to reveal the heavenly Father to mankind. This also meant that in His teaching He could make final and definitive statements about matters of faith and practice, including the afterlife.

John places God's Son in a category all by Himself up front in his first few lines. No other world religion can make the claim its founder has existed from eternity and is, in fact, the Son of God.

Interestingly, the New World Translation of Jehovah's Witnesses changes "the Word was God" to "the Word was *a god*." Jehovah's Witnesses reject the deity of Jesus Christ, asserting instead that Michael the archangel became a man in Jesus Christ.

> **Denying Jesus as the Son of God is very hard for people to do when they study with an open mind the "infallible proofs" Jesus provided, which the Apostle John and the other Gospel writers recorded (Acts 1:3).**

Jesus arrested Saul of Tarsus on the road to Damascus, transformed him into the Apostle Paul, and made him the apostle to the Gentiles (See Acts 9). Paul picked up the theme of Jesus' superiority in his letter to the Colossians. He celebrates in soaring language that Jesus Christ "is the head over every power and authority … the image of the invisible God … and the firstborn over all creation" (See Col. 1:15-20; 2:9, 10).

> **The Christian Universalist Association, the umbrella organization that seeks to represent and serve Christian universalist churches, publishes a Statement of Faith. Article One offers a definition of God that is far removed from the Good News in the Bible. It gives no recognition to the eternality of Jesus as God's Son and makes no provision for the Trinity. Nor does it offer teaching on the incarnation of Jesus, including His miraculous conception by the Holy Spirit and His Virgin Birth. Instead, Jesus is presented in Article One "as the human manifestation of God's nature and character." *(The full articles of faith can be accessed at www.Christianuniversalist.org.)***

Since Jesus is the living Word of God (John 1:1, 2), it naturally follows that His essence as the living Word would need to be translated into the written word of God. One manifestation of this is Moses having received the Ten Commandments on tablets of stone written with the finger of God (Deut. 9:9, 10). Stephen, in his address to the Sanhedrin some fifteen hundred years later, actually spoke of the commandments as "living words" that Moses passed on to us (Acts 7:38; Heb. 4:12). The Apostle Peter explained the inspiration of the Holy Spirit that translated the living Word into the written word as follows:

> Above all, you must understand that no prophecy of Scripture came about by the prophet's own interpretation of things. For prophecy never had its origin in the human will, but prophets, though human, spoke from God as they were carried along by the Holy Spirit (2 Pet. 1:20, 21).

The same Holy Spirit who inspired writing the Old and New Testaments also illuminates readers to experience the living Word as they read. The Bible that the two testaments form has become the grand revelation of God available to all generations. Jesus, the living Word, never wrote a book. The sole record about Him came from the writings of His disciples.

It is in this context that we turn next to a brief look at the impact of the Son of God on writing the New Testament.

## Authority to Write the Bible

When Jesus, the living Word of God, took on humanity in the incarnation, He had full inherent authority to say what each of the Old Testament writers originally intended. This was true even if the prophecy had lain dormant in the Scriptures for a millennium before finding its day on the stage of salvation history. And, if the text were first written for the coronation of an Israelite king, Jesus could speak authoritatively to the ultimate prophetic meaning of the passage in His own life as the King of kings, even a thousand years later. The Lord also had reason to expect that His interpretations would stand the test of time.

Jesus appeared to His disciples in a locked room on resurrection night after returning from Emmaus and bequeathed this special inspiration to them that was innate in Him. It was because Jesus opened the minds of His apostles that they were able to link inseparably the Old and the New Covenants (Luke 24:45).

> He said to them, "This is what I told you while I was still with you: Everything must be fulfilled that is written about me in the Law of Moses, the Prophets and the Psalms." Then he opened their minds so they could understand the Scriptures (Luke 24:44, 45).

## The Special Lens

Jesus' original apostles were empowered to interpret the Old Testament scriptures through the lens of the Lord's stunning triumph at His cross and the tomb He left shamed and empty. Transferring this anointing was critical to the spread of the gospel of Jesus Christ around the world.

The opening statement of John's Gospel illuminates this authority. John had a clear understanding of Jesus as the eternal Word and felt no need to seek permission from anyone to assert the claim. His many experiences with Jesus over the three years of Jesus' ministry constituted all the authority John needed. For example, Genesis 1:1 says, "In the beginning God created the heavens and the earth." The Apostle John interpreted the role of the eternal Word in the creation, saying, "In the beginning was the Word, and the Word was with God, and the Word was God. He was with God in the beginning. ... All things were made by him" (John 1:1-3).

> **The devil's *number one* deception is to lead people to misinterpret the Word of God. During Jesus' temptation in the wilderness it was Satan's chief tactic, albeit unsuccessful.**

On resurrection night Jesus enabled His apostles to begin to see these kinds of truths in the Old Testament. His doing so cleared the way for the disciples, as inspired by the Holy Spirit, to write the New Testament (2 Pet. 1:21). Their doing this bequeathed to history an infallible written record of Jesus to every generation.

At the same time, they corrected mistakes in interpretation in the Old Testament that begged to be refocused. It is worthy of repeating that Jesus was qualified to discern these errors and adjust them because He was the *logos*, making Him the:

Wisdom of God, the
Living Word of God, and the
Fountain of truth from which the Old Testament writers wrote
the Word of God.

This explains why the Lord knew the Old Testament scriptures perfectly, far better than any "expert in the law" (Matt. 22:35; Luke 10:25-37). It also meant Jesus was fully capable of silencing them in any debate.

The eternal Word came to His people Israel in an incarnation as their Messiah. "Messiah" is the Hebrew word for the *anointed one*, and "Christ" is its Greek translation. "Messiah" speaks to Jesus' office, while "Son of God" speaks to His essence or nature in the Godhead. Jesus is in essence the Son of God. This status qualifies Him to fill the office of Messiah. Hence, both terms, Son of God and Messiah, speak to Jesus' deity.

> **Without dispute, Golgotha was history's greatest game changer, and so was the tomb Jesus mortally humiliated, leaving it empty on resurrection morning.**

Jesus enabled the apostles to examine the Old Testament through the lens of His death and resurrection. It enabled them to discover how completely the prophets had set the stage for the New Covenant. Hence, the apostles could write the New Testament in true unity and harmony with the Old Testament. The death and resurrection of Jesus was the great unifier.

## The Role of the Old Testament in the Gospel

The Old Testament preserved the New Testament gospel for millennia, until the Lord's triumph at Calvary opened up the truth that had been in the first covenant all along. Understood from this perspective, the New Testament is the divinely inspired revelation of what was already in the Old Testament (Rom. 1:2; Gal. 1:11; 3:8). It became the responsibility of the New Testament writers, as inspired by the Holy Spirit, to mine these veins of golden truths in the Old Testament and express them in the context of the Lord's death and resurrection. The New Testament, therefore, shows how the crucifixion and resurrection of Jesus, the Lamb of God, unifies the two covenants into one message.

Jesus of Nazareth, the *logos* (Word) of God, is the central hope of the Old Covenant and the central dream come true of the New Covenant. In the power and anointing of His own essence, Jesus pulled the Old Testament and the New Testament into one unified Holy Bible. In the Old Covenant, Jesus is the Messiah who was to come. In the New Covenant, He is the Messiah who came. His mission as the Lamb of God was to take away the sin of the world (John 1:29, 35). The end result is that the two Testaments blend into one divinely inspired Sacred Canon. Each of the two covenants is just this closely interrelated and exists because of the inspiration of the Holy Spirit (2 Pet. 1:21). Because the Sacred Canon is inspired by God, it perpetuates itself as the book that has spread Jesus' message worldwide.

### "HE WROTE THE RULE BOOK!"

A number of years ago, when I was playing in a friendly men's softball game, the umpire made a call that incensed our coach. He didn't agree at all with the ump's interpretation of a specific league rule. The game stopped and a heated discussion ensued. Finally, the ump sighed as he pulled a rulebook from his back pocket and proceeded to read page 27, paragraph 3b, section 1.

"As you can clearly see," he concluded, "this rule means that my call must stand."

Unconvinced, my coach yelled, "But you're not interpreting that rule correctly!"

To which the ump replied, "Uh, excuse me, I think I should know: I wrote the rulebook."

After an awkward silence, my coach walked back to the bench. Shaking his head and pointing to the ref he told us, "Get ahold of that guy. He wrote the rulebook!"

Throughout his ministry, Jesus didn't just affirm and endorse the

words of Scripture; He talked with the authority of the one who had *authored* the Scriptures. He wrote the "rule book."
   *Matt Woodley, The Gospel of Matthew: God With Us (InterVarsity Press, 2011), pp. 68-69.*

This kind of understanding of Jesus the Messiah as the author of Scripture motivated the Apostle Paul, an avid disciple of Jesus Christ, to write with a refreshing joy that sprang from a deep well of appreciation:

[Give] thanks to the Father, who has qualified you to share in the inheritance of the saints in the kingdom of light. For he has rescued us from the dominion of darkness and brought us into the kingdom of the Son he loves, in whom we have redemption, the forgiveness of sins (Col. 1:12-14).

The New Testament developed precisely because Jesus gave the capability to the apostles to understand the scriptures in resurrection focus. This gift also proved to be a vitally important factor that aided the disciples in laying the foundation of the Lord's church (Eph. 2:20; Luke 24:25, 32).

**The Christian Universalist Association in Article 7 of its Statement of Faith affirms "the Bible to be the authoritative textual basis of their faith, a collection of writings that contain divine revelations and which, in some sense, is collectively a divine revelation." In contrast, the orthodox understanding of the scriptures affirms Jesus is the living Word and the Bible is the written revelation of God. The gap here is huge between "contains" and "is."**
   **Universalists also "recognize that the revelation of divine truth is not limited to the pages of the Bible. ... many Christian thinkers ... have written texts which are just as inspiring and valuable as canonized Biblical books." An orthodox understanding of the Bible affirms its 66 books are the revelation of God for all matters of faith and practice. No other books enjoy the inspiration of the Holy Spirit to the extent they can be added to the 66 books of the Bible.**

How important that we go back to the Apostle John, the original source, and permit him to show us Jesus Christ as the Son of God.

## God's Son, the Creator
**3 Through him all things were made; without him nothing was made that has been made.**

John also uses the Greek terms *logos* and *theos* to communicate the divine authority through which everything was made in the creative work of God. This links Jesus with the creation: "In the beginning God [the Hebrew *Elohim* = the supreme God] created the heavens and the earth" (Gen. 1:1). The name *Elohim* is in the plural here, hinting at a plurality in the Godhead. King David expressed it, "By the word of the LORD were the heavens made. ... he spoke and it came to be; he commanded, and it stood firm" (Ps. 33:6, 9; 147:4, 5, 15).

This Messiah, very God and perfect man, is the creative Word of the Godhead who spoke into being everything in the universe (Gen. 1:1-3; Ps. 33:6, 9). He also sustains His creation by the power of His Word (Heb. 1:2, 3).

What a claim! Jesus of Nazareth is the creator of all that is. It must have felt like a huge leap of faith for Israelites to look at Jesus, and then see this man from Galilee as maker and sustainer of all.

The truth is, for anyone to believe in Jesus, the light of revelation must shine in each person's heart, and each must choose to accept the revelation (Matt. 16:17). Without this revelation, no one can comprehend Jesus in His splendor, accepting Him as redeemer and the only path to the Father.

The Lord who is the maker of the heavens and the earth came to the earth He created to form a new order among men. We know it as the gospel—the good news birthed by the life, death and resurrection of Jesus Christ.

No other world religion claims its founder is the creator of all things. With Jesus Christ, it is not a hollow assertion. Jesus performed creative miracles in His ministry to back up the claim, and John records them.

Jesus in His own person makes the gospel exceptional, placing the Good News in a category other world religions cannot rival. In doing so, the gospel undercuts religious pluralism's view that no world religion possesses ultimate truth and that all religions lead to God.

## Jesus: Life and Light
**4 In him was life, and that life was the light of men.**
**⁵ The light shines in the darkness, but the darkness has not understood it.**

God the Son, who held life and light in His hands, spoke the creative word on the first day of creation: "Let there be light, and there was light. God saw that the light was good" (Gen. 1:3, 4). Then, on the fourth day "God made two great lights—the greater light to govern the day and the lesser light to govern the night" (Gen. 1:16).

John described Jesus as uniquely different, however, from the sunlight of creation; Jesus was the *Sonlight;* "the light of men." The prophet Isaiah spoke of the Messiah as the light to illuminate the human spirit hopelessly mired in the "thick darkness" of sin:

> Arise, shine, for your light has come, and the glory of the LORD rises upon you. See, darkness covers the earth and thick darkness is over the peoples, but the LORD rises upon you and his glory appears over you. Nations will come to your light, and kings to the brightness of your dawn (Isa. 60:1-3).

The word picture of the birth of a baby is appropriate. A child in the womb of its mother lives in darkness until the infant bursts into the bright light of our world. The penetrating light of the Holy Spirit flashes to the very bottom of the dark chasm of the soul and shines the light of Christ Jesus, making possible a new birth. In the brilliance of this light we are born into a new life.

The phrase in v. 5, "has not *understood* it," derives from a Greek word meaning *to take eagerly, to seize or possess.* The idea is that this luminary sent by the heavenly Father brought a bright and shining, life-giving message most of His own people willfully refused to assimilate and possess as their own. He should have been welcomed with hearts that eagerly seized the new light, but they did not take hold of it.

---

**Ah! to glory in the light Jesus brought to mankind. "If any man is in Christ, he is a new creation; the old has gone and the new has come" (2 Cor. 5:17).**

---

The Apostle John will give considerable attention to Jesus as the light of the world in chapters 8 and 9. For now, he introduces the subject and then presents how the Lord's forerunner introduced the Light (vv. 6-8).

## John the Baptist: "Sent From God"
**6 There came a man who was sent from God; his name was John.**

The Apostle John expressed the arrival of John the Baptist in a single sentence: "God sent John the Baptist as a witness to the fact that Jesus Christ is the true Light" (John 1:6 TLB). Luke the Physician gave expanded detail:

In the fifteenth year of the reign of Tiberius Caesar — when Pontius Pilate was governor of Judea ... during the high priesthood of Annas and Caiaphas, the word of God came to John son of Zechariah in the desert. He went into all the country around the Jordan, preaching a baptism of repentance for the forgiveness of sins. As is written in the book of the words of Isaiah the prophet:

"A voice of one calling in the desert,
'Prepare the way for the Lord,
    make straight paths for him.
Every valley shall be filled in,
    every mountain and hill made low.
The crooked roads shall become straight,
    the rough ways smooth.
And all mankind will see God's salvation'" (Luke 3:1-6).

**People to this day are fundamentally changed into powerful voices when "the word of God" comes to them. Contemporary John the Baptists with a distinct call from God are sorely needed today, and in every generation.**

**7 He came as a witness to testify concerning that light, so that through him all men might believe. 8 He himself was not the light; he came only as a witness to the light.**

John the Baptist was the son of Zechariah and his wife Elizabeth. John's father was a priest active in the worship at the temple. Reared by Godly parents, John grew up and became the star witness and forerunner of the light that beamed out of the life of Jesus Christ. Jesus illuminated the path to redemption and extended the offer worldly wisdom could never make—the free gift of eternal life to every person worldwide who believes in Him.

### The Messiah's Disguise
**9 The true light that gives light to every man was coming into the world. 10 He was in the world, and though the world was made through him, the world did not recognize him.**

## HIDDEN IDENTITY IN THE WORKPLACE
The first summer my wife and I were dating, she worked as a temp at a bank. In the first two weeks she had the job, she quickly noticed some

extremely unprofessional behavior among the team of four people she worked with and their supervisor. The supervisor, who was a generation older, was very friendly with the younger staff, taking long coffee breaks with them. College-aged staff would sit on her desk to chat and gossip.

The supervisor and her team were so friendly that the group's behavior toward one other new member of the team was a stark contrast. This person was shunned, a woman in her 30s who had come on staff just a week before my wife. If she walked up and tried to join the conversation during a coffee break, the conversation ended.

The group, including the supervisor, made jokes about her behind her back and laughed at the way she dressed. They rolled their eyes and winked at each other when she was present. It was obvious this middle management worker was perceived as an unnecessary intrusion.

Two weeks into the temp job, my wife walked into the office on Monday morning and was surprised to find a much different scenario. No gossiping, no kidding around, no long coffee breaks. All the workers had their eyes riveted on their work. The previous supervisor had been replaced. The cliquish team addressed the new supervisor with formal, businesslike respect. My wife thought she even saw fear in their eyes.

The new supervisor was not a stranger. It was the 30-something woman who had been shunned and mocked. It turned out the bank had hired her to be the new supervisor from the first day she came on the job three weeks before, but the bank had concealed her true identity so she could observe the work style of the team.

*Craig Brian Larson, editor of PreachingToday.com; cited from PreachingToday.Com.*

The disguise of humanity gave Jesus adequate time to grow up into manhood and to carry out His ministry, doing it amid the ever-growing hatred directed toward Him. Jesus' life was on a timeline that climaxed with His Passover sacrifice as the Lamb of God, occurring exactly as planned from eternity. In His true humanity Jesus won the heartfelt affection and loyalty of His followers, who launched His international vision after His resurrection (Heb. 4:15; 5:5; 6:20; 7:26; 8:1; Matt. 28:16-20; Acts 1:8). He compelled no one to follow Him; anyone who comes to Him in repentance does so by his own free choice. Not once did Jesus use force to motivate anyone to bow his knee, nor threat of punishment to win a coerced loyalty. The camouflage made it possible for this entire process to go forward.

The incarnation meant Jesus of Nazareth, *God the Son* veiled in flesh, was walking the dusty roads of Israel, sleeping in the homes of His own subjects, laughing and talking with them, and eating their food. In doing so, the Messiah saw only too well the pain on the faces of His chosen people. He understood fully the burdens they carried, the tears in their eyes, their unfulfilled hopes and crushed expectations, and the fearsome penalty of death reigning in their bodies.

## The Creator lived in the disguise of true humanity in the natural order His creative Word sculpted.

Jesus knew well His original creation had been a perfect paradise, and witnessed firsthand the destruction the curse of sin had wrought. With the fall of man it had become a vicious world in which death claimed the weak and the strong alike, every person born. The curse of death also permeated the whole of nature. In fact, in worldly wisdom the strong always seem to dominate the weak.

The living Word, the source of the Old Testament scriptures and the author of creation, visited the synagogues of Israel in disguise and read to them the very scriptures He had inspired their prophets to write. As He did so, He saw firsthand how far removed the hearts of His own people were from Him. In fact, on one occasion they actually wanted to throw Him over a cliff when He claimed He was their Messiah, the Anointed One (Luke 4:18-30; Isa. 61:1, 2).

## The Rejected Savior
### 11 He came to that which was his own, but his own did not receive him.

Jesus did not come as a triumphant conqueror, or as a monarch expecting to ascend his throne, or as a president ready to take the oath of office and the reins of power. He came instead as a humble servant cloaked in flesh and motivated by love (Mark 10:45; John 13:34; 15:12).

Interestingly, Jesus never required anyone to worship and serve Him. Not once.

The Messiah who was His Father's only begotten Son, the Lord of the universe and King of kings, put aside His privileges when He became a man—including His right to respect, loyalty and trust. Instead, He set out on the rocky and dusty roads of Israel to win the hearts of His own people, using only love as His weapon of choice. But the typical response to Jesus was to despise Him as a person and reject His teaching (Isa. 53:3).

Following Jesus in the 21st century assumes this same free choice: "Anyone who wants to approach God must believe He exists and cares enough to respond to those who seek him" (Heb. 11:6 MSG). Clearly, for love to be love, it must be free. The attractiveness of this freedom to choose helps to explain why love wins the hearts of people.

Jesus came doing the works of God, with a step-by-step plan ultimately to reach the hearts of people of all races and ethnicities, men and women, Jews and Gentiles, slaves and freemen (Col. 3:11; Gal. 3:11). Jesus' method was to motivate people with His teaching and convince them with His miracles. His strategy was to inspire them to confess His divinity and royalty, and do it voluntarily and freely. As for the response Jesus received, the overwhelming majority despised Him and categorically rejected Him. Even today many people feel the same way toward Jesus—they simply loathe Him and everything for which He stands.

> **When we embrace who Jesus is and sense His love for us, His personal care pulls us to Him and changes us into new people, from the inside out.**

Some in Jesus' Jewish family did make the confession, however. The problem was the overwhelming majority who did not. In their stubborn and hard-hearted pride, they chose to reject Jesus' claim to be the Son of God, which meant they also refused the gift of eternal life He offered.

As Jesus increasingly did the mighty works of God, one by one the sons of Abraham were compelled to make free choices. The Lord at Caesarea Philippi addressed the penetrating, all-important question to Peter, for example: "Who do you say that I the Son of Man am?" (Matt. 16:15). It is the universal question with which all people everywhere must grapple.

Yes, the love of God by its very nature requires all to choose, but love will not determine what the choice will be; love never dictates to free will. Those who accept or reject Him to this day do so deliberately, as a choice. The God who created Adam and Eve gave our first parents the great gift of freedom. He made the blessing so expansive they were empowered to say "Yes" or "No" even to their Creator, and so can all of their children (Gen. 2:15, 16).

The worst kind of contempt and loathing often comes from the house of one's friends. It is the Ahithophel story all over again.

> If an enemy had insulted me, then I could bear it.
> If someone who hated me had attacked me, then I could hide from him.
> But it is you, my equal, my best friend, one I knew so well!
> We used to talk to each other in complete confidence
>     and walk into God's house with the festival crowds. ...
> But I call on God, and the Lord saves me.
> Morning, noon, and night I complain and groan, and he listens to my voice.
> With his peace, he will rescue my soul ... (Ps. 55:12-14, 16-18 GW).

## The Redeeming Messiah
### 12 Yet to all who received him, to those who believed in his name, he gave the right to become children of God—

The Good News of Jesus Christ always advances in the midst of conflict. Jesus knew what was ahead and kept His eyes focused on Calvary as His goal. Only after His resurrection would He reap a great harvest worldwide of the "children of God" who receive Him. Jesus understood from eternity that everyone would not welcome Him.

The struggle started while He was in His mother's arms, and was chillingly fearsome:

> Then Simeon blessed them and said to Mary, his mother: "This child is destined to cause the falling and rising of many in Israel, and to be a sign that will be spoken against, so that the thoughts of many hearts will be revealed. And a sword will pierce your own soul too" (Luke 2:34, 35).

As the conflict was all too true, so was the ultimate triumph at Calvary. Jesus came to die. The religious leadership over time grew to despise Jesus passionately and wanted Him dead. Ultimately, they made good on their threats (Isa. 53:3; 60:14). Their bitter rejection sent Jesus to the cross and made Him the perfect sacrifice to communicate the love of God to all people.

The result has been God's love made it possible for everyone to repent and become sons of God. Jesus died as the substitute and sacrifice for every son of Adam. He is the personal Savior of all.

Charles Gabriel expressed it in the chorus of his beloved hymn (1905):

> O how marvelous; O how wonderful.
> And my song shall ever be, O how marvelous,
> O how wonderful, Is my Savior's love for me.

### 13 children born not of natural descent, nor of human decision or a husband's will, but born of God.

This is the Apostle John's introduction of Jesus' solution to the problem of sin deeply embedded in the hearts of all people. The power of a new birth would raise up "children of God." This solution is fully developed in John 3.

Jesus' method for doing this is to change people in their hearts, from the inside out. It is a change no one can make by his own initiative or work to earn. It is solely a gracious blessing from God.

People must have a way to start over, to be reborn, to make a new beginning yielding a new creation (Acts 4:12; 2 Cor. 5:17; Gal. 6:15).

**No provision is made in verse 13 for people to come to salvation after rejecting in this life Jesus' name and the new birth He offers. Therefore, John's powerful assertion undercuts the core of Christian universalism.**

**The road Jesus paved with His own sacrificial blood can be traveled only by those who believe in Jesus' name and are born of God. *They* have the right to become children of God. It can be understood in this context why Jesus' message differs from all other world religions. Each of them in its own way teaches people they must do the impossible—labor hard and earn their salvation.**

**Not the redemption that comes by Christ Jesus. This "so great salvation" comes by grace through faith alone. It is the gift of God (Eph. 2:8, 9; Acts 4:12).**

## Jesus: The Incarnate Messiah
### 14 The Word became flesh and made his dwelling among us.

As a member of the Lord's inner circle, the Apostle John had the ideal vantage point to ponder the death and resurrection of Jesus, as well as His many miracles and teaching. This also enabled John to make comparisons to the Old Testament. As he did so, he came to the conclusion it is self-evident and beyond dispute that Jesus of Nazareth was of the same divine essence Jehovah revealed in the Old Testament.

## John's Implicit Assumption
Simply put, John comprehended the revelation that the Nazarene was indeed the Son of God (John 20:31). Therefore, John's book assumes the Father-Son relationship revealed in Jesus' incarnation squared with Moses' teaching, "Hear O Israel, The LORD our God, the LORD is one" (Deut. 6:4).

This understanding is unstated by John and receives no explicit explanation or defense in John's Gospel. This should not minimize the appreciation that it was a very hot issue in Jesus' ministry that kept coming up in various ways. For example, the Apostle John refers to Moses 13 times, each in the first nine chapters of his Gospel. One of the Lord's many challenges was to redefine Moses so as to give the great emancipator and lawgiver the honor he was due, while correcting the inappropriate conclusions about Moses in Jewish thinking.

Our generation, 21 centuries removed from Jesus' earthly life, must also grapple with Deuteronomy 6:4. It is important to understand that what John assumes in verses 1, 2 and 14 is supported in the Old Testament and revealed in the New Testament. The effort to demonstrate this in a few condensed pages follows.

## The Problem

The scribes and doctors of the law over the 1,500 years from Moses to Christ held to a strict interpretation regarding Moses' statement, "The LORD our God, the LORD is one" (Deut. 6:4). Their teaching claimed God can be only one in substance or essence, and only one in personhood.

When Jesus came as God's Son in an incarnation (in flesh and blood), the scribes and doctors of the law of necessity had to deal with Jesus' identity. To them, Moses' teaching, "the LORD our God is one Lord" meant God can be no more than one in essence, and no more than one in personhood. Based on this definition, they chose to interpret Jesus of Nazareth as but a mere man and rejected Him as the Messiah who is God's Son.

The Apostle John's experience with Jesus led him to agree with the scribes and doctors of the law regarding the one substance or essence of God. At the same time, John discovered the God whom he had touched and handled in Jesus Christ required a new understanding of personhood (1 John 1:1). John lived with Jesus for three years. This closeness enabled him to comprehend that Jehovah God, whom Israel's forefathers had worshipped for so long and was indivisibly One, *is* indeed plural in persons.

One of the first revelations opening up this truth was Jesus' baptism in Jordan River. It showed the indivisible God of eternal being exists as a Triunity of persons—Father, Son and Holy Spirit. Jesus was standing in Jordan River, the Holy Spirit descended on Him in the form of a dove, and the Father spoke from heaven (Deut. 6:4; John 1:32-35; Matt. 3:16, 17; Mark 1:10, 11; Luke 3:21, 22).

The Gospel of John presupposes, therefore, the God of the Old Testament, the Son of God revealed in Jesus of Nazareth, and the Holy Spirit are indivisibly One in substance or essence. At the same time they are three in Triunity, distinct but inseparable as indivisible persons.

This conclusion is the foundation of the monotheistic view in salvation history that came to be identified by the term *Trinitarian*.

## Dangerously Off Course

The Jewish scribes and doctors of the law were way off course during Jesus' earthly life. Simply put, they were holding to a false and dogmatized explanation of Deuteronomy 6:4. The inaccurate conclusion taught by the Jewish leadership was ominously serious. These religious leaders, based on their strict interpretation of what Moses wrote, decided only one conclusion was possible: Jesus had to be a mere man. How could He be anything more, since God is One? It apparently never occurred to them that their understanding of Moses' teaching could be wrong. In their thinking, Jesus could not be the Messiah, even though they knew from the Old Testament that Messiah would come from God. When Jesus claimed equality with God, therefore, the religious rulers considered it blasphemous on its face and worthy of a death sentence (John 10:33; Matt. 26:65).

This interpretation of Deuteronomy 6:4: "the LORD our God, the LORD is one," in fact, was the single piece of evidence the Sanhedrin used to nail Jesus to a cross (Mark 14:64). False doctrine has been deadly in every generation.

The Apostle John adjusted this murderous misunderstanding of Moses' teaching in the positively stated first sentence of His book and affirmed it in verse 14. This correction is arguably John's single greatest legacy to understanding the identity of Jesus Christ.

No, John did not feel the need to cite Deuteronomy 6:4 directly, but it is certainly understood.

---

**Jehovah's Witnesses hold to a similarly strict interpretation of Deuteronomy 6:4: Jehovah of the Old Testament is the true God, Jesus is not the equal of Jehovah, and the Holy Spirit is merely God's power or active force in the earth. Hence, the Trinity is rejected.**

**Jehovah's Witnesses also deny the existence of hell. Death is identified as a state of nonexistence and unconsciousness.**

**This group further holds to a form of universalism: the people resurrected in the millennium will have another chance to prepare to live forever.**

**Jehovah's Witnesses reject so many of the foundational teachings of the gospel, its advocates are identified as heterodox (opposite of orthodox) and as a heretical sect.**

---

The following brief study of the Hebrew Scriptures further illuminates John's implicit conclusion.

## The Solution to the Problem

Moses would have been the first to accept Jesus as the Messianic prophet the great emancipator foretold: "The LORD your God will raise up for you a prophet like me from among your own brothers. You must listen to him" (Deut. 18:15; John 5:45, 46; Matt. 17:2; Mark 9:2; Luke 9:31). Jesus came to his own people, but they were not at all willing to obey Moses' prophetic instructions telling them they "must listen" to Jesus of Nazareth as their Messiah.

## Messiah in Psalm 2

Psalm 2 demonstrates the apostles' ability to interpret Old Testament scripture through the lens of Jesus' cross and resurrection. The Psalter does not name the author of Psalm 2, but Peter and John attributed it to King David, Israel's greatest king (Acts 4:25-28). We are not told how they came to this conclusion, but it is quite possible they heard it from Jesus. David was also a prophet. In this psalm David penned a royal edict in the name of God on the subject of the plurality of the Godhead: "I will declare the decree: the LORD [Jehovah] hath said unto me, 'Thou art my Son; this day have I begotten thee'" (Ps. 2:7 KJV).

A millennium later, after Peter and John were threatened by the Sanhedrin, they poured out their hearts to God in prayer. These apostles made Psalm 2 the foundation of their petition and attributed its authorship to King David (Acts 4:24-28; Ps. 2:1, 2).

The ultimate meaning of what David penned in Psalm 2 a thousand years earlier was intended for David's greater Son, the Messiah. This prophecy slumbered in the Psalter for a millennium before it found its fulfillment in the incarnation of Jesus Christ. Then it leaped on the stage of salvation history. Additional proof that this psalm was Messianic is found in the other times in the New Testament the prophecy is cited with a Messianic meaning (Acts 13:33; Rom. 5:10, 11; Heb. 1:5; 5:5).

Why is this so important?

The gospel calls on people of faith to place the destiny of their eternal souls in the hands of Jesus Christ. For this step to be taken, people deserve to know He really did have standing with God to carry out His mission to make atonement for all who accept His redeeming blood (Luke 1:6-8; Gal. 3:13, 14; Heb. 2:17; 1 Pet. 1:18; Rev. 5:9). The writer of Hebrews portrays Jesus as the express image of the Father and the High Priest of a new and better covenant. This high standing did in fact give Him the right and authority to make the atoning sacrifice for your sins and mine, and the sins of the whole world. He alone brings us into union with the heavenly Father (Heb. 1:3; 3:1; 4:14; 6:20). Our eternal souls are in good hands!

**As regards religious pluralism, why would Jesus voluntarily walk through all of the horrendous rigors of crucifixion if there were other valid paths to God? Such would mean Jesus died the death of a fool.**

**Further, if He were not the Son of God, the merciless jeers of the religious leaders who taunted Him while He was dying on the cross, although cruel under any circumstances, become a little more understandable (Luke 23:35).**

**The Gospel of John demonstrates Jesus is the Son of God who died for all. This endows Him with the final say as "the way, the truth and the life" (John 14:6). All people would be wise to heed Moses' injunction and "listen to him" (Deut. 18:15).**

## Psalms 2 and 3: A Contrast of Two Sons

When taken together, Psalms 2 and 3 offer additional insight into the nature of David's greater Son. Psalm 2, David's psalm about God's exalted Son, was positioned in the Jewish Psalter before David's psalm written while he was fleeing Jerusalem to escape the death trap of Absalom, his rebellious son (Psalm 3). Psalms 2 and 3, therefore, are the contrasting portraits of two very different sons.

In Psalm 2, David prophesied Jehovah was a Father who had a Son. This Son, Jehovah's Son, would one day be Israel's Messiah (the anointed one). This Son of God gave His Father implicit loyalty. In fact, the bond was never broken between them—no, not even once. In Psalm 3, David's flesh-and-blood son plotted to overthrow and kill his own father in what was possibly the darkest hour of David's 40-year reign (See 2 Sam. 15:25–16:14).

King David penned a "decree of the LORD" a millennium before Jesus' birth (Ps. 2:7). David's statement, "You *are* my son," therefore, is a prophetic affirmation of the eternality of the Son of Man from Nazareth. The verb "are" describes *being* and is *timeless*; this Son from heaven had no beginning, so there never was when He did not exist. He was Jehovah's son from eternity, who became Jehovah's *only begotten Son* in time and space in His incarnation. A virgin was His mother, God was His Father, and He was conceived by the Holy Spirit (Isa. 7:14; Luke 1:35; Matt. 1:18-20). King David predicted He would grow up and have the heathen nations for His inheritance in a kingdom extending to the uttermost parts of the earth (Ps. 2:8).

### No, God's Son was not an Absalom (Ps. 3).

### Moses as an Accuser

Jesus taught that the interpretations of Moses by the scribes and Pharisees were so skewed, they were in effect putting words in the great lawgiver's mouth he never spoke or prophesied. This meant they did not believe what Moses foretold. Their interpretation of what it meant to keep the Sabbath day holy is just one of many examples (John 5:9-18). Jesus said to them:

> Do not think I will accuse you before the Father. Your accuser is Moses, on whom your hopes are set. If you believed Moses, you would believe me, for he wrote about me. But since you do not believe what he wrote, how are you going to believe what I say? (John 5:45-47; see also Luke 20:37, 38).

When Jesus came as the fulfillment of the Messianic prophet the great lawgiver foretold, the religious leaders were categorically unwilling to learn from Jesus and follow Him (Deut. 18:15).

# The Messiah: Both Lord and Son

Jesus' exchange with the Pharisees at the temple also adds to this discussion:

> One of them, an expert in the law, tested him with this question: "Teacher, which is the greatest commandment in the Law?"
> Jesus replied: "'Love the Lord your God with all your heart and with all your soul and with all your mind.' This is the first and greatest commandment. And the second is like it: 'Love your neighbor as yourself.' All the Law and the Prophets hang on these two commandments."
> While the Pharisees were gathered together, Jesus asked them, "What do you think about the Christ? Whose son is he?"
> "The son of David," they replied.
> He said to them, "How is it then that David, speaking by the Spirit, calls him 'Lord'? For he says, "'The Lord said to my Lord: "Sit at my right hand until I put your enemies under your feet."'
> If then David calls him 'Lord,' how can he be his son?"
> No one could say a word in reply, and from that day no one dared to ask him any more questions (Matt. 22:35-46; see also Ps. 110:1).

In this discourse, Jesus quoted Moses' statements in Deuteronomy 6:5 and Leviticus 19:18 to show the unity of God is anchored in the love of God. He then quoted Psalm 110:1 in this exchange to demonstrate that King David spoke as a prophet. This means David interpreted Moses' teaching. "Speaking by the Spirit" in this passage, David affirmed Messiah would be both David's Lord and David's son.

=====================================================
**The force of the statement "the LORD said to my Lord" is compelling as expressed in Hebrew: "*Yahweh said to Adonai*," or "*God said to God*" (Ps. 110:1).**
=====================================================

Jesus told these Pharisees in the temple, therefore, that Psalm 110:1 was a Messianic prophecy about Himself. David specifically prophesied God the Heavenly Father has a Son who holds equality in rank and essence (Matt. 22:44).

This Son in His incarnation was Jesus Christ, Israel's Messiah. He came to earth with two whole and perfect natures (the human and the divine). Both were indivisibly combined in one person, truly man and very God. David also foretold after Jesus' work on earth ended, the Messiah would be received back in exaltation at His Father's right hand. In this lofty position He awaits His Father's placing all His enemies under His feet (Ps. 110:1).

Jesus did not see any contradiction between Moses' affirmation of the unity of God (Deut. 6:4) and His own teaching, foretold in the prophecy of King

David, "The LORD said to my Lord ..." (Ps. 110:1). Jesus was both Yahweh's Son and David's seed.

Jesus' reasoning silenced His critics. "From that day no one" had the nerve "to ask him any more questions" (Luke 20:40).

## The Transfigured Messiah

Four great Old Testament prophecies predicting the coming of the Messiah intersect with Jesus at the Mount of Transfiguration (Luke 9:28-36):

1.  Moses' prophecy of the coming Messiah (Deut. 18:15).
2.  Moses' declaration, "Hear O Israel, the LORD our God is One Lord" (Deut. 6:4). These are two of the great emancipator's most remembered proclamations.
3.  King David's prophecy asserting Jehovah God has a Son (Ps. 2:7).
4.  David's prophecy about this Son, "Yahweh said to ADONAI, sit at my right hand until I make your enemies your footstool" (Ps. 110:1). Jesus specifically interpreted this prophecy as applying to Himself (Matt. 22:44).

The Transfiguration should be understood as a great Biblical illustration of the identity of the Messianic prophet Moses and David foretold. It came eight days after Peter's confession at Caesarea Philippi. Jesus' question then was, "Who do people say the Son of Man is?" (Matt. 16:13-16). Peter answered with a faith statement confessing Jesus as the Son of God. The heavenly Father gave God's answer to this same question at the Transfiguration of Jesus (Luke 9:35, 36). He did it amid a dazzling display of divine glory.

The great event occurred while Jesus was praying on an unnamed mountain in Israel. He was transfigured there, with Peter, James and John as witnesses. Jesus' "face shined like the sun and his clothes became as white as the light" (Matt. 17:2). Moses and Elijah appeared with Jesus. They "were splendid in appearance" and "glorious to see" (Luke 9:31 TLB).

## The Afterlife

This account gives an illuminating peek into the afterlife. God had buried Moses on Mount Pisgah some 1,500 years before the Transfiguration, and Elijah had gone into heaven amid a whirlwind in a chariot of fire pulled by horses of fire some 800 years earlier (Deut. 34:5; 2 Kings 2:11). Both men were very much alive in the world of the spirit all of that time.

In this scene, they appeared together on the holy mountain. They knew each other and conversed intelligently, although their ministries were separated by some seven centuries. They were also visible in those miraculous moments to Peter, James and John, whose eyes were opened to see and recognize them.

The disciples listened to part of the conversation between Jesus and Moses and Elijah.

The Transfiguration, therefore, confirms intelligent life continues for the righteous after death. Jesus specifically taught that death to the child of God does not mean the end of existence, but is only a change in form of existence (John 5:25; 11:25). The Apostle Paul's comforting statement adds insight in this context: "to be absent from the body is to be present with the Lord" (2 Cor. 5:8). Paul also affirms the grand promise of eternal life will include a literal, bodily resurrection, with Jesus as the first fruits (1 Cor. 15:12-28). It is reasonable to conclude in the resurrection to come all of God's children, including each of our loved ones who died in Christ, will be "splendid in appearance" and "glorious to see."

## The Conversation

Moses and Elijah talked with Jesus about His "decease [*exodon*] he would accomplish in Jerusalem" (Luke 9:31). The English word *exodus* is a transliteration of this Greek term. Moses, the great emancipator and lawgiver, led an exodus of the children of Israel from Egypt to the Promised Land. Elijah, arguably the greatest of the prophets, dreamed of leading Israel away from idolatry and back to God.

The Greek word for *decease*, *exodon*, embraces the idea of a departure. As used in the Transfiguration, it foreshadowed Jesus' death by crucifixion in Jerusalem. It also anticipated Jesus' resurrection and its aftermath. Jesus would lead the ultimate exodus, taking His followers back to His heavenly home and to the companionship of His Father.

Moses and Elijah did not talk with Jesus about how many thousands of soldiers would be required to throw off the yoke of Rome. Nor did they discuss what it would take to break the domination of Greek culture with all of its idolatrous ways and the immoral social implications that went with it.

Instead, of all the many things they could have talked about, Moses and Elijah gave their time to only one theme. They talked with Jesus about His death that was so near.

**The conclusion should leap out at us. All ministers and teachers are responsible to follow the pattern of the conversation at the Transfiguration. The death and resurrection of Jesus and its implications must be the central theme of all ministry. Ah! The cross of Jesus demands a primary place in every sermon and Bible lesson!**

It is unthinkable that either Moses or Elijah would have been invited to the grand event had they not in their lifetime of ministry accepted the deity of the Messianic prophet Moses foretold. Moses met the pre-incarnate Christ several times. Two examples were at the burning bush and when Moses struck the rock in the wilderness and the life-saving water gushed out. At the burning bush, Moses saw the "angel of the LORD" identified as Jehovah (Exod. 3:1-5). In the wilderness during the exodus, Jehovah revealed Himself to Moses again (Exod. 17:6). The Apostle Paul said about Jehovah, whom Moses met: "the spiritual rock ... was Christ" (1 Cor. 10:4). While running from Jezebel after his Mount Carmel triumph, Elijah, too, met the angel of the Lord, who is identified as Jehovah (1 Kings 19:12-18).

When the conversation began on the holy mountain, Elijah, Moses and Jesus were not strangers. Not only Moses and Elijah, but all people in the Old Covenant who experienced forgiveness and peace with God did so because they placed their trust for salvation in the Messiah who was to come (Rom. 3:25).

In this mountain scene Moses and Elijah's visit with their Messiah was very different from their earthly visits. The Messiah, whom they had so longingly anticipated, was now incarnate in flesh and blood. He had come to take away the sin of the world (John 1:29). Their discussion with him focused on Jesus' death and resurrection and the exodus that would follow it. These events were all about to take place in Jerusalem (Luke 9:31). Moses and Elijah in the Transfiguration each obviously embraced Jesus' redemptive sacrifice.

The grand theme of the conversation between them presupposes that Moses would have also affirmed King David's prophecy that Jehovah has a Son (Ps. 2:7). In addition, he would have agreed with King David's statement: "The LORD said to my Lord [or "*Adonai* said to *Jehovah*"], sit at my right hand until I make your enemies your footstool" (Ps. 110:1).

The Apostle Peter said the prophets knew God was up to something big and it related to the salvation of all people. They "searched intently and with the greatest care, trying to find out the time and circumstances to which the Spirit of Christ in them was pointing when he predicted the sufferings of the Christ and the glories that would follow" (1 Pet. 1:10, 11).

The prophet Moses had been dead some 15 centuries, and Elijah, some eight centuries. Yet, they were blessed to be able to visit with Jesus on the mountain. They even received the latest information from the Messiah Himself on how it would all come to pass, and very soon.

While the Biblical record does not say it, undoubtedly both Moses and Elijah genuinely worshipped Jesus on the mountain, having no doubts about Messiah's identity. They surely thanked the Lord with overflowing gratitude for the redemptive sacrifice He would be making a few weeks up the road. Their worship might have even been recorded in the story, except that the disciples were "very sleepy"

(Luke 9:32). At a minimum, no one should doubt Moses and Elijah rejoiced in the high privilege of this visit with Messiah. Their deeply felt longing, the celebrated hope of the millennia for a kinsman-redeemer to make things right between God and man, was about to be fulfilled! (See Ruth 2:1; Job 9:33, 34; Isa. 54:5; 59:20).

This revelation further illustrates the Father and the Son as persons in the Godhead. Moses and Elijah were called to meet with *Jesus*. They participated in the discussion about Jesus' death and resurrection. Then, the voice of *God* spoke out of heaven with the Messiah standing on the mountain. The heavenly Father audibly claimed Jesus of Nazareth as His beloved Son. In doing so, the Father gave His own answer to Jesus' question at Caesarea Philippi.

The overriding purpose of the Transfiguration was to reveal Jesus as the singular object of their affection, who would soon triumph on Golgotha, the Hill of the Skull (John 19:17). As such, the Transfiguration explicitly reveals the Father and His incarnate Son. The Holy Spirit, who filled Jesus "without measure" at His Jordan River baptism, was also obviously present and participated in staging the grand event (John 3:34). It is the mission of the Holy Spirit, in fact, to make Jesus known (John 14:16, 26; 15:26).

Peter broke into the conversation:

> "Master, this is a great moment! What would you think if I built three memorials here on the mountain—one for you, one for Moses, one for Elijah?" While he was going on like this, babbling, a light-radiant cloud enveloped them, and sounding from deep in the cloud a voice: "This is my Son, marked by my love, focus of my delight. Listen to him" (Matt. 17:4, 5 MSG).

Peter, James and John were in a situation in which they did not know how to act or what to say. Hence, when hit with a blinding light, they fell to the ground. The voice of the Father in heaven that had spoken at Jesus' baptism boomed again in those moments. It was so overpowering, Peter, James and John were "terrified." When the disciples collected their senses enough to stand, "They saw no one except Jesus" (Matt. 17:7, 8). It must have been very comforting to them when they did open their eyes to see only the kind face of their Messiah.

---

**Ah! "No one except Jesus"—He is the whole point. Jesus is the Savior, in a league all by Himself; He has no competitors who are even close rivals (Acts 4:12).**

**All of Jesus' followers in every generation are admonished to live with their eyes fixed on the "altogether lovely" Jesus the Messiah, our Savior, who**

**leads the greatest exodus of all time (Song of Sol. 5:16; Acts 4:12; Heb. 12:2).**

**The Transfiguration is convincing verification indeed of the deity of Jesus Christ. The final proof is the Lord's death and resurrection.**

Jesus, again, is revealed as the "one and only" (John 1:14). It is a theme woven through a variety of settings in John's book.

## Conclusions

Four deductions stand out in this study:

1. Jesus possesses the same essence as the heavenly Father and is His "express image" (Heb. 1:1-3).
2. Both Moses and King David prophesied the deity of God's Son (Deut. 6:4; Ps. 2:7; 110:1). As such, the focus of our attention must be on Jesus alone (Luke 9:35). We must "listen to Him" (Deut. 18:15).
3. Moses and Elijah, great men that they were, would be the first to say they were not even close to Jesus' equals.
4. The eternal God is indivisibly One in essence and at the same time plural (triune) in persons. Moses' declaration, "the Lord is one," must be understood accordingly (Deut. 6:4; Luke 9:35).

Hence, neither Moses nor Elijah would have had trouble believing everything the Apostle John wrote about Jesus in his Prologue. Indeed, in the entire book!

## Peter's Applications

The Apostle Peter never forgot that experience. When he penned his second epistle some 35 years later, he made a particular application of the meaning of the Transfiguration. He first presented the awesome event as a defense of his apostolic credibility. Then he linked the "honor and glory" Jesus' Father gave His Son at the Transfiguration to the "power" of the Lord's second coming. Peter was emphatic that He, along with James and John, were "eyewitnesses." They saw Jesus' glory "on the sacred mountain." They also audibly heard the voice of the Father. God was delighted to claim Jesus of Nazareth as His beloved Son, who pleased Him fully. Peter was giving testimony, therefore, to what he had seen and heard. The implication is that Peter expected the Lord's second coming to occur with the same majesty as was the Lord's at the Transfiguration.

We did not follow cleverly devised stories when we told you about the coming of our Lord Jesus Christ in power, but we were eyewitnesses of his majesty. He received honor and glory from God the Father when the voice came to him from the Majestic Glory, saying, "This is my Son, whom I love; with him I am well pleased." We ourselves heard this voice that came from heaven when we were with him on the sacred mountain (2 Pet. 1:16-18).

The Apostle John made a valid assumption in the first two verses of His Gospel and verse 14: the deity of Jesus of Nazareth was self-evident and squares with Deuteronomy 6:4. John's conclusion is justified in the Old Testament and is explicit in the New Testament scriptures.

## Monotheism

The primary contribution of Jewish religion to mankind, and especially to Western civilization, is bringing Jesus Christ into the world. In doing so they bequeathed to mankind monotheism, the worship of one God. Decade after decade, century after century, for almost two millennia the Jewish people were willing to live by their interpretation, which advanced their strict interpretation of the essence of God. They maintained a strict monotheism even while their own prophets, like King David, foretold an expanded understanding (e.g., "You are my Son; today I have become your Father" [Ps. 2:7]).

Although many sons of Abraham turned to idol worship, many others never did. Men like Daniel did not budge, though they were surrounded by Babylonian culture totally given over to polytheism (the worship of many gods). They did not even adjust when Jesus came and gave "many convincing proofs" of His deity (Acts 1:3). Instead, they despised Jesus for making the claim and crucified Him (Acts 2:36; 4:10).

## The Story Line of the Gospel
## 14 The Word became flesh and made His dwelling among us.

John's teaching that the Word (the *logos*) that has existed from eternity has become a flesh-and-blood man in Jesus of Nazareth is the great story line of the gospel (John 1:14). In His incarnation, His humanity was an effective camouflage that made possible His sacrifice on the cross.

Arguably the following two are the anchor miracles of salvation history. No others recorded in the Bible rise to their level:

1.  Jesus was conceived by the Holy Spirit in the womb of a virgin, with God as His Father (Isa. 7:14; Matt. 1:23; Luke 1:35).
2.  Jesus was viciously crucified on a rugged Roman cross, died, was buried and arose from the dead on the third day according to the scriptures (1 Cor. 15:3, 4).

The plan, conceived in eternity, is the heavenly Father's solution to man's fall (1 Pet. 1:18-20). God-the-eternal-Word became truly man through a miracle of miracles, a sinless conception by the Holy Spirit in the womb of the Virgin Mary. Jesus was born without a sin nature and did not need a savior; God was His Father (Luke 1:26-38). Motivated by the great love of God, Jesus stepped on the human scene because all people in every generation desperately need a redeemer.

## The Messiah: Actually Dwelling Among Us

The idea of "dwelling among us" (v. 14) embraces Old Testament images of the Spirit, who lived first in the tabernacle and later in the temple. It is also illustrated by the Feast of Tabernacles that occurred on the Jewish calendar in September/October. For the seven-day celebration, the people made temporary dwellings out of "branches of palm trees, and the boughs of thick trees, and willows of the brook" to remember their wilderness sojourn (Lev. 23:29-43; see also Deut. 16:16, 17 KJV).

Each of these images has its ultimate meaning in the actual presence and anointing that accompanied the Lord Jesus, whose dwelling among us was truly in the flesh. It also prophetically looks forward to the gift of the Holy Spirit in the era of the church, when the Spirit dwells in the hearts of God's people. Jesus shouted out His great prophecy of the advent of the Holy Spirit on the last and greatest day of the Feast of Tabernacles in Jerusalem (John 7:37-39).

Messiah's tabernacle of flesh was temporary, however—only three short years of active ministry in a lifespan of 33 years. The eternal Word took on a human body to complete His work as Redeemer and Savior. "The Word became flesh and blood, and moved into the neighborhood" (John 1:14 MSG).

The Apostle John also used the concept "dwelt among us" four times in the Revelation. In each case the idea changes from short-lived to permanent (e.g., Rev. 7:15 KJV): "They are before the Throne of God, and serve Him day and night in His temple, and He that sitteth upon the Throne shall dwell among them." John also uses it in Revelation 21:3: "I heard a great voice out of heaven, saying, 'Behold, the tabernacle of God is with men, and He will dwell with them'" (See also Rev. 12:12; 13:6).

Jesus humbled Himself to become a man and associate closely with His disciples:

> Eating,
>> Sleeping,
>>> Walking,
>>>> Laughing,
>>>>> Living with them,
>>>>>> Growing tired, hungry and thirsty with them,
>>>>>> His dirty, hurting feet throbbing like theirs.

In His incarnate ministry, He offered full proof of His humanity. His miraculous deeds also opened people up to discover His divinity. While tenting with mankind, His many astounding works forced the people to lift their sights to God.

Jesus in His own person is the ultimate meaning of the Feast of Tabernacles (Lev. 23:34; Deut. 16:13-16), a celebration Jesus honored and kept. The Lord, who was the fulfillment of the Feast, humbly stepped unrecognized into one of the many thousands of booths that sprang up all over Jerusalem.

> **Jesus lived in a booth like everyone else, but without receiving any honor as the personal, grand fulfillment of the Feast of Tabernacles.**

When John 1:1 is blended with verse 14, they together form the strongest possible affirmation that Jesus is God's Son, Deity in flesh and blood: "In the beginning was the Word, and the Word was with God, and the Word was God. He was with God in the beginning. ... The Word became flesh and made his dwelling among us." These two, when connected, unmistakably establish John's intent to present Jesus as the Son of God.

### 14 We have seen his glory ...

The glory of Jesus in the Old Testament included the grandeur and aura of God's presence dwelling over the ark, between the cherubim in the Most Holy Place.

> There, above the cover between the two cherubim over the ark of the Testimony, I will meet with you and give you all my commands for the Israelites (Exod. 25:22).
> When Moses entered the Tent of Meeting to speak with the LORD, he heard the voice speaking to him from between the two cherubim above the atonement cover on the ark of the Testimony. And he spoke with him (Num. 7:89).

In the New Testament, one such occasion when Jesus "revealed his glory" was when He turned water into wine at the wedding in Cana of Galilee. The result was His disciples put their faith in Him (John 2:11; see also Matt. 14:33). Another was His Transfiguration, witnessed by the disciples in His inner circle, Peter, James and John (Matt. 17:1-8). Yet, the Lord said He did not come seeking glory for Himself; it was a mere by-product of His ministry (John 8:50).

This understanding of Jesus' glory in His incarnation establishes Him as unique and presents Him as "the one and only." The founder of no other world religion rises to the level of this kind of affirmation and splendor.

**Of course, this understanding upsets religious pluralists. Jesus *alone* just cannot be <u>the</u> answer, pluralists believe. But He is!**

## The One and Only
**14 ... the glory of the one and only who came from the Father, full of grace and truth.**

Jesus enjoyed from eternity a special glory in the Triunity of God (John 17:5). His glory was also expressed in His humanity. It was a stroke of divine wisdom, as well as of ultimate humility, when Jesus lowered Himself to become a human being. But that step also showed the genius of God, for the very fact that God became a man is one of the signal achievements of His holy life, demonstrating that He really is due the highest honor.

## A COLLEGE PRESIDENT STOOPED LOW
When pastor and writer Clark Cothern was five years old, he thought college presidents were powerful, frightening people. That is, until one stooped down to his level to spend time with him. He writes:

"What I saw of college presidents I saw from floor level, as I played on the other side of my mother's desk in the administration building at Grand Canyon College (now University) in Phoenix, Arizona. My mom was the dean of women at the time.

"I would watch as students walked slowly down the hall toward the president's office and stop. They would rub their sweaty palms on their pants or skirts, take a deep breath, straighten their shoulders, and knock. The door would creak open. That's when I would catch a glimpse of the president's shiny, black wingtip shoes. A steady, strong hand would reach through and shake the trembling hand of the student. The student would then disappear inside the mysterious chamber known as 'The President's Office.'

"I figured that walking into that room must be pretty much like going before the throne of judgment. It was a terrifying thought, that is, until the day the president stooped into my world.

"I was playing with my toy car in the hall outside his office when the door opened. There they were those shiny, black wingtip shoes. The next thing I knew, President Robert Sutherland, the biggest man on campus, dressed in his pinstriped, three-piece suit, knelt down. He placed the knee of his crisply creased trousers on the hallway floor. "'May I have a turn?' he asked.

"After we played cars together, President Sutherland asked if I would do him the favor of calling him 'Dr. Bob.'

"That's the day my opinion about college presidents changed.

"I can see how some people might think God is a powerful, frightening being. Yet after I met God, my opinion about Him changed, too. The Apostle John wrote, 'The Word became flesh and made his dwelling among us.'

"Dr. Bob stooped low into my world and the experience has stayed with me through life. It has certainly helped me understand that verse better."

*Clark Cothern, in the Christmas sermon, "When God Stooped." Cited in PreachingToday.Com.*

The Greek word for "the one and only" carries the meaning *only one of its kind.* The term does not imply God created the Son, so that the Son has not always existed. Instead, the Son has always been the very essence of His Father. He truly is the "one and only," and this reality defines the magnificence and splendor of His person and presence. The writer of Hebrews describes Jesus as the "express image" of the Father (Heb. 1:3).

Neither does "came from the Father" imply "*created* by the Father." Instead, it embraces "*sent* by the Father" (e.g. John 6:57). Jesus is the only person born of a woman whose human nature never came by parental generation; therefore, Jesus did not inherit the sin nature of Adam. Instead, the Lord was conceived in the womb of the virgin and given His sinless nature by the miraculous energy of the Holy Spirit. As Gabriel said, "[T]he baby born to you will be utterly holy—the Son of God" (Luke 1:35 TLB). Gabriel also affirmed, "Nothing is impossible with God" (Luke 1:37).

**Mormonism embraces a Trinity of three distinct persons (Father, Son and Holy Spirit). These three exist in a unity of purpose, but not of essence; hence a doctrine of tri-theism instead of monotheism. Mormonism rejects the unity of essence in the Biblical revelation of the Father, the Son and the Holy Spirit, one God in three persons.**

## "Full of Grace and Truth"

The characterization "full of grace and truth" shows but two of the many beautiful traits in the sterling character of Jesus Christ. *Grace* speaks to the liberality of God, who imparts acceptance and unearned benefits. It includes deliverance from danger and from temptation—recognizing how besetting sins so easily destroy a person's life (Heb. 12:1). The term further embraces the favor of God to give blessings. It also opens doors of opportunity, and then endows the confidence to step into them. Jesus freely did favors for people who sought them, as well as for those who did not seek them. He still does so today.

To witness Him in action compelled the exclamation that He was "full of grace!" Favors generously flowed out of Him. At the same time, He never compromised truth. The stories of the woman at the well, the woman caught in the act of adultery, and the thief on the cross are three examples of how He faultlessly blended grace and truth (John 4:6-42; 8:3-12).

The word picture of a vaccine is appropriate. Grace functions as the "vaccine" that stops the virus of sin before it can take hold inside us. Grace keeps us from sinning (Gen. 39:9; Titus 2:11, 12).

The word picture of an antibiotic also fits. Grace is the antibiotic that destroys the curse of sin if we fall into its trap and sin against God. Grace gives us the confidence to repent, get back up, and start over. Hence, this "antibiotic" releases people from the stronghold of the disease called sin (1 John 2:1-3; Ps. 51; 2 Sam. 12:13).

## The Voice in the Desert
**15 John testifies concerning him. He cries out, saying, "This was he of whom I said, 'He who comes after me has surpassed me because he was before me.'"**

It takes lots of grace to admit the ministry of another has outshined one's own. The Baptizer's successor was both his superior and his predecessor.

This verse also shows the passion John felt about his message. He was so fully convinced he had heard God that he spoke with compelling intensity: "He cries out ..." (*krazo = to call aloud, exclaim, entreat*).

**From the pages of the Bible, the Baptizer is still exclaiming today, "This is He!" John is yelling it out, entreating our generation, as well, to turn in repentance to the Messiah, the Christ of the Bible.**

The key to eternal life is not to be found in sincerely following the path of any world religion in which one finds oneself. Sincerity cannot be depended upon to establish truth; how easily a person can be "sincerely wrong"! The answer is found in "repentance toward God and faith toward our Lord Jesus Christ" (Acts 20:21; Rev. 1:18).

## The Final Sacrifice: Abundant Grace
**16 From the fullness of his grace we have all received one blessing after another. 17 For the law was given through Moses; grace and truth came through Jesus Christ.**

John was blessed with a Godly father and mother, Zechariah and Elizabeth. His father was a priest, who was serving in the temple when he saw a vision and received the message from the angel Gabriel that he and Elizabeth would have a child in their old age. As John grew up, no doubt his parents poured the Old Testament scriptures into him (Luke 1:5-25).

One is left to wonder if Zechariah ever talked with his son about the seemingly unending nature of animal sacrifices in the Mosaic system of worship. Did they ever dream together about Messiah's coming, and especially that He would end the sacrifices?

While the Biblical record does not answer these questions, it is clear John anticipated the sacrifice was near that would end all sacrifices. People would finally be liberated from the day after day bondage of the law's do's and don'ts and unending sacrifices. Just the 1,500 years of pouring out sacrificial blood, from Moses to Christ, sacrifice, after sacrifice, after sacrifice, is a long time. But in the new order John foresaw, Jesus' one sacrifice would stop the killing. Worship would flow out of peoples' hearts, with each believer becoming a tributary of the unending river of the grace of God:

Grace on top of grace.

Unmerited favor on top of unearned favor.

"Inoculating" grace to keep us from sin.

"Antibiotic" grace to destroy the virus of sin after it has set up its deadly grip in our lives.

Moses gave the Law, but the Son of God gave "the fullness of grace," so that we all receive "one blessing after another." The exclamation "fullness of grace" is an apt description. Even though Jesus was so very despised and lived with raw rejection daily, He continued to give blessing, after blessing, after blessing in His ministry. Jesus never stopped giving blessings, even on His cross. Amazingly, the Lord never tired of giving life even to ungrateful people, and the supply never ran out (Luke 23:43).

**The Lord continues to be this kind of magnanimous giver in our day! Wow! "Ask whatever you wish." The Bank of Grace will never go bankrupt.**

Writing to the church at Ephesus, Paul explained this grace as an unending quality in the Lord's character: "God ... is rich in mercy ..." (2:4), and mercy is one expression of grace. ("Rich" = *plousios* = *plutocrat.* The term carries the idea of copiously rich, aboundingly wealthy.) Paul is not writing here about the Lord's wealth in gold and silver, but in the grace of compassion. Even the term multibillionaire is inadequate to describe heaven's Bank of Mercy. So is multitrillionaire. Jesus Christ is so full of grace, in fact, no danger exists that heaven's bank will ever be depleted. The danger is greater that the oceans will go dry before God's supply of grace will be exhausted! In fact, the quantity of grace is so great, the Messiah can afford to send His rain on the righteous *and* the unrighteous (Matt. 5:45).

It is also true that the God who gives favors for which we do not ask is a Father who enjoys being asked: "If you remain in me and my words remain in you, ask whatever you wish, and it will be given you. This is to my Father's glory, that you bear much fruit, showing yourselves to be my disciples" (John 15:7, 8).

When Jesus pours out His blessings, however, He has the right to come looking for committed disciples who will bear fruit (Eph. 2:10). The Holy Spirit raises up followers with hearts so full of grace, they are pleased to become fruit-bearing channels of this generosity to hurting people (Luke 6:38).

Moses did give the Law, and law is good at prescribing right and wrong and setting penalties for wrongdoing. But law is limited. It can never balance grace and truth. "If a law had been given that could impart life," Paul wrote, "then righteousness would certainly have come by the law" (Gal. 3:21). Since law can only prescribe right from wrong, it lacks the power to redeem from wrongdoing. It can punish people who break the law, but it can never make people righteous.

The term *grace* defines this new mountain range in the character of God and reveals the abounding goodness of Jesus Christ, the Son of God. Many of God's favors come because we ask; others are unsolicited and unexpected divine favors, often becoming the greatest blessings of our lives.

## Forgiveness: The Superlative Quality of Christian Faith

The grace of God is most wonderful news, and God delights in sharing this benevolence broadly (John 1:6-18). The grandeur here is how Jesus took us to a much higher ethic than the Ten Commandments that are based on mandates and prescriptive lists of do's and don'ts. If the Law can be described as the beautiful foothills of the Rockies, then the Sermon on the Mount marks the picturesque vista of Mount McKinley. At the top of this mountain we discover how grace blends perfectly with truth.

Grace without truth breeds lawlessness, and truth without grace breeds legalism. For grace to do its work, it must never diminish truth; instead, each must always balance the other on the scales of justice.

The principle of forgiveness, understood in this context, is the consummate quality of the gospel of Jesus Christ, and forgiveness by its very nature balances grace and truth. This conclusion is appropriate because forgiveness always faces truth and admits it, never denying or whitewashing it. The very nature of asking for forgiveness assumes a person realizes what he has done wrong. And for forgiveness to be granted, the wounded person must comprehend the offense he is releasing. In both scenarios, truth must be faced.

**Forgiveness is grace extended when it is neither earned nor deserved, all the while honoring the demands of truth.**

## Balancing Grace and Truth in the Life of King David

King David's experience illustrates the principle well. Psalm 51 is David's deeply felt prayer of repentance after the prophet Nathan exposed his adulterous affair with Bathsheba (2 Sam. 12:7). David's case was sleazy and repugnant, and even led to the murder of Bathsheba's husband.

The wayward king faced what could have been the consequences of his sinful choices: the loss of his kingdom and execution (Lev. 20:10; Deut. 22:22). It was enough to drive him to his knees as he begged God for mercy and humbly confessed, "Against you, you only, have I sinned and done what is evil in your sight, so that you are proved right when you speak and justified when you judge" (Ps. 51:4). King David knew he was amenable to the great King, God Himself, and his sin had first and foremost violated God by despising His character (2 Sam. 12:10). David also understood the worst thing that could happen to him was for God to withdraw His Holy Spirit from him (Ps. 51:11).

David's prayer of repentance embraced a full admission of the implications of the affair. Because fidelity is a pillar in the moral character of God, faithfulness defines what God expects in the husband and wife relationship. To violate God's character with *infidelity* in marriage is both despicable and evil (See Gen. 39:9).

It is cause for profound gratitude that the goal of justice with God is to correct and not merely to punish. The heart of God is not set on destroying the wicked, but on wiping out their wickedness. The Apostle Peter said God does not want "anyone to perish, but everyone to come to repentance" (2 Pet. 3:9). And Jesus made clear, "unless you repent, you ... will all perish" (Luke 13:3, 5; John 3:16). He also told the Pharisees, "If you do not believe I am the one I claim to be, you will indeed die in your sins" (John 8:24).

King David repented. He turned around and got back on the right road. In his repentance he admitted his sin without any effort to gloss over it or diminish it. This meant truth was vindicated. In fact, the sincere cry of the broken and contrite king is one of the greatest models of repentance in all of salvation history and included petitions like this:

Have mercy on me, O God, according to your unfailing love; according to your great compassion blot out my transgressions. Wash away all my iniquity and cleanse me from my sin. For I know my transgressions, and my sin is always before me (Ps. 51:1-3).

David's repentance resonates with the rich meaning of the character of God revealed to Moses in the cleft of the rock (Exod. 34:5-8). In fact, Moses' experience was the supreme revelation in the Old Testament of the nature or moral fiber of God. The prophets kept looking back to it over the remainder of the Old Testament era (see Num. 14:18; Neh. 9:17; Ps. 86:15; 103:8; 145:8, 9; Joel 2:13; Jon. 4:2).

The LORD descended in the cloud and stood with him there, and proclaimed the name of the Lord. The LORD passed before him and proclaimed, "The LORD, the LORD, a God merciful and gracious, slow to anger, and abounding in steadfast love and faithfulness, keeping steadfast love for thousands, forgiving iniquity and transgression and sin, but who will by no means clear the guilty … ." And Moses quickly bowed his head toward the earth and worshiped (Exod. 34:5-8 ESV).

God always seeks David's kind of Godly sorrow because it produces a changed heart (2 Cor. 7:10). When this has occurred, it is time for the mercy and grace in God's character to do their work. The end result is the righteousness of God is exalted (Rom. 1:17; 3:25). King David expressed it, "[Y]ou are proved right [or righteous] when you speak and justified when you judge" (Ps. 51:4; Rom. 3:4).

## Forgiveness! Ah, forgiveness.

This new condition of King David's repentant heart opened the door for God to forgive the wayward ruler. Thus, the grace poured into David's soul became "antibodies" to conquer the "virus" of his lust. It was also "serum" to inoculate the king against future sin: "the one who was born of God [Jesus] keeps him safe, and the evil one cannot harm him" (1 John 5:18). But if a person does fall into sin:

There is someone to plead for you before the Father. His name is Jesus Christ, the one who is all that is good and who pleases God completely. He is the one who took God's wrath against our sins upon himself and brought us into fellowship with God; and he is the forgiveness for our sins, and not only ours but all the world's (1 John 2:1, 2 TLB).

The student of the Bible should always remember the objective of God's love is to redeem and restore, and not to destroy. Repentance, at its essence, demonstrates a person has turned around in his heart, gone back, and is now walking on the right road. The result is the offended God always releases the rebellious offender. It happens when repentance has completed its work and the perpetrator is changed from the inside out. When this takes place, the love of God has achieved its goal. Forgiveness, therefore, is the great stroke of genius in the message of Jesus Christ, and the term "gospel" expresses this indescribably good news.

People can sometimes deceive with false protestations of repentance, faking a changed heart. But God cannot be fooled. He knows what is in man, and He needs no one to tell Him anything about man (John 2:24, 25). He discerns "the thoughts and intents of the heart" (Heb. 4:12). Again, herein rests the brilliance of the gospel. Grace redeems, but not by denying truth. Instead, forgiveness by its very nature fully admits the truth, yet releases the offender who genuinely repents. This can happen because the demands of God's justice and the promise of grace blend to change an individual in his heart.

King David cried out to God for help. He admitted he had done wrong and pled for mercy. He turned around in the humility of repentance, shook off his shame, and went back to the roadway of right living. The king was a different man with a changed heart. Truth had been faced and admitted; now grace could forgive and forget. No evidence exists David ever committed adultery or murder again.

## Grace and Truth Out of Balance

King David did reap a host of problems in his government and his family, resulting from his sin (2 Sam. 12:10). In addition, people often want retribution, and they are not satisfied with the repentance that leads to forgiveness. This can include significant people in our lives, such as authority figures, and sometimes even our children.

People who look only for punishment (the demands of truth) and not the forgiveness that responds to a changed heart do not know the character of God (Exod. 34; John 8:4). This explains the difference between King David and Ahithophel, David's most trusted advisor. Bathsheba was Ahithophel's granddaughter. After the sickening tryst became public, Ahithophel nurtured a root of bitterness toward his king, obviously believing David did not deserve mercy. It continued to eat at him as the weeks turned into months and then years. Ahithophel comprehended truth, but did not understand grace. David *was*, in fact, an adulterer and a murderer. He no doubt always believed David escaped the punishment he deserved because he was the king. This also meant David's counselor could never forgive his king.

Ahithophel was a brilliant counselor, but not smart enough to balance grace and truth. After the affair, he continued to serve side by side with David in the kingdom, but with a bitter heart. He was intelligent enough to keep David from perceiving it, but not smart enough to keep the bitterness from eating up his soul.

Ahithophel probably ascribed sinister political motives to Nathan when, speaking for God, Nathan told David, "God has put away your sin; you will not die" (2 Sam. 12:13). He likely convinced himself Nathan was trying to curry favor with the king. But he woefully misunderstood the power of repentance to change the heart, as well as the gracious and merciful character traits of God revealed to Moses (Exod. 34).

Ahithophel saw his chance to turn on David when Absalom rebelled against his father with the goal to make himself king. This decision resulted in Ahithophel ending his own life as a victim of suicide. He is often referred to as the Judas of the Old Testament. (See 2 Sam. 11:3; 17; 23:34; 1 Chron. 3:5.)

Bathsheba's dad, Eliam, was one of David's 30 Mighty Men (2 Sam. 11:3; 23:34). Eliam was no doubt deeply offended, too, by the king's adultery with his daughter and the callous murder of her husband, including trying to cover his sin. But Eliam must have also understood the grace of forgiveness follows genuine repentance and balances truth. Nothing in the record indicates bitterness in Eliam's heart.

It is a compelling part of David's life that his firstborn son Amnon raped Tamar (his half-sister). When David learned of it, he was too lenient with Amnon. He related to Amnon solely with mercy and made no attempt to apply the consequences of truth to motivate Amnon to repent of his lust that so violated both God and his sister. The result was Amnon went free and faced no judgment.

David's son, Absalom, hated Amnon for raping Tamar, his sister. Absalom took matters into his own hands and related to Amnon only with the demands of truth that required the stiffest penalties (see 2 Sam. 13). Absalom no doubt convinced himself he was standing up for truth as his father should have done; after all, Amnon *was* a rapist. When he got his chance, therefore, he arranged his brother's murder. According to Absalom, Amnon had finally received what he had "deserved" all along!

Grace and truth were never balanced in this sad family crisis. The story does show, however, that for healing to take place, grace and truth must balance. Mercy alone does not heal and can breed hatred. Truth alone will not heal either. It will only punish and can easily become murderous.

> **Christian universalism makes the grievous error of not balancing grace and truth. Its advocates see only love and grace in God's character, but not justice and judgment, not even as the reward of the persistently wicked. However, God revealed when He placed Moses in the cleft of the rock that justice and judgment are part of His character. "[God] does not leave the guilty unpunished" (Exod. 34:7).**

King David's sad saga also has profound implications for parenting. Some fathers discipline with the demands of truth; others choose to show more grace. But neither alone will rear balanced children. In fact, truth alone can lead to grievous sin, as can grace alone. Parents must always remember the goal of discipline is to correct, and never merely to punish. When a child is led to genuine sorrow, truth has done its work and the door is open for grace to heal the wound. Then a parent must forgive and restore, and forget about it.

Yes, grace and truth must balance.

## Ah! Jesus: The Perfect Balance

David's greater Son, the Messiah, always balanced grace and truth so the demands of both were satisfied. The gospel of Jesus Christ does so with the pre-condition of heartfelt repentance for sin. This produces a changed heart and leads to forgiveness (2 Cor. 7:10, 11). Without this changed heart, there is no balance. When this change of heart happens and grace and truth are balanced, the forgiveness of God always results. Then, another attribute of God is exalted—His righteousness. King David celebrated it: "You are proved right [righteous] in your words and prevail in your judging" (Rom. 3:4; Ps. 51:4).

But there is more. The grace of God that forgives and forgets also adopts the penitent lawbreaker into the family of God (1 John 3:1-9). The result is he will continue to learn more and more of what it means to enjoy the lofty status of a son in the family of God. He has been transformed from the inside out by God's grace into an heir and joint heir with Christ.

## The Name: Jesus Christ

John 1:17 represents the Apostle John's first use of the compound name Jesus Christ (Savior-Messiah).

> From his abundance we have all received one gracious blessing after another. For the law was given through Moses, but God's unfailing love and faithfulness came through Jesus Christ (John 1:16, 17 NLT).

This affirmation of the rich grace that poured out of the life of the Lord can be understood as a parenthetical summary by the Apostle John of the implications of the Baptizer's message. Take, for example, the use of the two names that are merged here, "Jesus Christ" (Jesus the Messiah, the anointed one). It is reasonable "Jesus Christ" was not a name the Baptizer would have used when Jesus was launching His ministry. Over time, however, "Christ" did merge into the Lord's name as more and more people recognized the anointing in Jesus' life.

The name "Jesus Christ" [Jesus the Messiah] is used five times in the Gospels. Matthew used it twice, to introduce his genealogy and to begin his narrative about the incarnation and birth of Jesus (Matt. 1:1, 18). Mark used it to introduce his book: "The beginning of the gospel about Jesus Christ, the Son of God" (Mark 1:1). Neither of these statements demonstrates use of the name in Jesus' ministry years. Luke does not use the name at all, but he did record Simeon's prophesy saying the baby he held in his arms in the temple was the "Lord's Christ" (Luke 2:26). John used it in his introduction of the ministry of John the Baptist (John 1:17), and Jesus used it regarding Himself in His high priestly prayer: "This is eternal life: that they may know you, the only true God, and Jesus Christ, whom you have sent" (John 17:3, 4).

Jesus Christ is the common name for the Lord in Acts, where it is used 15 times. Clearly after the Lord's resurrection the name began to find widespread use. It always honors Jesus as the Messiah. Paul used the name "Jesus Christ" 26 times in Romans and 12 times in Ephesians. It is also reasonable John the Baptist first coined the name Jesus Christ (Jesus the Messiah) as a prophecy and spoke it months before Messiah made the final sacrifice. Taking into account how much gospel the Baptizer predicted, it is believable he foretold this too. From this perspective, when Jesus was just beginning His ministry, the Baptizer saw what was coming, although the full unveiling of Messiah (the Christ) as the great balancer of grace and truth had not yet unfolded.

> **Jesus Christ—such a lovely name! Why has a name so very precious been largely removed from the public square, taken off the airwaves and out of the secular print media? Why? Could it be that Jesus still claims He is the Son of God and does not bow to any other god or ideology?**

## Jesus: Revealing the Father
**18 No one has ever seen God, but God the One and Only, who is at the Father's side, has made him known.**

This verse wraps up the Prologue in the same way John began it, in the blazing light that reveals Jesus as the Son of God. The Greek is compelling here: "No one has ever seen God [*theós*] but God-the-one-and-Only [*monogenés theós = the only begotten God*] who is at the Father's side, has made him known." Jesus of Nazareth is this only begotten God. He is the fountainhead of the mercy that always brings grace and truth into harmony. "This one-of-a-kind God-Expression, who exists at the very heart of the Father has made him plain as day" (John 1:18 MSG). The Father's perfect illustration of His nature and character is His only begotten Son, Jesus of Nazareth. "Anyone who has seen me," Jesus said, "has seen the Father" (John 14:9).

John's statement compels the conclusion that the God who is One in substance or essence has a Son who is God the One and Only. His place is at His Father's right hand (Matt. 22:44). This Creator and Sustainer of the universe came into the world voluntarily to reconcile God and man. The invisible God who is Spirit became visible in Jesus Christ God's Son, but without a sinful nature. The only begotten of the Father, the "one and only," is the pure essence of the Father. In His visit to this earth, this Messiah showed grace at its best on His cross, where He did humankind the ultimate favor of dying in our place. "While we were yet sinners, Christ died for us" (Rom. 5:8). The result is our sins are forgiven when we repent and accept His death as our substitute.

It is this Son who became incarnate as Jesus the Messiah, the Christ (the anointed one). In doing so He unveiled a new revelation of the God of Abraham as *the heavenly Father*. A key element of Jesus' job description was to make His Father known. Out of this understanding springs the Christian concept of the family in which God is our Father and Jesus is our elder brother. All believers come into this family by Jesus Christ through adoption, with the full rights of sons, including being joint heirs with Christ (John 1:12; Rom. 8:17, 23, 24; Gal. 3:26; Mark 3:35; Matt. 28:10; Eph. 1:5; Heb. 2:11, 12, 17; 1 John 3:1, 2). This is best understood as a legal transaction which grants the person being adopted all the rights of a natural born son in his new family. In the eyes of the law, he is a new person in the new family so that all debts and obligations, as well as privileges, associated with the old family are abolished and treated as if they never existed. The past is expunged from the record and everything is new again.

## ROMAN PLURALISM

Ancient Rome was dominated by polytheism. The Roman method of handling its diversity of gods was to erect a pantheon in the city of Rome and place the gods of first the republic and then the empire in it. The pantheon embodied Rome's version of religious pluralism.

The gospel of Jesus Christ, being monotheistic, presented Jesus to people as "the one and only." This meant Rome interpreted Christians as atheistic because the gospel did not affirm this ancient pluralism and embrace polytheism.

Today, Christians are not viewed as atheistic, but they are cursed for being *dogmatic*!

Instead of the gospel ever gaining a place in the house of the gods of Rome, the good news that is Jesus Christ ultimately shut down the pantheon! Then, in 609 A.D., the old Pantheon building was consecrated as a Christian church dedicated to the memory of all the Christian martyrs.

The Pantheon remains a place of Christian worship even today.

## FOUR CONFESSIONS OF JESUS AS THE SON OF GOD
### John 1:19-51

The Apostle John next proceeds to tell the story of the first four people in the Lord's ministry to recognize Jesus as the Son of God. In doing so he places the primary focus on John the Baptist. Each of the four was drawn to Jesus by the Holy Spirit through the agency of a different kind of motivating influence:

1. John the Baptist — divine revelation by the Holy Spirit.
2. Andrew — a recommendation from John the Baptist.
3. Philip — a direct call from Jesus.
4. Nathanael — prophecy.

## John the Baptist

**19 Now this was John's testimony when the Jews of Jerusalem sent priests and Levites to ask him who he was. ²⁰ He did not fail to confess, but confessed freely, "I am not the Christ." ²¹ They asked him, "Then who are you? Are you Elijah?" He said, "I am not." "Are you the Prophet?" He answered, "No." ²² Finally they said, "Who are you? Give us an answer to take back to those who sent us. What do you say about yourself?"**

The Apostle John here frames the identity of John the Baptist, and by implication, of the Messiah soon to be revealed. When the Jewish leaders asked John if he was the Messiah, the Baptizer "denied it flatly" (v. 20 TLB). Neither was he Elijah or one of the prophets. An important factor in knowing who you are is knowing who you are not. John knew he was not Israel's Messiah. This helped him stay focused on his own mission in life. If Jesus had not had a forerunner, His redemptive work would have been much harder to achieve (Isa. 40:3).

**23 John replied in the words of Isaiah the prophet, "I am the voice of one calling in the desert, 'Make straight the way for the Lord.'"**

John was the trailblazer for the Messiah; the voice. Some 800 years earlier Isaiah foretold a prophet would one day call from the wilderness, "prepare the way for the LORD [Jehovah]" and "make straight in the wilderness a highway for our *God* [*Elohim*]" (Isa. 40:3). The Baptizer had the confidence, birthed by the Holy Spirit, to link his own ministry directly to this prophecy. He made the bold affirmation that the Messiah who was standing among them (v. 26) was indeed God. Jesus is specifically identified by Isaiah as "the LORD" (Jehovah, the "I am") and "our God" (*Elohim*—the supreme God). Isaiah's prophecy could not be clearer. He foretold the voice coming from the wilderness would be preparing the way for the Messiah.

**Obviously, Jesus needs John the Baptists in every generation.**

The Apostle John demonstrates here the authority Jesus gave His disciples on resurrection night to open up the Old Testament scriptures (Luke 24:45). The great apostle asserted fearlessly that Jesus Christ is this living Word, God's only begotten Son who fulfilled Isaiah's prophecy. It continues to be evident John saw no contradiction with what he was teaching and the proclamation of Moses, Israel's great emancipator and lawgiver, that "the LORD is one" (Deut. 6:4).

**24 Now some Pharisees who had been sent ²⁵ questioned him, "Why then do you baptize if you are not the Christ, nor Elijah, nor the Prophet?" ²⁶ "I baptize with water," John replied, "but among you stands one you do not know. ²⁷ He is the one who comes after me, the thongs of whose sandals I am not worthy to untie." ²⁸ This all happened at Bethany on the other side of the Jordan, where John was baptizing.**

The overriding point of John the Baptist's ministry was to announce the Son of God's arrival. In the way the forerunner did it, he set the bar high, proclaiming Jesus of Nazareth as his superior. John said, "I am not even fit to be his slave" (v. 27 TLB). Part of the job of slaves was to tie and untie the master's shoes. To this day, John's standard is the measuring tape for evaluating every person who fulfills the ministry of apostle, prophet, evangelist, pastor or teacher.

**Are you lovingly announcing Jesus Christ as both the Son of God and Messiah to the people in your sphere of influence, doing it without regard for the push back you might receive?**

## John the Baptist's *Rhema* Word

"The word of God came to John son of Zechariah in the desert" and it was a *rhema*, a specific word of God to him (Luke 3:2). John the Baptist was a bold, prophetic voice crying out in the wilderness. One should not conclude, however, that the Spirit was speaking only to John, and no one else. For one example, Luke recorded in his account of the birth of Jesus how the Holy Spirit, about 30 years earlier, told Simeon he would not die until he had seen the Lord's Christ (Luke 2:25-32).

John's revelation, however, was distinctive from Simeon's prophecy. The Baptizer had the *rhema* from the Holy Spirit and the anointing to announce it, and the crowds flocked to him. Simeon praised God, but had no anointing to proclaim widely what he knew. To have announced it then would have been premature.

**What Simeon saw in the future of Mary's Baby gave him peace to face his own death. Knowing Jesus always gives peace to die by! What hope in our generation do you see for God's Son?**

John's message was simple: the Messiah, embodied in the Man from Nazareth, was already on the scene, and John was His spokesman.

No one else had the message from God. The Baptizer stepped up on a pulpit of sand dunes and made an easily measurable affirmation—repent and get ready, for the Messiah is here among us; the time is now!

John's courage was monumental. If he had been wrong, what a laughingstock he would have become! But John confidently kept on repeating it. Repentance was the one and only acceptable preparation for Messiah's pending appearance.

John sealed the message of repentance with water baptism. He perceived baptism as a public testimony of a changed heart. Baptism was John's symbol for death to the former sinful way of life, because a person cannot live under water. Then, as the water flowed down Jordan River, it represented sins being washed away. Coming up out of fresh, clean water was the sign of beginning a new life, free from the crushing load of the sins that were washed away. Using water as his sign, John lived out his commission from God to get as many people as he could ready for the Messiah.

The Baptizer's role required urgency. John grew up under the influence of Spirit-filled parents and had himself been filled with the Holy Spirit from his mother's womb (Luke 1:15, 41, 67). He knew by the Spirit the time for Messiah's appearance was at hand (John 1:26-34). This meant the Holy Spirit talked with John and gave him his knowledge about Messiah and his sense of timing. John also knew with great confidence that he had heard from God and was saying to the people what God had told him.

This is all the more significant considering Israel had not heard a prophetic voice for 400 years. John's Godly parents no doubt taught him as best they could how to listen to God and handle what he heard. John's parents were elderly when he was born. The Gospel accounts do not show how long John had the opportunity to learn from them. No doubt, John did not have his father or his mother when he launched his ministry. He *did* have the guidance of the Holy Spirit, and that was enough!

After four long centuries of prophetic silence, John's task was to go it alone and open the hearts of the people to comprehend God was visiting them again. His role was to stimulate Israel's appetite with the sense of immediacy that was in his pronouncements. He was "preparing the way" for none other than the Messiah. In this sense, John's ministry blazed the trail and reached its pinnacle when he baptized Jesus at Jordan River. It was there, in that historic stream, John courageously made the big announcement.

**29 The next day John saw Jesus coming toward him and said, "Look, the Lamb of God, who takes away the sin of the world! ³⁰ This is the one I meant when I said, 'A man who comes after me has surpassed me because he was before me.'"**

John the Baptist was granted the high honor of presenting Israel's Messiah, who has no rival as the "big thinker" of all time. The Lord thought in universal terms with a mission so huge it can only be described today as an idea worthy of God Himself: "Look, the Lamb of God who takes away the sin of the world." No emperor, king, prime minister or president since Jesus lived on earth has ever tried to frame a vision close to Jesus' job description. No one. Jesus lives in history in a league all His own! At the same time, Jesus loved people as individuals and never tired of caring for just one person.

**John's cry, "Look, the Lamb of God..." is a bold and prophetic vision statement. In a few simple words it summarizes the international mission and job description of Jesus Christ. Don't try to tell Jesus He is only one way among many to His Father!**

The Prophet Isaiah picked up this dimension of Messiah's vision in the second of his four servant songs:

Before I was born the LORD called me; from my birth he has made mention of my name ... . He said to me, "You are my servant, Israel, in whom I will display my splendor." ... And now the LORD says—he who formed me in the womb to be his servant to bring Jacob back to him and gather Israel to himself ... he says: "It is too small a thing for you to be my servant to restore the tribes of Jacob and bring back those of Israel I have kept. I will also make you a light for the Gentiles, that you may bring my salvation to the ends of the earth" (Isa. 49:1-6; the other three songs of the servant are Isa. 42:1-4; 50:4-9; 52:13–53:12).

When no one else in the world had this specific word from God about Messiah's job description and the anointing to express it, John the Baptist comprehended it. He went on to announce it with the exclamation: "Look! There is the Lamb of God who takes away the world's sin!" (John 1:29 TLB).

This expansive, universal language—"takes away the *world's sin*"—can only be understood in Messianic terms. This man from Galilee was the God-man. His life would be sacrificial for all people and His blood redemptive worldwide.

He would forgive sins and provide the cure for the sin problem itself. His antidote would go to the root of the sin problem. He would "take away the *sin*" that yields individual acts of *sins*. The gospel solution really does dig to the bottom of the root of sin in the human heart and then uproots it. All who come to Jesus in repentance are changed from the inside out, removing this natural tendency to rebel against God in the heart of all who repent.

John surely would have known Isaiah's prophecy about the suffering Messiah and could have been thinking of what Isaiah wrote when He baptized Jesus: "He was oppressed and afflicted, yet he did not open his mouth; he was led like a lamb to the slaughter, and as a sheep before her shearers is silent, so he did not open his mouth" (Isa. 53:7). This Lamb, announced by John the Baptist, received His appointment from God. It made His sacrifice one-of-a-kind (Heb. 3:2; 5:5, 6).

In the tabernacle and later in the temple, every morning and every evening "at twilight" according to Jewish law, a lamb had to be offered (Num. 28:1-8). It was required day after day after day, for the 1,500 years from Moses to Christ. In addition, once yearly the High Priest at the Feast of Passover was responsible to go into the Holy of Holies to make sacrifice for his own sins and the sins of the people. He commemorated as he did so Israel's escape from Egypt. All this blood communicated the seriousness of the curse of sin. The great need called for continually pouring out more blood and the life that went with it, because mankind's rebellion against God has continued generation after generation. "Without the shedding of blood, there is no forgiveness of sins" (Heb. 9:22 TLB).

This river of blood stirred a longing in the hearts of faith-guided sons of Abraham for the day when a perfect sacrifice would be offered to end all sacrifices (Heb. 7:27; 8:8; 9:12-15; 12:24; see also Amos 5:21; Jer. 31:31-34).

> **A trail of blood from the veins of a million precious, little lambs soaked the road that ended at Calvary (see Exod. 12:4, 5; 29:38, 39; Heb. 9:12).**

Each of the lambs slain on the dyed-red road to Golgotha was chosen by men. Only Jesus the Messiah is described in Holy Writ as the "Lamb of *God*." Jesus volunteered for this specific role before the foundation of the world (1 Pet. 1:19, 20; Rev. 13:8). God's plan was for Jesus' sacrifice to be sufficient not only for Israel, but for the root of sin in all people.

The Apostle John, who lived into his 90s, penned the Revelation in his golden years. In John's first scene of heaven he saw "a Lamb, looking as if it had been slain, standing in the center of the throne" (5:6). Jesus is this glorified Lamb of God, and He will carry for all eternity the scars of His singular and unique, all-sufficient sacrifice. Those blemishes are His badges of triumph over the sin in *your life,* dear reader, and *mine* too.

So what about you? Does your life give testimony that you faithfully and consistently introduce Jesus to people as the "Lamb of God who takes away the sin of the world"? Is His sacrificial death at Golgotha the central theme of your witness?

> **Ah! The story of the cross of Jesus begs for the prominent place in every *sermon*—in *every* sermon. In fact, a Bible lesson is but a pep talk without it!**

Luke concluded his survey of the ministry of the Baptizer, saying, "With many other words John exhorted the people and preached the good news to them" (Luke 3:18).

John was faithful in preparing the way for Messiah, possessing as he did a broad understanding of the gospel. His life challenges all ministers to preach and teach focused on the sacrificial death of Jesus as the Lamb of God, even as they expound the wide range of gospel themes.

> **31 "I myself did not know him, but the reason I came baptizing with water was that he might be revealed to Israel." 32 Then John gave this testimony: "I saw the Spirit come down from heaven as a dove and remain on him. 33 I would not have known him, except that the one who sent me to baptize with water told me, 'The man on whom you see the Spirit come down and remain is he who will baptize with the Holy Spirit.' 34 I have seen and I testify that this is the Son of God."**

John the Baptist knew God speaks to people and developed a marvelous capacity to listen for the voice of God (1 Sam. 3:9). In fact, the revelation he enjoyed presumes these ongoing conversations. This shows up in John's emphatic statement about how he obtained the information. "The one who sent me," he said, explained to him what was about to happen.

The Apostle John did not record the actual story of the Lord's baptism in Jordan River, when the Father spoke from heaven and the Spirit descended on Jesus in the form of a dove. Matthew, Mark and Luke told this part of the narrative (Matt. 3:13-17; Mark 1:9-11; Luke 3:21, 22). John did, however, record the testimony of the forerunner. His account includes what the Holy Spirit told the Baptizer in advance, what John the Baptist saw at the baptism of Jesus, and how the Baptizer began to prophesy fearlessly after the grand occasion. John also knew what he heard and saw was based in Old Testament prophecy. Isaiah foretold it in the first of his Songs of the Servant: "Here is my servant, whom I uphold, my chosen one in whom I delight; I will put my Spirit on him." The result of that anointing by the Holy Spirit would be that "he will bring justice to the nations" (Isa. 42:1).

As a firsthand witness to these events, the Baptizer held to a New Testament understanding of the plurality of the God who is indivisibly One. He was emphatic, saying, "I have seen and I testify that this is the Son of God" (John 1:34). Clearly, John did not limit himself to the definitions of the religious establishment in Jerusalem. He heard in person the voice of the Father, saw the Spirit come down in the form of a dove, and witnessed the Son of God in the water. This revelation of the Father, Son and Holy Spirit has come to be recognized as a clear affirmation of the Trinitarian personhood of the God who is One in essence (Matt. 3:17; Mark 1:11; Luke 3:22).

The revelation of the gospel to John was broad. This shows up in his understanding of the work of the Holy Spirit. It was the Spirit, in fact, who told John how to recognize the Messiah. His testimony shows the Spirit communicated with John conversationally: "The man on whom you see the Spirit come down and remain is he." In the absence of this revelation, John said, he would not have recognized Jesus.

John witnessed exactly what he was told to expect. "The Spirit [came] down from heaven as a dove and [remained] on [Jesus]." The baptizer was confident of the revelation from God and proclaimed, "I have seen and I testify that this is the Son of God."

Another strand of this story is Jesus' mother, Mary, and John's mother, Elizabeth, were relatives, perhaps cousins. This made John the Baptist and Jesus relatives too. With John growing up in the hill country of Judea and Jesus in Nazareth, it is possible they had never met (Luke 1:39; 2:39, 51; 4:16). In an agrarian culture like first-century Israel, a person could live his entire lifetime and never travel more than a mile or two from home. One is left to wonder if, after Jesus' baptism, they excitedly traded stories about their childhood. The person John announced was his relative. John the Baptist knew and had the courage to say his relative was Israel's Messiah, God Himself!

Jordan River was Jesus' inauguration as the God-man who came into the world as Israel's Messiah and the world's Savior. When the Holy Spirit came on Jesus, He launched His ministry. John the Baptist baptized with water unto repentance. The anointing of the Holy Spirit on Jesus foreshadowed Jesus' intent to baptize all of His followers with the same Holy Spirit who empowered His own life.

John's earliest memories included awareness of the Holy Spirit in his life (Luke 1:15). It is reasonable to believe he talked to the Holy Spirit from childhood, and the Spirit to him. Then, as a young man, the word of the Lord came to him, appointing him Messiah's forerunner.

Many in the body of Christ have yet to discover the great power of the Holy Spirit to reveal Jesus to people. One thing is for sure: as long as the Holy Spirit is actively engaged and working in the earth, He will present Jesus as the "one and only," and never one among many.

**Jesus, as the first fruits of Spirit-filled men, is still begging for His message to be heard, never forgotten or watered down. This pluralistic and politically correct generation must be confronted directly, in the love and authority of Jesus' name.**

### Andrew

**35 The next day John was there again with two of his disciples. ³⁶ When he saw Jesus passing by, he said, "Look, the Lamb of God!"**

Pastors and church leaders today introduce Jesus in a myriad of ways: as a great teacher, as one who has high moral values, as the Lord who cares for social needs. The list is long. John the Baptist introduced Jesus with a singular and exclamatory focus: "Look, the Lamb of God!" Two of the Baptizer's disciples, Andrew and John, caught the message. This joyful affirmation went to the heart of Jesus' mission as the atoning sacrifice for the sins of all people. It continues to do so to this day.

The Lord must feel crucified afresh and put to open shame when so many pulpits present him as something less than the Son of God. Some ignore altogether His atoning sacrifice (Heb. 6:6). Jesus Himself expressed it: "'And I, if I be lifted up from the earth, will draw all men unto me.' This he said, signifying what death he should die" (John 12:32, 33 KJV).

The writer of Hebrews gives a stern warning about the kind of falling away that diminishes the Lord's sacrifice (6:4-8). He used a word picture of a barren field: "[L]and that produces thorns and thistles is worthless and is in danger of being cursed. In the end it will be burned" (v. 8). The great goal of all apostolic ministry is to tell compellingly the story of Jesus' crucifixion and resurrection, sharing it over and over and over, without ever tiring of telling it.

**If Jesus' gripping story is told passionately—"Look, the Lamb of God!"—the Holy Spirit will continue to draw people to God, just as He attracted Andrew and John.**

**37 When the two disciples heard him say this, they followed Jesus. ³⁸ Turning around, Jesus saw them following and asked, "What do you want?" They said, "Rabbi" (which means "Teacher"), "where are you staying?"**

When Jesus addressed them, Andrew and John knew exactly what they wanted, and it was implied in their question, "Where are you staying?" Their desire was to switch their loyalty from John the Baptist to Jesus and be with Him, becoming His disciples. John followed Jesus along with Andrew, and both went on to become the Lord's apostles. John earned a place in the Lord's inner circle with Peter and James. In his ministry years, John wrote five New Testament books: the Gospel of John, three letters carrying his name, and the Revelation.

It deserves to be restated, John the Baptist's introduction, "Look, the Lamb of God," was so compelling it motivated Andrew and John to end their relationship with him and follow Jesus. To his credit, the Baptizer was willing for them to switch their loyalty to Jesus. The Lord is always attractive to people when He is presented from a heart full of deep appreciation for His atoning sacrifice as the Lamb of God.

**39 "Come," he replied, "and you will see." So they went and saw where he was staying, and spent that day with him. It was about the tenth hour.**

To this day when people are introduced to Jesus—like John the Baptist introduced Andrew and John—and they respond with a sincere and hungry heart, the Lord will receive them and make them His disciples.

On one occasion, James and John, these sons of thunder, wanted to call down fire from heaven to consume some Samaritans who did not welcome the Lord. "But Jesus rebuked them" (Luke 9:54, 55). In the years following, God's grace did its work in John's heart and he ended his ministry recognized as the apostle of love. (See John's three general epistles, where the character change is vivid; e.g., I John 4:7-12.)

**40 Andrew, Simon Peter's brother, was one of the two who heard what John had said and who had followed Jesus.**

John the Baptist discovered Jesus' identity by *revelation*. Andrew's choice resulted from the *testimony* of John the Baptist. John, too, followed Jesus on the Baptizer's recommendation.

**41 The first thing Andrew did was find his brother Simon and tell him, "We have found the Messiah" (that is, the Christ). ⁴² And he brought him to Jesus. Jesus looked at him and said, "You are Simon son of John. You will be called Cephas" (which, when translated, is Peter).**

"The first thing" for Andrew was to reach out to his brother, best known as Simon Peter. John's wording abounds with Andrew's enthusiasm, which is characteristic of new believers' excitement: "We have found the Messiah!" How important that all followers of Jesus retain their fervor and first love as they grow in Christ (Rev. 2:4)!

Jesus expressed a two-fold prophecy to Peter. Jesus correctly identified his name and foretold the change in character to result from the new name Jesus gave him: Cephas, the rock.

John could have easily made the claim he was the first to confess Jesus as Messiah, but he did not. John's account does not show Peter "bought in" immediately either, affirming Jesus' deity. Andrew certainly did, but we are not told Peter did. Neither does John confess that he affirmed Jesus up front as the Son of God.

### Philip and Nathanael
**43 The next day Jesus decided to leave for Galilee. Finding Philip, he said to him, "Follow me."**

No invitation equals one extended by Jesus Christ!

The Apostle John used the wording "Finding Philip," which indicates Jesus gave time to seeking Philip; Jesus searched until He found him. As the Son of Man, Jesus lived with the limitations of time and space, as do all of us. Finding Philip was not automatic; seeking him out was required. When the Lord located him in Bethsaida, just north of the Sea of Galilee, He extended the invitation, "Follow me." To his eternal credit, Philip accepted Jesus' invitation.

Do you regularly receive counsel and direction from the Holy Spirit?

### RECEIVING GUIDANCE

"Pastor, could I talk to you for a minute?"

Her voice was low; she wasn't sure of herself. She looked to be in her early 20s, a girl I'd never seen at our church before.

It was my first year as senior pastor at Full Gospel Tabernacle in downtown Fresno, California. I was greeting people after the Wednesday night Bible study.

"What can I do for you?"

"Would you please talk with my husband? He moved out from our home and into an apartment with two women. I don't know what to do."

"Is he a Christian?"

"He's the one who led me to a relationship with Christ."

"I'll be glad to talk with him. How can I get in touch with him?"

"That's the problem. I can't reach him. If he wants to talk, he calls me."

There was little I could do. I asked her to have him call me if he talked with her again.

I remember the look of despair in her eyes as she walked away.

Friday was my day off. I got up early. We were landscaping our front yard, and I wanted it finished. By late morning the end was in sight. It was hot. I was muddy, aching, and thoroughly tired of the whole project. To add to my woes, I ran out of ornamental plants. I drove to the store for more.

The first store had the right kind, but the price had gone up. A store a mile down the road had them, and the price was right. I loaded my cart and headed to the checkout.

As I waited in line, I glanced at the cashier's nametag. It looked familiar. As he began to ring up the plants, I motioned to his nametag.

"Is that your name?" (Dumb question, but I wanted to be sure.)

He looked at me blankly, going on full *village idiot* alert. "Yes."

"Are you married to _____?" and I named the woman who had talked with me on Wednesday night.

He looked wary. "Yes?"

I drew myself up to my full 6 feet, 5 inches—unshaven, messy, sweaty, and muddy. I gave him my happiest smile.

"God has sent me here to talk to you about your marriage!"

Some 300,000 people lived in the Fresno area then. Out of all of them, the first person I had talked to—other than family and staff—since Wednesday night was this husband.

In a lifetime of seeking to be led by the Lord, that is the most powerful example I have experienced. I had heard many stories of people led by the Spirit to go to unusual places or to say unusual things. I always wondered what that would be like. At times I've really needed guidance and have prayed earnestly for it. God has helped me. But my unerring, no-wasted-step trip to that husband remains my most remarkable example. Not only was I not trying to be led, I wasn't conscious of God's leading. I just wanted the yard finished.

C. David Gable, "He Leadeth Me," *Pentecostal Evangel* (5-30-10), p. 15.

**44 Philip, like Andrew and Peter, was from the town of Bethsaida. 45 Philip found Nathanael and told him, "We have found the one Moses wrote about in the Law, and about whom the prophets also wrote—Jesus of Nazareth, the son of Joseph." 46 "Nazareth! Can anything good come from there?" Nathanael asked. "Come and see," said Philip.**

Three of Jesus' disciples came from the fishing town of Bethsaida: Philip, Andrew and Peter. Philip was the third of the four people in this chapter to confess Jesus as the Messiah, expressing it in his witness to Nathanael. Philip saying, "We have found the one Moses wrote about in the Law, and about whom the prophets also wrote" is an affirmation of Jesus as the Christ. This is the same confession Andrew made.

The exchange between Philip and Nathanael gives insight into Nathanael's personality. He was witty, for example, and used sarcasm to express his wit: "Nazareth! Can anything good come from there?"

**47 When Jesus saw Nathanael approaching, he said of him, "Here is a true Israelite, in whom there is nothing false." 48 "How do you know me?" Nathanael asked. Jesus answered, "I saw you while you were still under the fig tree before Philip called you." 49 Then Nathanael declared, "Rabbi, you are the Son of God; you are the King of Israel."**

Nathanael's confession occurred because of Jesus' amazing accuracy in speaking prophecy. One aspect of prophetic ministry is how prophets obtain specific information about the past and/or future of people's lives. They possess facts they could know only if disclosed by the Spirit of God. This gift makes prophecy a powerful tool for motivating people to follow Jesus. Jesus Himself, the greatest prophet who has ever lived, used prophecy to win people. Nathanael's story is a case in point.

Jesus accurately affirmed Nathanael's identity and his character: "A true Israelite in whom there is nothing false." The Greek word here for *false* carries the idea of *deceit* or *subtilty*. With this statement, Jesus gave Nathanael a huge compliment. Nathanael did not have a heart like his forefather Jacob, who was highly skilled in the practice of deceit. In fact, *Jacob* means *deceiver*. But Jacob wrestled all night with the Angel of the Lord at the brook, Jabbok, and prevailed. Right there, his character changed. The transformation was expressed in the Angel's gift to him of a new name. He became *Israel*, meaning *a prince with God* (see Gen. 32). Nathanael had the character of his forefather, the patriarch Israel. Jesus knew this when He gave Nathanael the compliment, and its significance went to the core of Nathanael's identity. He must have thought, "Wow! This man really does know me!"

Jesus also prophetically gave Nathanael the facts about his physical circumstances when Philip talked to him: "I saw you while you were under the fig tree before Philip called you."

*"I saw you"*—How could Jesus have "seen" Nathanael if He, as Mary's Baby and the Son of Man, were not also the Son of God who was guided by the Holy Spirit? (See Ps. 33:13-15.)

*"You were under"*—Nathanael was not standing near, or beside, or even some distance away from the tree.

*"the fig tree"*—not an olive tree, for example.

*"[B]efore Philip called you"*—This statement nailed down the exact time. The prophecy motivated Nathanael to respond, "Sir, you *are* the Son of God— the King of Israel!" (John 1:49 TLB). This prophecy was so factually specific it motivated Nathanael to put His trust in Jesus on the spot.

**If Jesus had said, "I saw you under a sycamore tree," Nathanael would have rejected Him on the spot. But Jesus' prophecies are always accurate.**

**Interestingly, Jesus did not rebuke Nathanael for his questions, but commended him as a man with no malice in his honest desire to learn from Jesus.**

**50 Jesus said, "You believe because I told you I saw you under the fig tree. You shall see greater things than that." ⁵¹ He then added, "I tell you the truth, you shall see heaven open, and the angels of God ascending and descending on the Son of Man."**

Nathanael would have understood instinctively the Lord's comment about "angels of God ascending and descending." It is the story of Jacob's dream when he fled from his brother. Esau wanted to kill Jacob after he deceived Esau and stole his birthright. When Jacob escaped to the north and reached the area he gave the name Bethel, he saw in a dream that night a ladder extending up to heaven. Angels were ascending and descending on the ladder (Gen. 28:12-16). Nathanael no doubt also understood when Jesus used the name "Son of Man" to speak about Himself that He was claiming to be Deity.

The difference between what Jacob dreamed and what Jesus said to Nathanael is noteworthy. The Lord expressed the "Son of Man" *is* the ladder. Jesus is the Messiah, the door, the way and the path. The angels of God ascend and descend "on the Son of Man." He is the one-and-only road reaching all the way up to God's throne.

**Prophecy was strikingly powerful in the ministry of the Lord, and anticipated this ability would become a gift of the Spirit in the Lord's church (Eph. 4:11). Prophecy is such a complement to evangelism, but it is not a guarantee people will confess Jesus as the Son of God.**

## SEVEN MIRACLES, SEVEN DISCOURSES, AND SEVEN "I AM" STATEMENTS

The Apostle John builds the case for Jesus as the Son of God around seven of the Lord's Deity proving miracles, the seven discourses associated with the miracles, and seven "I AM" statements. Each is powerful in bringing people to faith in Christ.

The seven miracles are:
1. Turning water into wine at the wedding in Cana of Galilee (John 2:1-12).
2. Healing the nobleman's son (John 4:46-53).
3. Healing the man at the Pool of Bethesda (John 5:1-9).
4. Feeding the 5,000 (John 6:4-13).
5. Walking on water (John 6:16-21).
6. Healing the man born blind (John 9:1-12).
7. Raising Lazarus from the dead (John 11:30-53).

The miracles of Jesus throughout salvation history have always opened people's hearts to come to the Lord in repentance as well as receive His teachings.
Seven discourses are also included in John 1-11:
1. The exchange during this first Passover to Jerusalem after the Lord's baptism in Jordan River. It was the first of many confrontations between the leadership operating the temple system and Jesus (John 2:12-22).
2. The new birth and Nicodemus (John 3:1-21).
3. The new birth illustrated: The woman at Jacob's well (John 4:1-42).
4. The discourse following Jesus' healing the man at the Pool of Bethesda (John 5:16-47).
5. Jesus presents Himself as the Bread of Life (John 6:22-71).
6. The discourses at the Feast of Tabernacles (John 7:14–10:42).
7. The story of the death and resurrection of Lazarus (John 11:1-57).

The seven "I AM" statements begin in Chapter 6, and the first five of the seven will follow in Book Two:
1. I am the bread of life (John 6:35).
2. I am the light of the world (John 8:12).
3. I am the gate (John 10:9).
4. I am the Good Shepherd (John 10:11).
5. I am the Resurrection and the Life (John 11:25, 26).
6. I am the Way, the Truth, and the Life (John 14:6).
7. I am the Vine (John 15:5).

The astounding miracle at the wedding in Cana of Galilee (recorded only by John) is the first of the seven miracles and follows in Chapter 2. This chapter will also begin to tell the story of Jesus' first visit of His active ministry to Jerusalem for a Passover Feast.
We now turn our attention to the first of the seven miracles.

# CHAPTER 2

## JESUS: THE SON OF MAN
### The Wedding at Cana of Galilee

*Chapter 2 presents the Son of God in His true humanity, on the scene and reporting for duty. This is demonstrated in His first miracle at the wedding in Cana of Galilee. John also tells the story of Jesus' trip to Jerusalem in this chapter. It was His initial temple visit after His inauguration as Messiah at His Jordan River baptism, and it includes the first of Jesus' seven discourses.*

## THE FIRST CHRISTIAN WEDDING
### John 2:1-11

**1 On the third day a wedding took place at Cana in Galilee. Jesus' mother was there, 2 and Jesus and his disciples had also been invited to the wedding.**

The best decision this couple ever made was to invite Jesus to their wedding. These young adults obviously did not comprehend just how prestigious a guest they had invited. In addition, they had no way to know their marriage was about to become the symbol for marriage in the Christian era. The presence of Jesus of Nazareth made it so.

It is possible these young people did not come from wealthy families and were unable to plan a large wedding with hundreds of guests. Their modest means and humble families did not hinder Jesus from attending their wedding and bringing His disciples.

Today this couple is honored around the world, and Cana of Galilee, in the ancient tribe of Asher, is a village with enduring, worldwide fame.

### LONGER WITHOUT HER!

Mary Francis Meyers died today, a great woman in our church. Her husband Ken died two or three years ago.

I'll never forget being in the Fireside Room when they celebrated their fiftieth wedding anniversary. I said, "Ken, fifty years is a long time."

He immediately responded, "Not nearly as long as it would have been without her."

*Robert L. Russell, "God's Design for Marriage," Preaching Today, Tape No. 166. Cited in PreachingToday.Com.*

Marriage is God's idea; He birthed the institution, making the family the basic building block of society. The Lord who was present at Cana also had been present at history's first wedding in the Garden of Eden.

It is important to study the life of Jesus—both for what He said and for what He did. His presence at this Jewish wedding made its own statement about what the Lord considered important. The Messiah's first miracle there extended the model of the wedding in the Garden of Eden to the whole of the Christian era.

Moses interpreted the first wedding in Eden saying, "A man will leave his father and mother and be united to his wife and they will become one flesh" (Gen. 2:24). This language is so focused, in fact, that any other model of a "wedding" cannot carry the blessing of "Christian." Not only is God the Father the originator of marriage; He is also its protector.

> **Oh! That every bride and groom today would consciously and prayerfully invite Jesus to their wedding, as well as seek His aid in making their marriage successful.**

## Jesus as the First Apostle
**3 When the wine was gone, Jesus' mother said to him, "They have no more wine."**

Running out of wine could suggest the limited financial means of this young man and his family. It would have been embarrassing to them and offensive to their guests. This miracle also helped to open the door to see the apostolic nature of the work of Jesus. In this case, His apostolic function was to help this young couple, and in doing so, set the example for what would become the place of the wedding in the Lord's church that He would birth not many months down the road.

This wedding is only one illustration of how Jesus' life mirrored the ministry of apostle par excellence, creating new sunrises and launching new beginnings. The totality of Jesus' incarnate life, in fact, was given to changing millennia-old paradigms, blazing new trails, and introducing new ways of thinking. The writer of Hebrews expressed it, "[H]oly brothers who share in the heavenly calling, fix your thoughts on Jesus, the apostle and high priest whom we confess" (Heb. 3:1).

Jesus is the first apostle of the gospel era. An apostle is a person who is sent on a mission. As the Son of God, Jesus was commissioned by His Father to take away the sin of the world. Jesus was also the High Priest of the New Covenant. His blueprint for achieving His priestly ministry was to offer Himself as the Lamb of God in a sacrifice to redeem all people who repent and believe the gospel.

After the crucifixion and resurrection of Jesus, the ministry of the Lord's disciples transitioned into sent ones, or apostles. Their job description was to fulfill Jesus' Great Commission (Matt. 28:16-20). They first waited in the Upper Room until they were filled with the Holy Spirit. Then, in the power of the Spirit, they launched a new organism in salvation history known as the church. The Day of Pentecost was its birthday.

Apostles are:

...selected by God,

...commissioned and empowered by the Holy Spirit to make happen a vision in the heart of God that in some significant way is new to a culture, and then

... equipped with the spiritual gifts to bring the vision to fruition.

## Sanctifying Marriage

Marriage and the family are very important to God. Jesus' presence at this Jewish wedding guaranteed marriage between a man and a woman would have the highest importance in the New Covenant. Jesus' attendance and the miracle He graciously extended to this couple guaranteed marriage would be a cornerstone value in the church Jesus was soon to launch. This wedding also modeled that the divine ideal is for children to be reared by a father and a mother.

John further demonstrated the special significance of weddings with the timeline of this wedding in Jesus' ministry. Jesus actually set apart the institution of marriage before the Lord's encounter with Nicodemus that introduced the New Birth (Chapter 3).

Jesus, the "apostle ... of our profession" set the bar high, performing His first miracle not at a sick bed, but at a wedding celebration (Heb. 3:1 KJV). The institution of marriage is foundational in building Godly homes, and God-fearing families develop Biblically based cultures. As goes the family, so goes the nation.

Everywhere the gospel has gone worldwide, no matter how pagan the culture, the example Jesus set at Cana of Galilee has exalted monogamous marriage as the divine plan: one man for one woman until death parts them.

Doing this also shows the Lord's genius in action. Marriage as a lifetime covenant requires commitment and truthfulness in the ups and downs of life. In fact, commitment sustains marriages; feelings of love can come and go, and they must always be secondary to commitment. This faithfulness builds into a culture the fidelity that makes for a strong nation. Any society is weak that does not have fidelity as a basic building block of fathers and mothers in marriage.

## Mothers: Moving the Heart of God
**4 "Dear woman, why do you involve me?" Jesus replied. "My time has not yet come."**

This kind of phrase was not out of the ordinary in the culture, and it would not have come through to Mary as harsh. Jesus' answer to His mother was not spoken in disrespect, but most probably with a twinkle in His eyes that Mary understood fully. A big, knowing smile may have broken on her face as she interpreted His response and watched Him move into action.

Was Jesus motivated by this appeal from His mother? Of course He was! Since this wedding, millions of mothers have moved the heart of God with their petitions. Acknowledging this, however, does not endorse the teaching of Mariolatry (worship of Mary). Mary's position as Jesus' mother did not give her superior intercessory powers that justify veneration of Mary as an object of worship.

Believers in Christ in every generation should pray directly to Jesus and in His name, without appealing to Mary with pressing needs. We do not plead with Mary to ask Jesus on our behalf; instead, we pray to Jesus Himself (John 14:14; 15:7; 16:23).

> **Jesus listens just as quickly today to the sincere cry of the least of His followers as He did to His own mother! (See John 14:13, 14; Rom. 5:2; Eph. 2:18; Heb. 4:16.)**

Jesus' response to His mother at the wedding illustrated the classic graciousness that characterized His holy life. From the beginning of His ministry, He delighted to give gifts to people. The miracle at Cana shows Jesus was so full of grace, He did gracious things when the beneficiaries did not realize their need, had not sought His help, and did not know He could help.

A true follower of Jesus will have a gracious heart like Him. How appropriate to look for needs and fill them. To follow the example of Jesus is to have a heart to serve the needs of people, even when they do not know to ask. The good news of the gospel shows any believer has direct access to Jesus.

### 5 His mother said to the servants, "Do whatever he tells you."

This was wisdom then and it remains wisdom today: "Whatever he says to you, do it" (NKJV).

**6 Nearby stood six stone water jars, the kind used by the Jews for ceremonial washing, each holding from twenty to thirty gallons. 7 Jesus said to the servants, "Fill the jars with water"; so they filled them to the brim. 8 Then he told them, "Now draw some out and take it to the master of the banquet." They did so, 9 and the master of the banquet**

**tasted the water that had been turned into wine. He did not realize where it had come from, though the servants who had drawn the water knew. Then he called the bridegroom aside and said, ¹⁰ "Everyone brings out the choice wine first and then the cheaper wine after the guests have had too much to drink; but you have saved the best till now."**

Ceremonial washing was intended to demonstrate the need for a clean heart. Such cleansing can easily devolve into a cold ritual, however, when done out of habit and without feeling. Many Jews, for example, could splash a little water and move on, giving little attention, if any, to why this ceremonial cleansing was in the Law (John 3:25; Mark 7:3; Ps. 26:6).

The servants did as Jesus instructed. The result was the best wine and more than enough—perhaps 150 gallons of the finest wine! (2:6 GW). How important to obey the Lord implicitly!

### A New Glory
**11 This, the first of his miraculous signs, Jesus performed at Cana in Galilee. He thus revealed his glory, and his disciples put their faith in him.**

In His incarnation, the Lord surrendered to His Father and to the Holy Spirit the heavenly glory He had enjoyed in the Trinity from eternity (Phil. 2:4-13). This miracle at the wedding in Cana, however, opened up a whole new dimension of awe that rightly belonged to Israel's Messiah. Jesus showed Himself that day as sensitive, caring and generous as He created a blessing to meet the newlyweds' need. The gospel has gone around the world in the centuries since then. From this story people everywhere have perceived Jesus' affirmation of the institution of marriage and the family. In addition, this story demonstrates Jesus' loving care for young couples just starting their lives together.

This story also shows Jesus' power to create. For water to become wine in an instant required a huge creative miracle. When a believer absorbs its magnitude, he can also begin to picture Jesus as the creator who spoke all life forms into being, including creating Adam and Eve, the father and mother of the human family.

**This young couple needed help, and Jesus gave them the best wine as a creative gift without their even asking. Religious pluralism holds Jesus is only one path to God among many. Yet, not a single founder of the world's religions has ever been even a distant rival to Jesus' creative authority and ability.**

The Messiah, who gave this young couple the gift of a lifetime in a matter of seconds, is in a league all by Himself. How much wiser to recognize and admit Jesus is the Son of God and "the one and only." The word of this awesome Lord is final for all matters of creation, as well as for faith and practice!

## A Miraculous Wedding Present

In beautiful fashion, by showing love to this couple, Jesus demonstrated His great love for all young adults. Yes, when Jesus' story is shared faithfully and creatively, young men and women will perceive Jesus is very concerned about them and is well able and willing to add blessing to the homes and families they build.

Jesus graciously honored this couple with what they could not provide themselves, and He did it requiring nothing in return. The servants and Jesus' disciples knew immediately what had happened, although the bridegroom did not. One can imagine the awe on their faces when they witnessed such creative power. The response of the master of the banquet about saving the best wine until last must have left the bridegroom wondering what he was talking about—until they both learned what had taken place.

No doubt the master of the banquet quickly realized who was the Master of the banquet!

Many people look at the miracles of Jesus and try to offer rational explanations for how they could have happened. Others deny them out of hand, dismissing them as impossible.

## TURNING WINE BACK INTO WATER

"C.S. Lewis may have become the chief Christian tutor to the twentieth century because he refused the perennial temptation to turn the wine back into water!"

*Ralph C. Wood, in a review of Lewis biographies in "Books & Religion" (Spring 1991), Christianity Today, Vol. 35, no. 9. Cited in PreachingToday.com.*

Rational thinking, however, falls flat at Cana of Galilee. It takes years and meticulous, diligent work to develop a vineyard to the point it is ready to produce a harvest of mouthwatering grapes. Then a husbandman works a whole growing season caring for the vineyard and protecting it from the little foxes that can so easily spoil the vines (Song of Sol. 2:15). Without this abundant attention, a vineyard will not grow and ripen into fruit. The grapes also had to be picked, crushed and filtered, and allowed the months, even years needed to age into choice wine.

Jesus understood the predicament of these young people before they did, and He chose to bless them. The Messiah attending their wedding spoke a creative

Word, and it superseded the cycle of seedtime and harvest. Jesus gave these young people a wedding gift they talked about the remainder of their lives. In doing so, the Son of God demonstrated He was Lord over time and seasons.

In seconds, pots full of water became jars full of the best aged wine! This miracle wedding present stands out because it showed God could do in a flash of time what took years to accomplish in the stages of a vineyard.

The miracle also glows in its manifold graciousness: Jesus was willing to do this for the young couple. The glory proceeding from such a miracle resulted in a new faith in Jesus that blossomed in His disciples. This great miracle demonstrated:

1.  Jesus' special care for a young couple who did not know they had a need.
2.  The sanctity of Christian marriage as the basic building block of society. While wedding customs differ from culture to culture, the union of one man and one woman becoming one flesh in a lifetime relationship—monogamous marriage—has become the Christian standard throughout the world.
3.  In the new order Jesus was beginning to launch, miracles would be a powerful tool as one of the gifts of the Spirit to bring people to faith in Christ.
4.  God's Son was on the scene—in their house, enjoying their wedding.

This miracle was a major indicator to Jesus' disciples that He was indeed the Son of God. At Cana of Galilee Jesus also made the big switch from acting out of John's testimony to making His own works His testimony. Faith in Jesus took a leap that day.

Jesus' miracle at Cana was also a demonstration of what was to come in the Lord's church. The Apostle Paul, for example, later identified *working of miracles* as a gift of the Spirit (1 Cor. 12:10, 28, 29).

---

**This couple was facing major embarrassment. Their need would not wait! Do you have a need that can't wait? Jesus is your answer too!**

---

After Jesus' crucifixion and resurrection, His disciples began to express a deep and abiding knowledge that God had come to man in Jesus Christ, and had chosen them as His disciples.

His glory at Cana was His marvelous ability to bless, extending agape love to a couple at their wedding feast. It goes without saying, they did not perceive their invitation to Jesus of Nazareth meant they would witness such a miracle.

## A Miracle of Agape Love

This miracle was all about *agape*, the love of God sparkling in the rich wine of grace. The couple at Cana of Galilee had done nothing to merit the blessing they received, yet Jesus gave them an astoundingly miraculous gift at their wedding, and He did it without asking, "Do they deserve it?" Once this young couple figured it all out, they surely never tired of telling it to their children and grandchildren. The miracle was of a magnitude only God, the maker of heaven and earth, could perform—create the finest wine from water, and do it in the few seconds of His spoken word. The phenomenon was so out of the ordinary that people were forced to ask, "Who is this man?" and admit only God could perform such a miracle. John also adds it was "the first glimpse of his glory" (John 2:11 MSG).

Agape is the love of God that flows out of the rich storehouse of divine grace. It extends kindnesses to people and acts on their behalf as God understands their need. In doing so, agape:

1. Sets no pre-conditions.
2. Comes in unlimited supply (always more than enough to meet the need).
3. Is unrelenting. It will pursue a person until it hems him in and forces him to say "Yes" or "No" to the invitation of God (Ps. 139:4). Even if he says "NO!" this love will not relent. It will continue to pursue until God knows one's heart is hardened beyond any hope of repentance.

## Miracles Bring "the Presence" and Show the Glory

When the miracle occurred at Cana, the aura of heavenly *Sonlight*—the Shekinah presence, the anointing of the Spirit—entered the house. The word quickly spread as the guests began to learn what had happened. No doubt, some refused to believe the testimony of the servants even in the face of the evidence. Yet, it could not be denied something huge had taken place.

Yes, Jesus, being rich in grace, gave them a wedding present of the best wine so that the couple had some left over to sell as they began their lives together.

> **Some 150 gallons of fine wine do not all of a sudden appear out of nowhere. There had to be a cause, and it was Jesus. What a wedding present!**

Pastors and parents should never forget to teach how Jesus loves to attend weddings. But all too often, Jesus comes and stands over in a corner, deeply in love with us, but feeling sad, rejected, unwelcome and totally unrecognized. Jesus yearns for the invitation and can add untold blessing to newlyweds.

## OUR SECRET ADMIRER

How many times Jesus has positioned Himself right in the middle of our circumstances as our doting fan!

Many movies have been filmed around a plot in which an actress receives a dozen roses after her performance. The card is signed, "Secret Admirer." The tension of the plot lay in discovering the secret admirer.

Finally, he reveals himself, they go out for dinner, fall in love, get married, and in the good old days, live happily ever after.

From the beginning, people have been hungry to know, "Who is this 'Secret Admirer,' this God who made me?"

God revealed who he is and what he is like by sending his Son.

We know God because of Jesus.

Jim Henry, "If Jesus Had Never Been Born," *Preaching Today*, Tape No. 159. Cited in PreachingToday.Com.

## Recognizing God in the House

Jesus' creative miracle at Cana has precedent in the Old Testament and accents how the anointing of the Spirit comes into peoples' lives and changes them for the better.

1. Elisha the prophet of God miraculously ministered to the need of a widow whose husband had died and left her with debts she could not pay. He did it by turning water into oil, and the widow sold it to pay the debt (2 Kings 4:1-7).

2. When Jacob fled from the wrath of his brother Esau, on his journey from Beersheba to Haran, Jacob laid down to rest at the end of the day, and had a life-changing dream:

> When Jacob awoke from his sleep, he thought, "Surely the LORD is in this place, and I was not aware of it." He was afraid and said, "How awesome is this place! This is none other than the house of God; this is the gate of heaven" (Gen. 28:16, 17).

3. Before Moses smote the rock in the wilderness, he cried out to the Lord:

> "What am I to do with these people? They are almost ready to stone me." The LORD answered Moses, "Walk on ahead of the people. Take with you some of the elders of Israel and take in your hand the staff with which you struck the Nile, and go. I will stand there before you by the rock at Horeb. Strike the rock, and water will come out of it for the people to drink" (Exod. 17:4-7).

It is reasonable most of the people of Israel did not see whom Moses saw. Moses discovered the Messiah standing there before him. The people got their water to quench their thirst, but probably very few perceived that Living Water was standing right there in front of each of them. They totally missed the eternal message of the water from the rock.

4. The Apostle Paul made very clear that Jesus Christ was Israel's rock in the wilderness:

> I do not want you to be ignorant of the fact, brothers, that our forefathers were all under the cloud and that they all passed through the sea. They were all baptized into Moses in the cloud and in the sea. They all ate the same spiritual food and drank the same spiritual drink; for they drank from the spiritual rock that accompanied them, and that rock was Christ. Nevertheless, God was not pleased with most of them; their bodies were scattered over the desert (1 Cor. 10:1-5).

5. When the upset king of Aram sent soldiers to arrest Elisha, they surrounded Dothan in the night. The next morning the hills were full of invading troops with their horses and chariots. Elisha's servant awoke to start the new day, and seeing them, was scared out of his wits:

> "Oh, my lord, what shall we do?" the servant asked. "Don't be afraid," the prophet answered. "Those who are with us are more than those who are with them." And Elisha prayed, "O LORD, open his eyes so he may see." Then the LORD opened the servant's eyes, and he looked and saw the hills full of horses and chariots of fire all around Elisha (2 Kings 6:15-17).

**Aram's "horses and chariots" were no match for Jehovah's "horses and chariots of fire." Lord, open our eyes!**

This couple at their wedding totally missed recognizing their Messiah. In fact, neither the bridegroom nor the master of the banquet knew who was in the house.

# A SHORT VISIT TO CAPERNAUM
## John 2:12

**12 After this he went down to Capernaum with his mother and brothers and his disciples. There they stayed for a few days.**

Capernaum, on the north end of the Sea of Galilee, was a hub for commerce. The city also boasted a large synagogue, the ruins of which remain to this day.

This particular stopover in Capernaum was quite a mix—Jesus' mother, His brothers and His disciples; a house full indeed! Can you imagine the laughter, the fun, the practical jokes and the storytelling? The fellowship was no doubt restful to Jesus before He started on the journey to Jerusalem. This gathering also had a sad note. Joseph's name is not in the group. Jesus' stepfather, a good and faithful man who fulfilled his part so well in the incarnation of Jesus, had already gone on to his reward.

## JESUS VISITS JERUSALEM
### John 2:13-17

**13 When it was almost time for the Jewish Passover, Jesus went up to Jerusalem. 14 In the temple courts he found men selling cattle, sheep and doves, and others sitting at tables exchanging money. 15 So he made a whip out of cords, and drove all from the temple area, both sheep and cattle; he scattered the coins of the money changers and overturned their tables. 16 To those who sold doves he said, "Get these out of here! How dare you turn my Father's house into a market!" 17 His disciples remembered that it is written: "Zeal for your house will consume me."**

This was the Lord's first Passover visit to the City of David after His investiture at Jordan River.

### TERRIFING ZEAL

"President Teddy Roosevelt's mother, Mittie, found young Teddy was so afraid of the Madison Square Church he refused to set foot inside alone. Her lad was terrified, she discovered, of something called the 'zeal.' It was crouched in the dark corners of the church ready to jump at him, he said.

"When Mittie asked what a zeal might be, Teddy said he was not sure, but thought it was probably a large animal like an alligator or a dragon. He had heard the minister read about it from the Bible.

"Using a concordance, she read him the passages containing the word 'zeal' until suddenly, very excitedly, he asked her to stop. The line was from John 2:17: 'And his disciples remembered that it was written, "The zeal of thine house hath eaten me up."'"

"Many people are still justifiably afraid to come near the zeal of the Lord, for they are perfectly aware it could eat them up if they aren't one of his."
Greg Webb, Leadership, Vol. 10, no. 1. From the book Mornings on Horseback by David McCullough. Cited in PreachingToday.Com.

Jesus' emotions had to be mixed on this visit. On the road up to Jerusalem, Jesus' disciples detected His bubbling enthusiasm as they headed toward the Holy City. It is reasonable to believe Jesus talked with His disciples about how, some 1,500 years earlier, the death angel had smitten all the Egyptian firstborn, both people and animals. That same angel of death had spared all Israelite families in Goshen who had covered themselves by placing blood on the doorposts of their homes. From that earliest beginning, Passover commemorated how the Israelite firstborn escaped death, and how Abraham's seed under Moses' leadership escaped from Egypt and headed to the Promised Land (See Exod. 12; Num. 9; Deut. 16).

Passover also had another meaning, although no record exists Jesus talked to His disciples about it on this trip. Jesus knew He would be rejected by His own people and they would sentence Him to death by crucifixion, making Him the Lamb of God. The verdict against Him would be carried out simultaneously with the High Priest's slaying the Passover lamb about three short years up the road.

**Think about the implications. The Messiah was going to Jerusalem to claim His Father's house! Is Jesus welcome—truly welcome—in your house of worship?**

At the time of Jesus' visit, the high priesthood was controlled by Roman authority. Rome retained for itself the power to appoint Israel's high priests. This meant, of course, the high priests were beholden to Roman power for their posts, making them committed to currying Roman favor. During the Roman occupation, the high priests were political figures in the land as well as spiritual leaders.

The Ark of the Covenant was lost to history about the time of the Babylonian invasion of Jerusalem six centuries earlier. Therefore, the Most Holy Place of the temple had been empty of the principle symbol of the Shekinah, the Presence of God, for centuries. While there were always priests who genuinely feared God—like Zechariah, John the Baptist's father—the priestly religious establishment was clearly corrupt.

What Jesus witnessed, at a time when He was consumed with zeal, was anything but what temple worship was intended to be. Instead, He saw a carnal, highly skilled marketing system. Men were selling sheep, doves and cattle for the sacrifices at handsome profits. Since they could only be bought with Jewish money, money changers were also more than willing to operate businesses exchanging foreign money for a handsome fee.

Sadly, the couple and their guests at the wedding in Cana of Galilee did not know their Messiah was at their wedding. But it must have been heartbreaking for the Messiah, who had attended the dedication of Solomon's temple a millennium earlier, to walk into His Father's house in Jerusalem and find it buzzing with activity, but doing all the wrong things. The great sin of the day was the priestly establishment had their hearts set on making another shekel, and prayer was not at all a priority in the temple (Mark 11:17). This meant nobody perceived their Messiah had entered the temple to claim it as His Father's house.

Nobody!

Talk about missed opportunities! Instead of humbly making their prayerful petitions of the Great King, they ignored Him until, in His zeal, He started overturning their tables and releasing their doves and pigeons. Then they cursed Him!

This temple visit demonstrated these Israelites, led by their religious leaders, held to a standard of righteousness far removed from the heart of their Messiah. It is even proper to say they sincerely believed their standard was the revelation of God and the right interpretation of the Law of Moses. Their commitment was so strong they would kill to preserve it, and even die for it themselves.

It meant they had framed their own righteousness.

## Self-Righteousness

Paul presented in Romans 1 the teaching that nature gives witness to God's creative greatness. "Since the creation of the world," Paul wrote, "God's invisible qualities—his eternal power and divine nature—have been clearly seen, being understood from what has been made." The sons of Abraham were also a shining lamp amid the nations (albeit at times only a candle). Paul concluded that these lights through the centuries were bright enough so that "all men are without excuse" (Rom. 1:20; see also 2 Pet. 1:19; Acts 14:17; 17:28, 29).

> Although they knew God, they neither glorified him as God nor gave thanks to him, but their thinking became futile and their foolish hearts were darkened. Although they claimed to be wise, they became fools and exchanged the glory of the immortal God for images made to look like mortal man and birds and animals and reptiles (Rom. 1:21-23).

When men cease to worship God and give Him the honor He is due, they always make a huge substitution of worldly wisdom for God's wisdom, as they seek to frame their own righteousness. This, then, is the seedbed of self-righteousness.

## Both religious pluralism and Christian universalism are self-righteous substitutes for the good news of salvation and eternal life presented in the Bible.

For example, man's wisdom can develop family structures, build great cities with magnificent buildings, design wealth-building commerce, martial powerful armies, and devise long-lasting political institutions. Some of these governments have lasted for hundreds of years, erecting one after another their monuments and shrines. But they always crumble into the dust of history. This is because they, of necessity, choose a flawed worldly wisdom. It never lasts and eventually expires from inner decay.

Because the core moral problem of humanity is the corrupt rebellion against God pulsing from man's heart, worldly wisdom never cures and restores the sinful sanctuary in man's inner self. This wisdom, in fact, cuts people off from God, and in the process, vehemently opposes God's Son. They perceive that Jesus threatens their system. Man's pride is far too colossal to admit he is wrong and humbly turn to God for help.

Knowing this, the Apostle Paul wrote to the believers at Rome a specific indictment of his own people, the nation of Israel. It explains why the national leaders in the religious system of the land and their followers rejected their Messiah and ultimately nailed Him to a cross: "Since they did not know the righteousness that comes from God and sought to establish their own, they did not submit to God's righteousness" (Rom. 10:3).

In framing their plan, they became self-righteous, all the while holding tightly to Abraham, Moses and the prophets, as well as the Old Testament scriptures—but as their self-righteousness redefined them. The ultimate outcome was they despised their Messiah when He came to them doing God-sized miracles and fulfilling all of the prophets. Paul said they responded to Jesus by refusing to "submit to God's righteousness."

Paul added:

> The righteousness that is by faith says: "... The word is near you; it is in your mouth and in your heart," that is, the word of faith we are proclaiming: That if you confess with your mouth, "Jesus is Lord," and believe in your heart that God raised him from the dead, you will be saved. For it is with your heart that you believe and are justified, and it is with your mouth that you confess and are saved" (Rom. 10:6-10).

## How important that the gospel message be heard around the world! According to the Joshua Project,

**of the 16,442 people groups in the world, 7,062 are unreached. These ethnic groups represent 43% of the world's population.**

## Zeal for His Father's House

Psalm 69 is one of the most quoted Old Testament psalms in the New Testament, second only to Psalm 22. King David was at his best as a prophet when he listened to the Holy Spirit and wrote Psalm 69. It is a storehouse of predictions about the suffering Messiah. As an example, King David wrote what a millennium latter would be his Messiah's actual words: "Zeal for your house consumes me, and the insults of those who insult you fall on me" (Ps. 69:9).

It was this same Messiah who planted the idea in David's mind to build the first temple. At the time, David was troubled because he was living in a house of cedar while the ark dwelt in a tent. The king's solution was to build God a house. Nathan gave David a prophecy informing him that in the name of God he could cast the vision and collect materials for the construction, but his son would be the builder. David's problem was his hands were too bloody from his many conquests (2 Sam. 7:12, 13; 1 Kings 5:3).

When David's son, Solomon, constructed the temple, the wise king humbly asked the God of his fathers to make it His own. At the dedication of the temple, Solomon led the nation in giving the house to God as His dwelling place. Jehovah accepted the invitation and showed up in such strength that the priests could not enter the house because of the power of the *Shekinah*, God's manifest Presence. [The Hebrew word *shekinah* refers to *living in* or *inhabiting*.] Jehovah moved in and settled down, claiming the house as His own (1 Kings 8:10, 11).

The Spirit had done the same thing some 500 years earlier in Moses' day. The Presence filled the tabernacle as God took up His abode there when Moses dedicated the tabernacle in the wilderness (Exod. 40:35). Moses had welcomed Jehovah into the tabernacle, and Solomon embraced His coming into the temple, each inviting God to claim it as the dwelling place for His Name (1 Kings 5:5).

As the passing decades grew into almost four centuries, spanning from Solomon's dedication to the Babylonian Captivity, the temple was God's home in the mindset of the Jewish people. Fathers handed down to their children the stories of how the Presence had taken possession at the dedication. The false conclusion the people of Israel drew, however, was that God was obligated to defend His home and no one would be able to conquer it. Some even advanced the argument that God would defend Jerusalem no matter how sinfully the people lived (e.g., Jer. 5:11-19; 14:13-16).

Solomon knew better, for the king who built the magnificent temple and dedicated it to God perceived the temple was far too small to house the great

Ruler of the universe. "Heaven, even the highest heaven, cannot contain [God]," Solomon said in his prayer of dedication. And "how much less this house I have built" (I Kings 8:27). Yet, Solomon gave his best and spared no wealth in the construction of the home for the Great King, the God of Abraham, Isaac and Jacob.

The priestly and prophetic institutions in the land knew the house belonged to God, too, and were zealous for its preservation. In addition, the people in the land felt great zeal for the magnificent building standing on Mount Moriah, where Abraham had been willing to offer Isaac. The Authorized Version says the building towered 120 cubits high, making it perhaps twenty stories tall (2 Chron. 3:4, KJV). (The current building on the site, the Dome of the Rock, is about seven stories tall.) One needs only read Solomon's dedicatory prayer and take note of the 142,000 animals sacrificed during the days of dedication to realize Solomon's zeal for the house (I Kings 8:62, 63).

**God Himself accepted the home and expressed great zeal for it.**

When the Lord apeared to Solomon a second time at Gibeon, God said to him, "My eyes and my heart will always be there" (I Kings 9:3). This is the language of passion: God Himself felt fervently about the place. Although "the earth is the Lord's and the fullness thereof" (I Cor. 10:26), the Jerusalem Temple was uniquely God's house; His special spot on the earth.

## THE TEMPLE SWITCH
## John 2:18–25

This initial visit after Jesus' Jordan River baptism shows the first indication of how disappointed Jesus was with the temple He claimed as His Father's house. His displeasure culminated in the months ahead in one of the greatest paradigm changes of his ministry—the temple switch. The dwelling place of God transferred from a temple of stone and gold and silver to the fleshly temple of the heart of each of Jesus' followers (I Cor. 3:17; 6:19; Jer. 31:31-33; Ezek. 11:19; 36:26).

It became increasingly clear as Jesus' ministry progressed, it would be out of the question for Him to achieve His worldwide vision if He made the Jewish temple His center of gravity. The religious system did not even *consider* making the changes necessary to position Jesus as Lord of the temple. Instead, they flatly refused to entertain He was their Messiah.

**Jesus had no choice but to change the paradigm!**

Temple worship would have to be bypassed, and Jesus set out to do just that. The sacrificial death of Jesus was absolutely necessary for mankind's redemption. The temple switch meant His sacrifice would be made away from the temple and outside the city limits.

Adore Jesus and make Him the center of temple worship? It was not going to happen. Instead, the road ahead for Him was paved with the most wretched rejection, horrible in its hate and bloody in its viciousness. Isaiah's prophecy would come true: "We despised him and rejected him—a man of sorrows, acquainted with bitterest grief. We turned our backs on him and looked the other way when he went by" (Isa. 53:4 TLB).

## "He came to his own people, but they didn't want him" (John 1:11 MSG).

### The Lord of the Temple Unwelcome in the Temple

The pre-incarnate Messiah knew every square inch of Solomon's temple and was there when Solomon gave it to God as His house. The Messiah also knew all about the second inferior temple built by Zerubbabel some four hundred years later (Ezra 2; 3:8; Neh. 7:7). Herod the Great launched the construction of the third temple, the one Jesus visited, about 500 years after Zerubbabel's Temple. It is part of the mystery of Godliness that Jesus, the God-man, made the trip to visit the temple as the Son of Man from Nazareth and claim it as His Father's house.

The issue goes deeper still. The high priest in the temple Jesus had just partially cleansed would sacrifice the Passover lamb in a few more days according to the ancient ritual. Think about it. Messiah was standing in the temple that was the successor structure to what Solomon so clearly had dedicated to God a millennium earlier.

Solomon and the religious order in his day warmly welcomed the manifest Presence as it moved into the temple God claimed as His dwelling place. The cloud of the Presence was so thick, the priests could not walk into the temple to offer their sacrifices. But when the incarnate Messiah, about whom both Moses and David prophesied, stepped into the temple and zealously claimed it as His "Father's house," the people working in the religious system simply ignored Him. Then, when He overturned their tables, they poured on Him the venom in their hearts, overwhelmingly rejecting Him.

The questions that had to be paramount in Jesus' mind on this visit included:

1. Could Jesus win to His vision the voluntary heart-and-soul loyalty of the religious leadership of Israel?

2. Could Jesus depend on the Jewish religious establishment centered in the temple to change and turn the temple into a house of prayer?

3. Would they see in Jesus the very epitome of the manifest Presence, which was the thick cloud in Moses' tabernacle and Solomon's temple? For example, when Jesus walked in, the Shekinah walked in. Jesus in His own person was the purest essence of the Shekinah.

4. Would they voluntarily accept Jesus as their Messianic sacrifice and stop making the offerings? Could they accept that slaying animals would no longer be needed with the Messiah taking His seat in God's dwelling place, between the cherubim in the Most Holy Place?

5. Would they encourage the people in the land to choose to adore their Messiah, who had come to them in flesh and blood, and make *Him* the center of their worship?

Jesus received no welcome at the temple in His first visit after His investiture at Jordan River. This response spoke a resounding "No!" to each of these questions.

The Jerusalem temple was destroyed in 70 A.D. when a Roman general, Titus, led a successful invasion of the city and destroyed the temple stone by stone. Jesus foretold it in one of His most famous prophecies (Matt. 24:2; Mark 13:2; Luke 21:6). With that decisive conquest, the offering of animal sacrifices ended.

The first of the seven discourses follows, along with its implications.

**18 Then the Jews demanded of him, "What miraculous sign can you show us to prove your authority to do all this?" 19 Jesus answered them, "Destroy this temple, and I will raise it again in three days."**

Jesus' visit demonstrated the die was already cast. Jesus could expect no cooperation at all from the Temple establishment. Instead, the Temple would continue to be a den of thieves and certainly not a house of prayer for all nations.

So what did Jesus accomplish with His zealous burst of righteous indignation? His visit made clear the religious leaders were much too dedicated to their interpretation of Moses' Law and to political survival. This prevented them from giving heartfelt attention to welcoming the manifest Presence back into the temple. Jesus did succeed for a few fleeting minutes, in His own person, in restoring the Shekinah in the temple. This happened because the spirit of Jesus is the essence of the Shekinah Presence. But the overall result was Jesus saw how far the temple establishment had moved away from the heart of His Father.

## The Predictable End Game

How this would conclude was already certain. In order for the Good News to go to all nations around the world, Jesus would have to bypass the religious order centered in the temple. It would take Jesus' death on the cross to launch the New Covenant; hence, His prophetic answer: "Destroy this temple [His body], and I will raise it again in three days" (John 2:19-21).

The religious leaders at the temple would become willing, though unwittingly, to make Jesus' sacrifice happen.

Jesus' strategy was to move away from the ornate temple made with hands to the fleshly temple in the heart of each of His followers (Acts 2:4; 1 Cor. 6:19, 20; Heb. 8:12; 10:17; Jer. 31:31). As John the Baptist prophesied, He would fill each of these warm, walking, talking temples with the manifest Presence—first with saving grace, and then with the baptism in the Holy Spirit (Matt. 3:11; John 1:33). This would mean wherever His followers went, this new temple-in-the-heart went with them. It also meant the very same Spirit that filled Moses' tabernacle and Solomon's temple would manifest in the lives of Jesus' followers, wherever they give witness to Jesus' death and resurrection, in any nation or ethnicity anywhere in the world.

Yes, the temple switch was one of the greatest paradigm changes in Jesus' ministry. But strikingly, the zeal of God's Son did not diminish with the switch; instead, the same divine passion transferred to the new temple-of-the-heart in His followers. In this New Testament focus, Jesus' fervor for His Father's house moved into the hearts of His followers. The Lord's zeal remains even today just as real, driven and determined as it was when He entered Herod's temple two millennia ago.

A key element of Jesus' mission was to make this temple switch. But before doing it, the Lord went into the temple on several occasions to give the leaders opportunities to open up to Him. They never did. In the three years Jesus was in their streets, at times physically in the temple, many sacrifices were offered, but nothing at all was ever done in His honor. The religious system did not even entertain the idea Messiah was in the temple. Instead of giving Jesus worship, they flooded Him with hate and jealousy. They rightly perceived Jesus had become a threat to their way of doing things, and ultimately, in their value system, an enemy of the nation.

## Prove Your Authority

The deep suspicion and mistrust in the hearts of Jesus' questioners came out in their words: "What miraculous sign can you show us to prove your authority to do all this?" Jesus knew well what would be required, and so His answer: "Destroy this temple, and I will raise it up again in three days." The heavenly Father gave a clear sign to authenticate the mission of His Son, including the new order of worship to follow Jesus' crucifixion and resurrection. As Jesus in His own Person is the purest essence of the temple, the sanctuary of the new order would be believers themselves, who are filled with the Holy Spirit.

This sign, of course, was misunderstood because their hearts had moved far, far away from the heart of God.

## 20 The Jews replied, "It has taken forty-six years to build this temple, and you are going to raise it in three days?"

The casual reader might conclude the narrative reads like Jesus was purposefully trying to make these leaders angry. He wasn't. They asked Him for a sign, and He gave them the prophecy of what was going to happen. His answer was very much on point. A new order was coming, and getting there would involve much pain.

Interestingly, instead of asking the Lord to explain what He meant, they jumped to their own conclusion. Their response was condescending and said with a snarl: "It has taken forty-six years to build this temple, and you are going to raise it in three days?" If only they had given Him a warm opportunity to explain!

Every time Jesus went into the temple, in fact, the result was loathing contradiction, confrontation, name-calling, insults and argument. According to the eternal plan of redemption, the sovereignty of God used the free will of these very threatened priests to bring about the sacrificial death and resurrection of His only begotten Son.

## 21 But the temple he had spoken of was his body. ²² After he was raised from the dead, his disciples recalled what he had said. Then they believed the Scripture and the words that Jesus had spoken.

Ezekiel the prophet caught the vision of the movement and relocation of the Shekinah, as God departed the temple in Jerusalem at the time of the Babylonian Captivity (Ezek. 10:18, 19). The Apostle John in this scene recorded the Presence in the Person of the Messiah walking back into the temple for an all too short visit—not more than an hour. Yes, embodied in God's Son is the sum total of the temple. But the Presence that is Jesus Christ did not settle down and make His dwelling this time in Herod's temple; instead, He was unwanted. Completely rejected, the Messiah walked out of the temple. Jesus had no choice but to build a new "temple-of-the-heart." Jesus' body was the essence of the temple, and Jesus' followers who patterned after Him would become temples too! Jesus Himself, in his own person, received the Holy Spirit without measure at His Jordan River baptism. He is the first fruits of this new temple of the New Covenant.

Jesus left the temple deeply disappointed after His short visit. His immediate alternative was to reveal the Presence among the people in the streets of

Jerusalem. Everything the Shekinah demonstrated in the temple at Solomon's dedication, for example, Jesus manifested (and more) in the streets of Jerusalem as the pending Passover celebration dawned.

> **Could the Holy Spirit be working in the streets of your city in ways most people in the church do not recognize?**
>
> **Do *you* hunger to see what God is doing so you can do that, and hear what God is saying so you can say that? (John 5:19, 20).**
>
> **Are you worshipping in a church which welcomes and regularly experiences the presence and power of the Holy Spirit in its services?**
>
> **If not, can you help make it one?**

Yes, in Jesus Christ, the same Shekinah that had made His dwelling in Moses' tabernacle and then in Solomon's temple—this very same Presence and Spirit—moved back out of the temple into the streets of Jerusalem.

Today the same Spirit flows to the nations out of the temple-of-the-heart through the baptism in the Holy Spirit. This means everywhere Spirit-filled believers go, the Shekinah Presence goes with them, anywhere in the world.

## Seeing and Believing
**23 Now while he was in Jerusalem at the Passover Feast, many people saw the miraculous signs he was doing and believed in his name.**

Jesus' visit to the City of David and its temple was not a totally wasted trip. Instead, "During the time he was in Jerusalem, those days of the Passover Feast, many people noticed the signs He was displaying and, seeing they pointed straight to God, entrusted their lives to him" (John 2:23, 24, MSG).

"Many people saw" Jesus' mighty works that served as street signs pointing straight to God. The Presence was there. The aura of divine glory was among the people again. In vivid Shekinah language, "the Word became flesh" in Jerusalem in the days of Jesus' visit "and made His dwelling" among the people. They saw "his glory, the glory of the One and Only, who came from the Father, full of grace and truth" (John 1:14).

Although "many" believed in Him, this early following did not include the religious establishment in the land or even a majority of the people. In fact, the closest Jesus came to being welcomed into the temple was when He was an infant, and again when He was about 12 years old.

Joseph and Mary took baby Jesus to the temple to present Him to the Lord and to carry out the purification rites described in the Law of Moses (Exod. 13:2, 12; Lev. 12; Luke 2:22). Two people, Simeon and Anna, recognized His identity at that time and celebrated His arrival. Neither was a priest.

Simeon was a "righteous and devout" man who "was waiting for the consolation of Israel, and the Holy Spirit was upon him." When the Holy Spirit led him into the temple at just the right moment in a divine appointment, Simeon recognized baby Jesus, took Him in His arms and praised God (Luke 2:25-32).

Anna the prophetess, of the tribe of Asher, also welcomed Him:

> She was very old; she had lived with her husband seven years after her marriage, and then was a widow until she was eighty-four. She never left the temple but worshiped night and day, fasting and praying. Coming up to them at that very moment, she gave thanks to God and spoke about the child to all who were looking forward to the redemption of Jerusalem (Luke 2:36-38).

Simeon and Anna did accept the Messianic revelation. No record exists, however, that the priest who did the ceremony presenting the infant Jesus to the Lord realized whom he held in His arms. To him, baby Jesus was just another of the many infants for whom almost every day he carried out the ancient ceremony.

## How easily the routine of "It's all in a day's work" can blind us to our golden opportunities of divine visitation!

When Jesus' parents brought Him to the temple at the age of 12, He amazed the priests and doctors of the Law with His questions, but each of the religious leaders who talked with Him saw Him as only an especially bright and intelligent child. The Holy Spirit gave none of them a revelation of what was ahead for the youngster with whom they were talking (Luke 2:41-52).

It is a sad commentary: when Jesus visited the temple, apparently there was not another lay person like "Simeon" or "Anna" in the temple with a heart to look for the Messiah and welcome Him. Neither was there a priest who walked in the Spirit and could recognize and welcome Him (Gal. 5:16, 25). There had been one priest, John the Baptist's father, who received some 30 years earlier a revelation about John's birth and the pending arrival of Messiah. But when Jesus launched His ministry, Zechariah had no doubt gone on to his reward (Luke 1:5-25).

To this day, until people become willing to embrace Jesus as "the one and only who came from the Father," they will never discover the liberating power of His redeeming grace, regarding which He is so "full."

He was in the world, and the world came into existence through him. Yet, the world didn't recognize him. He went to his own people, and his own people didn't accept him. However, he gave the right to become God's children to everyone who believed in him (John 1:10-13 GW).

## Jesus: Knowing Men's Hearts
**24 But Jesus would not entrust himself to them, for he knew all men. ²⁵ He did not need man's testimony about man, for he knew what was in a man.**

Jesus did not need the affirmation of these leaders for His own well-being because He put no stock in the praise of people. Jesus also knew all too well the evil in the heart of man and the power of the flesh to rule the choices of people. Consequently, Jesus did not "entrust his life to them. He knew them inside and out, knew how untrustworthy they were. He didn't need any help in seeing right through them" (John 2:24, 25 MSG).

## FRITZ HABER – AMMONIA FERTILIZER AND GAS

Fritz Haber is probably the most important person in your life that you've never heard of. He was a secularized Jew in Germany, who started to make his mark just prior to World War I. Haber was a chemist, who was married to a brilliant woman named Clara. Before World War I, in the midst of a looming food shortage in Germany, Haber discovered a way to separate the nitrogen out of the air that produced an ammonia drip. This ammonia could be put into fertilizer. Fritz Haber is one of the main reasons the world today can support almost seven billion people through fertilizer.

If this is all you know about Fritz Haber's life you might think, *This man was good because he made a tremendous difference in the world.* But there's more to Fritz Haber's life. He was also a very loyal German who signed up to fight in World War I. As the war progressed, he made an ammonia gas that could kill enemy soldiers.

In 1915 at Ypres, Belgium, Haber turned on his gas machine and a great, green cloud about the size of a whale emerged. The soldiers on the other side could see it coming across the no-man's land. As it approached, every living thing in its path dried up and died. Then it hit the Allied soldiers on the frontlines, and it killed every last soldier. The lingering gas even hurt innocent civilians.

Haber thought this was a grand success and the German officials agreed.

Haber went back home to visit Clara, and she was outraged at his gas machine. The very thing that he had used to save lives was now an instrument of death. Clara confronted him, but he did not want to listen to her. So, in the middle of the night, she took his service revolver, walked out into their garden, and shot herself in the heart. The next morning Haber put on his uniform and went back to the frontlines to unleash more of his deadly gas.

After the war Haber tried to help Germany pay the tremendous war reparations by devising a process to distill gold from seawater. But when Hitler rose to power, he decreed that all the Jews who worked for Haber had to be fired. Haber resigned in protest and left Germany, but no one would receive him.

He died alone, unloved.

*Adapted from Hershael York, from the sermon "Why Can't You Be Like Your Brother?" Cited from PreachingToday.Com.*

Are you and I different from Fritz Haber? The Bible answers, we might not go to the depths of evil to which he went, but we all come into this world with evil hearts. And, like Faber, we can still do some good things. Our "good things" do not change the fact that at the core of our being, we are in rebellion against God. The relationship is broken between us and the condition is terminal. Scripture is very clear: God has declared us all unrighteous. Like Haber, even the good things we do are tainted by underlying wickedness.

Is there a cure?

The wonderful news of the incarnation is Jesus knew the evil in our hearts and loved us enough to die for us anyway, changing us from the inside out.

The record of Jesus' first visit to Jerusalem in His ministry years to celebrate the Passover Feast continues in Chapter 3. The Apostle John presents the story of Jesus' solution to man's core problem with the account of Nicodemus' nighttime visit to Jesus.

# CHAPTER 3
# JESUS: THE MASTER TEACHER
## Nicodemus' Nighttime Visit

*This chapter shows the Lord, while in Jerusalem for the Passover Feast, in dialogue with a religious leader named Nicodemus. Jesus gave him the message of the new birth. The discussion between them is the second of the seven major discourses the Apostle John records. This chapter also shows Jesus taking His disciples apart for a rest after His visit to Jerusalem and concludes the Apostle John's record of John the Baptist's testimony about Jesus.*

## NICODEMUS COMES CALLING
## John 3:1-13

**1 Now there was a man of the Pharisees named Nicodemus, a member of the Jewish ruling council. 2 He came to Jesus at night and said, "Rabbi, we know you are a teacher who has come from God. For no one could perform the miraculous signs you are doing if God were not with him."**

This discussion is a great example of Jesus as both apostle and prophet (Heb. 3:1). As the *apostle* sent from God, Jesus in this conversation introduced the word picture of a new birth. It unveiled a new understanding of the path to a right relationship with God. Nicodemus was the first person in salvation history to hear it. As the *prophet*, Jesus revealed the agape love of God for all people, which is the core value in the heart of God, and predicted the worldwide harvest this understanding would make possible (John 3:16; 1 John 4:8, 16).

**We should never minimize the importance of our witness to a single individual!**

### Only "a Teacher Come From God"

Most believe Nicodemus came to Jesus at night to inquire secretly of the Lord because he honestly wanted to know more about God. This might well have been the case. But there is also another and more plausible explanation. It is possible Nicodemus went to Jesus out of his sympathetic belief Jesus was "a teacher come from God," with the goal to do Jesus a favor. Nicodemus' desire might have been to bring Jesus into fellowship with the Sanhedrin. It could have been a *"Jesus, I want to be your friend and open doors for you"* kind of visit. It is also plausible both motivations were at work.

Nicodemus obviously came to Jesus out of at least some admiration for His ministry. He acknowledged Jesus as a respected rabbi and believed Jesus had a message from God. He also used "We"—"We know you are a teacher come from God" (NKJV). This was an admission that others in the Sanhedrin knew it, too, but were not willing to admit it publicly.

The story of Jesus' visit to the temple in Chapter 2 has already shown Jesus was not going to be recognized as Israel's Messiah and the Son of God. But if Jesus would be willing to let the elders in the Sanhedrin define Him as "a teacher ... from God," there might be a way to welcome Him as another in the long line of Hebrew prophets. Such an invitation, however, would have required Jesus to settle for less than His Father's will and become part of their system; in other words, submit to the authority of the Sanhedrin. This line of reasoning means the ruling elders chose with full knowledge how they responded to the Lord. Nicodemus' statement was, "We know." This situation was an actual replay of the temptation in the wilderness:

"All [these kingdoms] I will give you if you will bow down and worship me." "Away with you, Satan!" Yeshua told him, "... 'Worship ADONAI your God, and serve only him'" (Matt. 4:9, 10 CJB).

The stumbling block for the Sanhedrin came when Jesus claimed to be much more than "a teacher come from God." [It remains the stumbling block for so many today!] What Nicodemus intended as a compliment said it all: "No man could do the miraculous signs you are doing if God were not with him." Nicodemus' statement would have been a high compliment to any Hebrew prophet in the Old Covenant, but it fell woefully short when he said it to His Messiah.

The paramount issue with Nicodemus and his priestly friends was the level of affirmation they were willing to give to Jesus. Their choice was to accept him only as a "man" and as a "teacher come from God." They were not at all willing to receive Jesus as the Messianic Son of Man foretold by the prophets (Dan. 7:13; Matt. 26:64, 65; Mark 14:62, 63). But the Lord Jesus demanded they take exactly this final leap of faith and acknowledge Him as Jehovah's Son and equal.

How people handle this ultimate conclusion about Jesus—then and now—is fundamental to understanding what the book of John is all about. Since Jesus would not take a shortcut, Nicodemus probably went home disappointed saying, "I tried."

Ultimately, the matter would be settled at Jesus' cruel crucifixion and victorious resurrection.

**This teaching of the new birth shows how the message of Jesus differs from all other world religions. The redemption that comes by Christ Jesus is not based on what we merit, or our works of righteousness. This so great salvation follows**

**repentance and comes by grace through faith alone. It is
the gift of God, with the righteousness of Jesus credited to
our accounts (Acts 4:12; Eph. 2:8, 9; Rom. 3:22, 23).**

**On the other hand, each world religion in its own way
requires people to do the impossible—earn their salvation
with their good works. But how do you ever know when
you have done enough?**

**The plan of salvation Jesus died to establish elevated
grace as the gift of God and is clearly superior to a works-
based sacrificial system, such as the Law of Moses.**

**In addition, each world religion, other than the good
news of Jesus Christ, is also works based.**

## Jesus' Diagnosis and the Antidote
**3 In reply Jesus declared, "I tell you the truth, no one can
see the kingdom of God unless he is born again."**

The Holy Spirit had inspired the Old Testament prophets to understand
well that man's fallen spiritual condition is internal and rooted deeply inside all
people in every generation:

* Moses gave the nation the Law and the sacrificial system, for example,
knowing as he did that the problem was deeper than the blood of lambs
and pigeons could penetrate. This helps explain why the great emancipator
told his people: "And now, Israel, what does the LORD your God ask of you
but to fear the LORD your God, to walk in obedience to him, to love him,
to serve the LORD your God with all your heart and with all your soul. ...
Circumcise your hearts, therefore" (Deut. 10:12-16; 30:6).
* David prayed, "Create in me a new, clean heart, O God, filled with clean
thoughts and right desires" (Ps. 51:10 TLB). The emphasis here is on the
word "create." David knew he could not develop a new heart himself.
In this sense, the prayer was prophetic. David's greater Son would one
day achieve this impossibility by making provision with His own blood to
create a guiltless heart with "clean thoughts and right desires."
* Jeremiah also perceived the depth of the problem and understood it was
inward and not external or environmental. "The human mind is the most
deceitful of all things," he penned. "It is incurable. No one can understand
how deceitful it is" (Jer. 17:9 GW; see also 4:2).
* Isaiah, too, had keen insight into the role of repentance: "Let the wicked forsake
his way and the evil man his thoughts. Let him turn to the LORD, and he will
have mercy on him, and to our God, for he will freely pardon" (Isa. 55:7).

- John the Baptist came preaching the same message of repentance for the remission of sins. He sealed this inward work of grace with a very public symbol of water baptism (Matt. 3:1, 11).
- After Jesus' baptism, Jesus preached exactly the same message, offering the same diagnosis: "Repent, for the kingdom of heaven is near" (Matt. 4:17).

The Jewish people had been offering their sacrifices for sins for two millennia, since Abraham fathered the nation (Gen. 15:1-6; Heb. 7:26-28). [Animal sacrifices actually pre-dated Abraham and went back to the first sacrifice in Eden (Gen. 3:15, 21).] The goal was for the blood of bulls and goats, pigeons and turtledoves—the death of innocent animals—to atone for guilty people and change their hearts. But animals cannot atone for people—they are not equal. This explains why this plan always lacked permanence and never could quite get the job done. Hence, "tomorrow's sin" would require a person to take the life of another animal. This reality meant the need continued, tomorrow after tomorrow after tomorrow, in an unending chain of tomorrows.

These sacrifices were like bandages covering up a wound, but having no power to go underneath it and heal the injury. The primary purpose of Moses' Law, therefore, was to serve as a schoolmaster showing the overriding need of a permanent sacrifice. It would ultimately take the sacrifice of the Messiah Himself to end all animal sacrifices (Gal. 3:24, 25; Heb. 9:8-15; 10:8-17).

Taking this same reasoning further, if Jesus were created by the heavenly Father (as Mormonism teaches), could His sacrifice be trusted as adequate to redeem all people? How would we know the sacrifice of a created Son satisfied all of the demands of God the Father for man's salvation? Would the death of a "created Jesus" be *fully adequate* to save "whosoever will"?

The great lesson of the Bible is Jesus of Nazareth was of the same essence as the one true God. As the uncreated Son of God and the second person of the Trinity, Jesus the God-man made the sacrifice on the cross; He was clothed in true humanity, in flesh and blood. Jesus Christ, the spoken Word of creation, was *God Himself* atoning for man's sins. As Isaac Watts, the great hymn writer, expressed it in one of his most beloved hymns, "At the Cross" (1707): "God the mighty maker died for man the creature's sin."

All too often, however, people buy in to the lie that they can heal themselves with their good works and their own efforts at self-improvement.

## A FEW SQUIRTS OF PERFUME

In a TV commercial by a credit card company, Capital One, a couple is making a purchase in a shopping center. When the clerk tells how much it will cost, the woman says she will pay the bill with her credit card.

Suddenly hordes of barbarians begin surging into the store. They run down the store aisles yelling, with weapons drawn, toward the couple making the credit card purchase. The point of the ad is that making yourself liable to the finance charges on credit cards is like bringing on the barbarians.

One quick scene in the ad gives a potent spiritual metaphor. As the barbarians charge past one store clerk at the perfume counter, she sprays perfume on them.

Trying to civilize a horde of bloodthirsty barbarians to get rid of their foul aroma with a few squirts of perfume is what we are doing when we hope to transform sinners by squirting them with religion.

Religion cannot change the barbarian at the heart of every person. Only a relationship with Christ brings the soul conversion that changes a sinner into a saint.

*Craig Brian Larson, Arlington Heights, Illinois. Cited in PreachingToday.Com.*

## Jesus' Solution: From the Inside Out

What makes this conversation with Nicodemus historic is the way Jesus framed the solution. He used the word picture of a new birth, grounded in the agape love in the heart of the heavenly Father. Although Nicodemus had earned his place as a respected religious leader in Israel, Jesus recognized the unredeemed condition of his heart. He also offered him exactly what he needed—a new birth that would give him a right relationship with God. Jesus' antidote redeems people from the inside out. Paul the apostle later expressed just how radical this spiritual heart transplant is: "If anyone is in Christ, he is a new creation; the old has gone, the new has come! All this is from God, who reconciled us to himself through Christ" (2 Cor. 5:17, 18).

The term "born again" derives from the word *anothen*, and it carries the idea of "born from above" (see this same usage in John 3:31; 19:11, 23). Jesus' point was a fundamental change that is generated in the heart of God must take place within a person, deep inside him. Like the birth of a baby, it begins with a seed and grows from the inside out. The solution demands a spiritual *birth* "from above" if anyone is to enter the Kingdom of God.

Matthew recorded a story about the Pharisees demanding Jesus explain why His disciples did not wash their hands before they ate. The Lord used the occasion to give insightful teaching about the inherently sinful and evil condition of the hearts of all people:

Out of the heart come evil thoughts, murder, adultery, sexual immorality, theft, false testimony, slander. These are what make a man 'unclean'; but eating with unwashed hands does not make him 'unclean' (Matt. 15:19, 20).

It is an eye-opener:
- The circumstances of a person's environment are not the primary causes of murders.
- The lewd images of the pornography industry do not predetermine adultery and sexual immorality.
- The attraction of *things*, be they ever so appealing, is not the root cause of theft.
- If you lie on your neighbor, even slander his good name, you will *not* do it because he said or did something that offended you, but because lying and slander are in the spiritual condition of your own heart.

The Pharisees understood cleaning the outside of the dish (external righteousness), but their *soap* left "the inside ... full of greed and self-indulgence" (Matt. 23:25).

Indeed! Man's problem is inner; the root issue is the evil condition at the core of his being. All people since Adam's fall in Eden have been "wired" to rebel against God and seek to replace God with their own God-rejecting self-righteousness.

> **Nicodemus saw Jesus as a God-anointed man who was performing many "miraculous signs," but not as the Son of God. In our generation, with so many following Nicodemus' example, how are you handling this "ultimate conclusion" about Jesus?**

This dialogue between Jesus and Nicodemus shows religious leaders at the highest levels of responsibility can know a lot about the scriptures, but in their hearts be light years away from the righteousness that comes by faith in Jesus Christ (Rom. 4:13). Nicodemus had no comprehension, for example, that Jesus stood magnanimously ready to pour out His sinless blood for him at Golgotha. Jesus also was willing to credit His own righteousness to Nicodemus' account, if he would only repent and turn to Jesus for help (Rom. 3:21, 22; 4:3).

Nicodemus was the first person in the Christian era to whom Jesus presented the prophecy of a new birth, and he could have been the first recorded person to experience it. Jesus opened up to this respected religious ruler a solution that would have given him a permanent cure, including the gift of eternal life. Since that conversation, this word picture of being "born again" or "from above" has become one of the most widely accepted truths Jesus presented in His ministry. It is a solution that goes to the core of man's rebellion against God and establishes Jesus as the ultimate apostolic thinker and prophet sent from God.

## A BRIAR AND A ROSE

A gardener walking by with his spade in hand noticed a briar growing in a ditch. The gardener looked at the briar carefully and decided to dig around it. Then he lifted up the briar to take it with him.

"What is he doing?" the briar asked himself. "Doesn't he know I'm a worthless briar?"

The gardener took the briar into his garden and planted it with his flowers. This time the briar said, "What a mistake he has made planting me among these beautiful roses!"

Then the gardener came once more and made a slit in the briar with his sharp knife and grafted it with a rose. The briar complained again: "What are you doing? You're hurting me!"

When summer came, lovely roses were blooming on the briar!

Then the gardener said to the briar, "Your beauty is not due to what came out of you, but to what I put inside you. You couldn't make yourself lovely and fragrant. But I could, and did!"

*Selected, author unknown.*

The Apostle Paul later wrote:

[N]ot many wise men after the flesh, not many mighty, not many noble, are called: But God hath chosen the foolish things of the world to confound the wise; and God hath chosen the weak things of the world to confound the things which are mighty; And base things of the world, and things which are despised, hath God chosen, yea, and things which are not, to bring to nought things that are: That no flesh should glory in his presence (1 Cor. 1:26-29 KJV).

Jesus did not announce this grand cure to multitudes on national television, but to one person. This reality points to the conclusion that all people hungry for peace with God must come to Jesus one at a time. God has no grandchildren, only sons and daughters. Not only did Nicodemus have the opportunity to be the first to experience eternal, from-the-inside-out redemption, but he also could have become a great evangelist of the new order by taking the good news back to the other members of the ruling council.

## BEHAVIORS OF A BLIND MAN

In his book, *An Anthropologist on Mars*, neurologist Oliver Sacks tells the story of Virgil, a man who had been blind from early childhood. When he was 50, Virgil underwent surgery and was given the gift of sight. But as he and Dr. Sacks found out, having the physical capacity for sight is not the same as seeing.

Virgil's first experiences with sight were confusing. He was able to make out colors and movements, but arranging them into a coherent picture was more difficult. Over time he learned to identify various objects, but his habits—his behaviors—were still those of a blind man.

Dr. Sacks asserts, "One must die as a blind person to be born again as a seeing person. It is the interim, the limbo … that is so terrible."

*Cited from Sermons.Com.*

Baby Christians, too, must be born of the Spirit so they can grow and learn the ways of God. To truly see Jesus and his truth means more than merely acknowledging what He did or said. It also embraces a total change of identity. The Apostle Paul expressed it when He penned: "If anyone is in Christ, he is a new creation; the old has gone and the new has come" (2 Cor. 5:17).

Nicodemus' visit was the historic first time the solution to the problem of evil in the human heart was expressed with such simple clarity. The word picture of the birth of a baby is common to all people worldwide. Yet not a single one of the Old Testament prophets had ever been able to say it like Jesus: "No one can see the kingdom of God unless he is born again." The statement is categorical: "*No one*"—not one individual—can find peace with God by any other path.

"No one"—this is a universal truth—no one anywhere in the world is the meaning. Jews, yes, but not only Jews; this truth is applicable to all Gentiles too. The Lord allowed for only one path into the kingdom of God—a new birth. This new birth comes solely through Jesus' sacrificial death on the cross for all people who repent and believe the gospel.

**With this "no one," the Lord sealed the case against religious pluralism, which claims all religions lead to God. It also helps to explain why Jesus is hated in our generation too!**

Jesus' solution springs from the inside out and works marvelously. This is also what sets the Christian message of Jesus' death on the cross apart from all other world religions. All of them propose a solution from the *outside in*: a person must earn his salvation by what he does. But by this standard, an individual can never be certain he has done enough. So how can you ever have peace with God?

## FIRE THE COMMITTEE!

You and I are not integrated, unified, whole persons. Our hearts are multi-divided. It's like we have a board room in every heart. Imagine: a big table, leather chairs, coffee, bottled water, a whiteboard and a video screen. A committee sits around the table in your heart. The members' names are the social self, the private self, the work self, the sexual self, the recreational self, the religious self, and others. The committee is arguing and debating and voting, constantly agitated and upset. Rarely can they come to a unanimous, wholehearted decision. We tell ourselves we're this way because we're so busy with so many responsibilities. But the truth is we're just divided, unfocused, hesitant, and not free.

This kind of person can "accept Jesus" in two ways. One way is to invite him as a member of the committee. Give him a vote too. But then he becomes just one more complication.

The other way to "accept Jesus" is to say to him, "My life isn't working. Please come in and fire my committee, every last one of them. I hand myself over to you. I am your responsibility now. Please run my whole life for me."

*Ray Ortund, "#9: What Does It Mean to Accept Jesus?" Ray Ortlund: Christ Is Deeper Still (blog), (6-4-10). Cited in PreachingToday.Com.*

The path to peace with God always embraces both accepting Jesus and removing the idols. All too often, however, like Rachel of old, we will go to any lengths to try to hold on to our false gods (Gen. 31:19-35). The result is always double-mindedness that stymies maturity in Christ (James 1:8).

## 4 "How can a man be born when he is old?" Nicodemus asked. "Surely he cannot enter a second time into his mother's womb to be born!"

Jesus agreed with the diagnosis of the Old Testament prophets. But He went further by rounding out the diagnosis with the universally understood word picture of a new birth. Then, He did what the prophets could not do by becoming the sacrifice to cure the problem (Heb. 7:27). This achievement is Jesus' supreme contribution to mankind's salvation.

In achieving this, Jesus offered a refreshing, new way of understanding the antidote to the deadly poison of sin in man's heart. For any person to attain a right relationship with God, he must experience through repentance and faith in Jesus Christ a new birth, giving him a spiritual heart transplant. Without this new heart, man's condition is hopeless, so that he will never find peace with God and eternal life.

Think about it! A new birth, a miraculous spiritual birth from above, by the Holy Spirit, creates a new heart: "If anyone is in Christ, he is a new creation; the old has gone, the new has come! All this is from God, who reconciled us to himself through Christ" (2 Cor. 5:17, 18).

## Abraham's Faith

Jesus, the ultimate prophet, presented His solution with an easily understood word picture. What Jesus expressed has its roots anchored solidly in the Old Testament, particularly the story of Abraham.

"Abram believed the LORD, and it was credited to him as righteousness" (Gen. 15:6). Abraham had done nothing to merit the righteousness that God awarded him; nothing, that is, except believe the promise of God to make his descendants into a great nation like the stars in the sky (Gen. 15:1-5). The blessing came solely as an act of grace. Abraham received a gift from God that changed him at the core of his being, transforming him into a faithful follower of God and making him the father of "all who believe" (See Ps. 32:1, 2; Rom. 3:21-28; 4:1-12; Gal. 3:6-9; James 2:23). Abraham's faith saw more, however, than the future of his offspring. He also met the pre-incarnate Messiah and believed the Messiah-to-come for his own salvation. Jesus' witness is that "Abraham rejoiced at the thought of seeing my day; he saw it and was glad" (John 8:56).

The gross pride in the human heart opposes fiercely Jesus' diagnosis and His antidote for man's salvation. Yet, peace with God comes only by grace through faith when we repent and take Jesus at His word.

How different the message of salvation God revealed to Abraham! Jesus unveiled the same plan to Nicodemus, adding the vivid imagery and reality of a new birth.

---

**Will you, dear reader, faithfully keep teaching Jesus' diagnosis and His cure?**

---

## Nicodemus' Response

If Nicodemus went to Jesus expecting to listen to His teaching and then do Him a favor by opening the door for Jesus to gain personal affirmation from the Sanhedrin, Jesus certainly turned the tables. Nicodemus was probably caught off guard dealing with Jesus' diagnosis of the human problem and the antidote Jesus offered.

Nicodemus was a highly respected teacher in Israel, but he was not a true son of Abraham that historic night (Luke 3:8; John 8:39-58). Nicodemus met in a great revelation the same Messiah whom Abraham experienced and believed (Gen. 15:6; John 8:56). Even though the Son of God was physically standing face-to-face and verbally talking with Nicodemus, Israel's teacher chose not to respond with Abraham-like faith. If Abraham had enjoyed the same opportunity Nicodemus had, the great patriarch would have been quick to open his heart and bow his knee, fully embracing Jesus and His teaching.

Why did Nicodemus not respond the same way? He had far more evidence than did Abraham. For only two examples, Abraham did not have the Old Testament scriptures, including the many prophecies of Messiah's coming, and had not experienced the "miraculous signs" that followed Jesus' ministry. At a minimum, Nicodemus could have said something like: "Jesus, wow! We know you are a teacher come from God and we've been seeing the 'miraculous signs.' But I don't understand how this can be. Yet, it is a refreshingly new way of looking at the problem. So, please tell me more. And how can it happen to me?"

Nicodemus most probably thought it was in his power to help Jesus gain what Nicodemus thought Jesus needed most, respect from the religious leaders of the land. Nicodemus did not seize the moment, his chance of a lifetime. He stumbled badly when he heard the good news of a redemptive second birth. Do you crave the praise of men more than God's praise? (John 12:43).

Nicodemus comprehended physical birth, but his question shows how he totally missed Jesus' point: "How can a grown man be 'born'? Can he go back into his mother's womb and be born a second time?" (John 3:4, 5 CJB).

**5 Jesus answered, "I tell you the truth, no one can enter the kingdom of God unless he is born of water and the Spirit. ⁶ Flesh gives birth to flesh, but the Spirit gives birth to spirit."**

Jesus did not directly rebuke Nicodemus for his response, although He did speak specifically to Nicodemus' question. Jesus' reasoning is easy to follow. The flesh can bring babies into the world; this all started with Adam and Eve. Standing in front of Nicodemus was the last Adam, the source of the "life-giving spirit," and "the Spirit gives birth to spirit" (1 Cor. 15:45).

Jesus' death and resurrection were the final demonstrations that He has the power to accomplish a second, spiritual birth. This "delivery" from above is as real as physical birth. It involves the birth pains of repentance, followed by the forgiveness of God. The new birth also sparks awesome celebration and feelings of acceptance "in the beloved" (Eph. 1:6). In this process, a person who was dead in trespasses and sins jubilantly experiences a new birth. New life is inside him. As the gospel seed absorbs the Sonlight and the refreshing water of the Spirit, it quickly blossoms from the inside out into a new life with a new heart that has new innocence before God (see Eph. 2:1-10).

The phrase "born of water" indicates the new birth is to be followed by water baptism, a symbolic act to give public testimony of the change that has occurred in a person's heart.

**Please note Jesus' statement again, "No one" (v. 5). Some religious pluralists will say, "OK, you go ahead and believe that, but don't try to take your message around the world and change people of other religions."**

**To concede this wipes out the meaning of "no one" and essentially cancels the Lord's Great Commission. While we can never compromise here, at the same time, our Lord allows for no haughtiness or superiority.**

**Instead, we must obey His Commission humbly, motivated by His great love for all people.**

We should not miss that Jesus' international vision is portrayed best on His cross. His death embraces all people everywhere. The mission of the Lord's church must first and foremost be about leading people to faith in Christ. Social action, such as digging wells in tribal areas and helping to start new businesses, can be important supplements to missionary activity around the world. The primary goal of the Great Commission, however, is to lead people to Christ so that they experience the new birth. Then, the goal is to organize and assimilate them in churches. Why would we make the effort to give a community clean water from the earth without helping them discover the living water that gives eternal life?

## The Spirit: Like the Wind

**7 "You should not be surprised at my saying, 'You must be born again.' 8 The wind blows wherever it pleases. You hear its sound, but you cannot tell where it comes from or where it is going. So it is with everyone born of the Spirit."**

Nicodemus should not have been caught off guard, but he was, even though he had sufficient knowledge of the Old Testament not to be. When we pause to think about it, Jesus' solution to the problem makes plenty of sense and should not have been unexpected. Jesus' inside-out explanation of the curse of evil that resides in all people should have been evident to Nicodemus; the gospel candle should have illuminated his heart.

The core problem worldwide is this rebellion against God inside every person. The great lessons of the centuries form a loud chorus of evil:

Wars won't fix the problem.

New rules and new laws cannot bridge the gap.

Reforming man's old heart never does achieve the goal, except for maybe a short time.

Education alone cannot resolve the issue.

Neither wealth nor poverty offers a solution.

Sacrifices, the blood of bulls and goats, won't do the job either.

Man's only hope for salvation and peace with God is a spiritual heart transplant, so that he gains a new heart that ceases to be an enemy of God. This is exactly the new life Jesus offers "from above" in the new birth.

## "So it is with everyone born of the Spirit."

### The Unshackled Wind

The word picture linking the Holy Spirit to the freely blowing wind is instructive, too, and further unveils the genius of Jesus Christ, showing how people experience God in the New Covenant. (The Greek word for spirit, *pneuma*, can also be translated as *wind*.) The Holy Spirit is God, the third Person in the Triunity of God (e.g., John 1:32; 14:16, 26; 16:7; Acts 5:3-5). The Spirit works in the earth to make Jesus known to people everywhere. The Holy Spirit brings people to salvation and peace with God, birthing saving faith. Jesus foretold the Holy Spirit "lives with you and will be in you." The Lord shows by this statement, "[Y]ou are in me, and I am in you" (John 14:17-20).

The job description of the Holy Spirit includes convicting people of their sins while convincing them Jesus is the Son of God and Savior of the world (John 16:8). We can be certain the Spirit was working in Nicodemus' heart that evening, encouraging him to respond, as Abraham had, and accept Jesus as His Messiah. The wooing of the Holy Spirit is very persuasive as he urges and pursues. But God is not looking for robots, and the Holy Spirit does not force people to act outside their free will. People can say, "No!"—even to their Creator (Acts 7:51). Hence, the Spirit can be resisted as He presents Jesus to people. As the story continues to unfold, it will become clear on this special night, Nicodemus did just that. He made the choice and said, "No!"

Every person, therefore, must come to Christ in repentance as an individual, one at a time. Jesus in His incarnation would never have been able to meet personally with each new follower while in the flesh as the gospel spread around the world. But the Holy Spirit can work one-on-one and make Jesus known to everyone who comes to Christ. The Spirit enables every person who repents to experience Jesus so that Jesus becomes his personal Savior and Lord. This individual relationship with Jesus happens because the Holy Spirit is not limited by time and space. For this reason, Jesus has only children, and no grandchildren.

**In the great genius of God, every born-again believer is bonded directly to Jesus Christ, who gave His life on the cross!**

Yes, the Spirit is unshackled like the wind! A person does not need to see the wind to feel its effects, nor must he understand its source or its direction. A newborn baby does not come into the world with mature knowledge of the birthing process, and experiencing the new birth does not depend on knowing the detailed meaning of the experience.

Calvary shows this blessing is all about the grace of God. How can anyone ever do enough righteous works to get to the place he can say to the Lord, "Jesus, you owed me your brutal death on the cross because I have worked for it and earned it"? The Apostle Paul picked up this theme and taught this blessing is experienced only one way, by grace through faith as a gift of God (Eph. 2:1-10).

The Holy Spirit is sovereign in His desire to care for each of Jesus' followers (John 14:26). He has never applied for a passport at any state department or asked permission from a single secretary of state to enter a country. Instead, like the wind, the Spirit steps across all barriers to make Christ known and give a new birth to each person who cries out to Him in repentance, anywhere in the world. The "word of God is living and active" and cannot be chained (Heb. 4:12).

This understanding shows the prophetic nature of the Lord's statement that the wind of God blows anywhere it pleases (v. 8). In doing so, it further unveils the great genius of Jesus' solution to every man's problem. No enemy has been able to stop the sovereign spread of the gospel worldwide (Matt. 16:18). The Holy Spirit, like the wind, goes where He pleases, in all nations and ethnic groups, everywhere. The Spirit is continually doing His redemptive work around the clock, bringing people to Jesus. They are adopted one-at-a-time as sons of God and brought into the eternal family of God. "My Father is always at his work to this very day," Jesus said, "and I, too, am working" (John 5:17).

Jesus' vision for all humanity took Him ultimately to Golgotha, where Roman soldiers nailed Him to a cross. They did it in cooperation with Jewish religious leaders, who looked on and mocked. But the grave could not hold Him; He stepped out of the jaws of death on the third day.

## The Wind Accepts No Barriers

The Roman Empire battled Jesus for some 300 years after His resurrection before ultimately giving up the fight and bowing the knee to the lowly Nazarene. (The Roman Emperor Constantine issued the edict of Milan in 313 A.D., which recognized Christianity as a legal religion in the Empire. Christianity became the state church of the empire 67 years later.) Over all those many decades of struggle, the church kept growing amid every wave of persecution and bloodshed. The Wind that is the Holy Spirit continued to blow, honoring no strategies proudly crafted to stop Jesus' advance. This was true even when the Wind was reaching for a single person living in the humblest shack in the farthest reaches of the Empire (Matt. 28:16-20).

**How do you stop such a Savior? Who can compel the Holy Spirit to cease and desist?**

## Nicodemus: Rejecting the Obvious
## 9 "How can this be?" Nicodemus asked.

Nicodemus did not respond with exclamation and delight at the good news. Instead, he reacted with skepticism. This probably meant Nicodemus did not visit Jesus expecting the Lord to be his teacher; after all, *he* was "Israel's teacher." The young couple in the wedding at Cana did not comprehend who the guest was they had invited. Neither did Nicodemus perceive whom He was visiting. He seemed to have no awareness he was in a conversation with the Master Teacher, the Son of God, his Messiah.

**10 "You are Israel's teacher," said Jesus, "and do you not understand these things? 11 I tell you the truth, we speak of what we know, and we testify to what we have seen, but still you people do not accept our testimony."**

Jesus responded to Nicodemus with amazement because He discerned what was in his heart. Jesus knew Nicodemus was capable of a response of faith and trust and could have been the gateway to the religious leadership of Israel. Nicodemus knew enough about the faith of Abraham and the Old Testament scriptures that he should have listened to Jesus' voice and accepted its ring of authority. After all, he had already complimented Jesus as a teacher sent by God, who was doing His miraculous ministry because "God was with him."

One is left to wonder what might have been the most painful part of this conversation for Jesus. Was it awareness Nicodemus and his associates were, simply put, not acting out of ignorance but *unwillingness?* It was a bold and compelling indictment. Yes, it becomes increasingly obvious as the story unfolds, "Israel's teacher" chose not to be teachable.

Jesus had honored Nicodemus with a new and prophetic revelation and blessed him to be the first person in history ever to hear it expressed in such a redemptive way. The Lord was confident about what He had said: "we speak of what we know, and we testify to what we have seen." The new birth would, in fact, permanently heal the great rift between God and man. The chasm could finally be bridged because Jesus was the bridge. But such wonderful news was met with willful rejection: "you won't believe our testimony"(John 3:11 NLT). Nicodemus' problem was he simply refused—willfully refused—to accept the obvious. It was a telling indictment.

Jesus' use of "we" and "our" (v. 10, "we know" and "our testimony") is instructive. Jesus was not speaking solo in this declaration that was so significant for Nicodemus' tomorrows and the future of Jesus' followers worldwide. This was an apostolic proclamation and prophecy. It had the full backing of His heavenly Father and was spoken in the authority of the Holy Spirit. Jesus later explained this dynamic when He said to the unbelieving Jews who were persecuting Him:

I tell you the truth, the Son can do nothing by himself; he can do only what he sees his Father doing, because whatever the Father does the Son also does. For the Father loves the Son and shows him all he does (John 5:19, 20).

As Jesus neared His cross, He also said:

I did not speak of my own accord, but the Father who sent me commanded me what to say and how to say it. I know that his command leads to eternal life. So whatever I say is just what the Father has told me to say (John 12:49, 50).

## Jesus' Gospel and the Ethic of Love

Jesus built the foundation of His ministry on the love of God that so totally characterizes the Godhead. Nicodemus should not have been surprised here either, because Moses had made the agape love of God the foundation of the Law. Moses wrote, "Love the LORD your God with all your heart and with all your soul and with all your strength" (Deut. 6:5). And in all interactions with your fellow men, he penned, "Love your neighbor as yourself" (Lev. 19:18). Jesus Himself affirmed "all the Law and the Prophets hang on these two commandments" (Matt. 22:40). The ethic of love, therefore, has a clear basis in the Old Testament.

Legalism, however, is always birthed by man's self-righteousness that has no roots in the revelation of God. Legalism tries to change people from the outside inward. But it always comes up short and is never able even to get close to finishing the job.

Love changes people from the inside out and marvelously achieves the goal.

The prophet Jeremiah foretold the day when God would "make a New Covenant with the house of Israel." It would be very different from the old Mosaic order, although grounded in the same love ethic. "I will put my law in their minds," God promised, "and write it on their hearts" (Jer. 31:31, 33; see also Ezek. 11:19; 18:31; 36:26). For this to happen, it required the followers of Jesus to have new hearts. Jesus explained it to Nicodemus as being "born again."

## 12 "I have spoken to you of earthly things and you do not believe; how then will you believe if I speak of heavenly things?"

Nicodemus, although a ruler in the nation whom Jesus complimented as "Israel's teacher," made the decision on the spot to let Jesus' teaching fly over his head. "You do not believe," *by your own choice*, is the sense of the statement, and the difference could not be more distinct between Nicodemus' lack of faith and Abraham's true faith in God. Jesus clearly expressed the root of Nicodemus' problem was not a lack of evidence. Instead, in the face of all of the abundant confirmations, Nicodemus spoke a resounding "No!" to his own Messiah. He did so although the proof was demonstrated in the authority of Jesus' teaching and in the Old Testament scriptures.

**13 "No one has ever gone into heaven except the one who came from heaven—the Son of Man."**

Jesus further disclosed His credentials to Nicodemus in this statement that authorized Him to give this teaching a distinctiveness no one else on earth could claim. Jesus as the Son of Man had come from heaven. Nicodemus no doubt understood immediately Jesus' use of the name Son of Man meant He was claiming to be Deity.

> **"Israel's teacher" was not willing to comprehend the word picture of a second birth. And he certainly did not acknowledge Jesus' identity as the Son of Man (a synonym for Messiah and Son of God). Nicodemus has many students in the 21st century!**

It is plausible Nicodemus came to Jesus with admiration for His ministry and wanted to bring Him into the religious system. Nicodemus did not, however, view Jesus as a teacher before whom he must bow. After all, Nicodemus knew a lot of the Old Testament; he had most probably memorized at least the Torah. But a man who knew word for word the five books of Moses did not stand a chance when he matched wits with the Son of Man, who is the living word on whom the Pentateuch is based. This "teacher come from God"—the Master Teacher—turned the tables on "Israel's teacher" so radically Nicodemus' head must have been spinning. But more was to come.

Jesus next brought up a 1,500-year-old story to illustrate the rebellion against God in the hearts of all Adam's children. Nicodemus knew the narrative well. It is the account of the plague of the poisonous vipers in the desert during Israel's 40 years of wandering, before they finally marched into the land of promise.

## LEARNING FROM SNAKES IN THE WILDERNESS
## John 3:14–21

### An Ancient But Temporary Cure
**14 "Just as Moses lifted up the snake in the desert, so the Son of Man must be lifted up, ¹⁵ that everyone who believes in him may have eternal life."**

As the Israelites traveled in their exodus from Egypt toward the Red Sea, they put God to the test (I Cor. 10:9; Matt. 4:7; Exod. 17:2; Ps. 78:41).

> The people grew impatient on the way; they spoke against God and against Moses, and said, "Why have you brought us up out of Egypt to die in the desert? There is no bread! There is no water! And we detest this miserable food!" (Num. 21:4, 5).

In spite of every miracle they had seen, the people began to grumble against God and Moses. It was a significant rebellion. Had it been successful, it would have destroyed the nation. The penalty for the insurrection was the people were smitten with a plague of venomous snakes and many died from the snake bites. In their desperation, the congregation turned to Moses in repentance, saying, "We sinned when we spoke against the LORD and against you. Pray that the LORD will take the snakes away from us" (Num. 21:7).

The people saw the snakes as their most immediate problem. But the fatal flaw in their hearts that produced the rebellion was by far their primary issue. The evil inside them motivated them to rebel against God and against Moses.

Moses did pray, and the Lord told him what to do:

> "Make a snake and put it up on a pole; anyone who is bitten can look at it and live." So Moses made a bronze snake and put it up on a pole. Then when anyone was bitten by a snake and looked at the bronze snake, he lived (Num. 21:8, 9).

By bringing this story into the conversation, Jesus connected with Moses, whom Nicodemus and the religious leadership of Israel held in the highest regard. In doing this, Jesus chose a chapter from Israel's national history that was common knowledge to remind Nicodemus of the poisonous root of deadly rebellion against God in the hearts of all people. The fact of introducing this story should also have reminded Nicodemus of something "Israel's teacher" surely understood. Although as many as a million lambs may have been offered in the 1,500 years from Moses to Christ, a permanent cure was never found for man's enmity against God. (This number does not count the many sacrifices slain in the millennia between the first animal that died in Eden up to the era of the Law.)

**To diagnose the spiritual condition of every man worldwide, Jesus used the term "no one" twice (in vv. 3 and 5). In verse 7 Jesus used an equally emphatic term, "You must be born again." In verse 14 Jesus gives the cure: "the Son of Man must be lifted up." Jesus is the**

**Father's one and only answer to man's rebellion against God. Yes, the situation begged for a final resolution— and Jesus offered it, paying the full price.**

## The Permanent Solution

A number of applications should be made from this story.

**1. The brass snake was itself prophetic.** Jesus spoke a prophecy to Nicodemus when He compared His own death to the viper Moses lifted up on the pole (Num. 21:8, 9). The Lord was emphatic in making the application:

> In the same way that Moses lifted the serpent in the desert so that people could have something to see and then believe, it is necessary for the Son of Man to be lifted up—and everyone who looks up to him, trusting and expectant, will gain a real life, eternal life (John 3:14 MSG).

To make the new birth possible, Calvary could not be bypassed. When this happened, Jesus was treated by His enemies as worse than a snake.

**2. The serpent was cursed for his role in the fall of Adam and Eve in Eden.** Jesus, the last Adam, was made a curse in our stead by being hanged on a tree (Gen. 3:14; Deut. 21:13).

**3. How serious is the illness?** This word picture of a snake, in fact, illustrates the extent to which Jesus accepted shame in order to provide the antidote for the viper's deadly venom (Matt. 10:16; Phil. 2:8; Heb. 12:2). The price Jesus paid also shows how evil the problem really is in the hearts of all people. Many recoil at the thought their hearts are this wicked before God. But the scriptures show the rebellion is as deadly as a den of coiled cobras that will not "heed the tune of the charmer, however skillful the enchanter may be" (Ps. 58:5).

**The revelation of Holy Scripture says the problem is indeed this bad. Yet, in Christ all who repent are made alive (2 Cor. 5:17).**

**Christian universalists reject the seriousness of man's fallen condition as revealed in the Bible. According to Article Four of the Christian Universalist Association's Statement of Faith, "No human being is totally bad," hence, "no human will perish eternally." Article Four goes on to say, "It is through purgatorial 'fires' of tests and trials that the human spirit is cleansed of negative attributes and attains a character that is compatible**

**with the Presence of God. This is the goal, the essence of salvation."**

**4. The universal application.** The snake called sin has sunk its venomous fangs into the soul of every individual on earth, and "the wages of sin is death." Looking to Jesus Christ, the last Adam, in heartfelt repentance is the sole cure for the deadly venom. "The gift of God is eternal life *through Jesus Christ our Lord*" (Rom. 6:23; 1 Cor. 15:45).

**5. The verb "lifted up" is a prophecy** in which Jesus predicted the extent of His humiliation (v. 14). It also anticipates His glorification (John 8:28; 12:32-34). The term *humiliation* speaks of Jesus' life from His conception in the womb of the Virgin until His shame peaked with His death by crucifixion. The term *glorification* begins with Jesus' resurrection and includes His 40 days of teaching before His ascension. It also embraces His exalted state at God's right hand after His ascension. In John 12:23-27, the apostle shows Jesus' crucifixion produced His glorification (see also Acts 2:33).

**6. Jesus' cross ultimately became His crown.** This is true because the cross is His crowning achievement, by which He is most remembered (Gal. 6:14). His enemies were convinced the Son of God would not be able to get off the cross (Matt. 27:32; Mark 15:32, 36). But for all people who believe in Jesus, the fact that He stayed on the cross until he died fulfilled John the Baptist's prophecy (John 19:30): Jesus was indeed the Lamb of God who takes away the sin of the world (John 1:29, 36).

On His cross, the Lord set the pattern for dealing with suffering. When a person bears his personal cross in faith and with good attitude, ultimately it becomes his crown too (2 Tim. 4:8; 1 Pet. 5:4; Rev. 2:10; 3:4). The path Jesus walked included gross humiliation, but it led to ultimate glorification. This same journey assures everyone who believes in him they will have eternal life.

**7. The solution.** God did not instruct Moses to start a program to kill all of the vipers in the desert. The venom of the snakes was tragic and painful, but it was a secondary bitter pill that sprang out of the rebellion in the Israelites' hearts. The venom called sin inside them was their much bigger concern.

The purpose of the snake on the pole was for the people to look at it as a symbol and be reminded it was the rebellion inside them that was causing all of the suffering and grief. This, in fact, is what the people confessed: "We sinned when we spoke against the LORD and against you" (Num. 21:7).

Putting a snake on a pole was also a visual prophecy of what would happen to Israel's Messiah when He came. Jesus would be lifted up on a pole too. Those who look to Him in faith, recognizing their own rebellion did in fact help to nail Jesus to the cross, are healed from sin's deadly poison by a new birth.

William Ogden expressed this great truth in poetry (1887):

Look and live, my brother, live!
Look to Jesus now, and live;
'Tis recorded in His word, hallelujah!
It is only that you "look and live."

**8. Only one remedy.** God provided a singular solution for the snake-bitten Israelites. He also offers only one plan of salvation, and it comes through faith in the blood of His Son Jesus, the Messiah (See Acts 4:12).

**9. The true antidote.** One can wonder if any Israelite, including Moses, fully perceived Israel's Messiah as the fulfillment of the snake on the pole. But Jesus, knowing what was ahead for Him, identified very closely with that bronze snake. When we come to Calvary in repentance and look with faith at Jesus on His cross as He poured out His blood in our place, we, too, receive forgiveness and experience a second birth.

Clearly, the brass serpent on the pole held no healing or redemptive power. Looking at a piece of bronze metal held no antidote for the venom of snakebite or for the rebellion against God that was more deadly than snake poison. Looking in repentance at the bronze serpent on the pole while believing God's word to Moses, however, made it possible to be healed.

In prophetic hindsight we know the pre-incarnate Messiah, Jesus the Son of God, was with His chosen people in the wilderness (1 Cor. 10:4). Hence, it is easy to look back and picture Israel's Messiah on the pole along with the bronze viper. It is by looking at Jesus in faith that we discover the gift of life. The Lord's ministry shows it is not required that we always perceive the actual source to experience God's gracious gifts. The miracle at the wedding in Cana of Galilee makes the point.

> **We will never appreciate the full depth of the Lord's humiliation until we can picture Jesus' willingness to stoop lower in His death than the deepest pit of sin. This is true even when it meant accepting worse treatment than a den of deadly cobras would get from a loving father protecting his children.**

Hence, the cure the Israelites experienced in the wilderness resulted from looking at the bronze snake, then at the same time believing the Lord who was with them. He was willing to forgive their rebellion and heal them. The cure was all about saving grace and healing faith.

For us today, we accept that Jesus voluntarily gave His precious blood as the atoning sacrifice for our sins. He paid the price for our pardon. We know this is true because it is Jesus' specific promise (John 3:14, 15). When the Holy Spirit applies Jesus' blood to our hearts, we feel with great emotion the blessing of the pardon, and it gives us the unimaginable—a new status as sons of God. The power of Jesus' blood is so potent, it does not merely reform our hearts; instead, Jesus gives each of us a new heart capable of loving God. We are made a new creation (2 Cor. 5:17).

**10. Curing the terminal illness.** The prophets understood well the lethal illness in the heart of every man. All humanity is in rebellion against God and needs a redeemer who can heal by removing the root of sin at the core of every person's heart.

Moses' remedy of pouring out the blood of animals such as bulls and goats was only a temporary solution for the Israelites' condition. The need was unending and everything was temporary. The blood of turtledoves, pigeons and lambs never climbed to the high level of the perfect sacrifice (Isa. 1:11; Heb. 10:1-10).

The Israelites depended on the revelation of God to Moses century after century. Hence, the Old Testament seers continued to identify the diagnosis, but could only wait for the Messiah to provide an effective antidote to cure a heart in rebellion against God. Yes, the law was a schoolmaster to bring men to Christ (Gal. 3:24, 25).

Jesus, the last Adam, made provision for all people to have a new beginning (1 Cor. 15:45; 2 Cor. 5:17). He did it with the offer of a new birth. Jesus' solution is easily understood in all cultures and illustrates the results of Jesus' sacrifice on Golgotha. Jesus became the Lamb of God by giving His life as the final and perfect sacrifice on Calvary's knoll. His death and resurrection turned the word picture of a new birth into reality.

With these applications in mind, it becomes obvious the dialogue between the Nazarene and Nicodemus was a classic demonstration of apostolic authority at work by Jesus. He is indeed the apostle sent from God (Heb. 3:1). Jesus opened up to Nicodemus in simple language the grand and final solution to the deadly problem of man's insurrection against his Lord.

Jesus' message was destined to circle the globe.

**Jesus' solution on the cross was permanent, eternal, and magnificently potent for "whosoever" (1 Cor. 15:45; Heb. 10:12-14). Religious pluralism can never offer a better antidote. All must stand back in awe at the genius of the plan.**

Whatever were Nicodemus' motivating factors when he came to Jesus that history-making night, he realized quickly Jesus was in charge of the visit and the conversation, and not him. But Jesus is always in charge. It was Jesus alone who made the night of Nicodemus' visit so memorable and significant.

Experiencing healing by looking at a snake on a pole, it should be pointed out, occurred only once in Jewish history and has never been repeated. The event that triggered the crisis has been remembered ever since as *the* rebellion in the wilderness. The death of Jesus Christ will never be repeated either.

After the plague ended, Moses preserved the brass snake on the pole, and Israel's religious leaders held it in safekeeping for the next 750 years. Some 500 years after the rebellion, it is likely Solomon gave it a place in the temple. We know the day came when the people began to venerate the bronze snake and burn incense to it. Then, some 250 years after Solomon's reign, good King Hezekiah stopped the practice. He removed the metal snake and broke it into pieces (2 Kings 18:3-7).

This history of the bronze viper shows vividly the evolving nature of idolatry. What is a valid symbol of God's miracle power in one generation, in the next can become an idolatrous false god. In the case of these Israelites, the temptation to create an idol was all the more real because reptiles were widely worshipped in ancient culture (see Rom. 1:23).

## The Solution in Simple Words
**16 For God so loved the world that he gave his one and only Son, that whoever believes in him shall not perish but have eternal life.**

The word "For" in verse 16 connects directly to Nicodemus' visit with Jesus. The conversation includes the discussion about mankind's fallen condition that was crying out for a permanent solution. This need is illustrated by the story of the poisonous snakebites in the desert that ended the rebellion against God and Moses, but offered no long-term cure. Other rebellions certainly followed. Verse 16, therefore, is all about the antidote the heavenly Father sent Jesus to provide as a permanent cure for the rebellion at the core of man's heart. The result in this brief sentence is a summary of the gospel profound in its simplicity. It explains in the plain language of the common man the good news Jesus brought into the world.

Abraham Lincoln's most remembered speech is his Gettysburg Address. Spoken in fewer than 300 simple words, it stated the reasons for the American Civil War. The speech may have had more impact on the outcome of the war than the Battle of Gettysburg.

Jesus Christ revealed the heart of God in 26 simple words (John 3:16 NIV). The heavenly Father sent His only Son into the world to redeem "whoever believes in him" through a second birth. It is the good news of God's "inside-out" solution. In expressing those few words, Jesus spoke one of His most memorized sentences worldwide.

The statement is also profound for its portrait of Jesus' Father in heaven who "so loved the world." The Greeks prided in being able to put an ocean of meaning in a simple word, but Jesus excelled them all with His use of the particle *houtoos* = "so."

> **Eternal life for "whoever believes" is wrapped up in this little word "so," and it expresses the unlimited extent of the love of God.**

Agape love will act in the best interests of another even when it is not deserved and the person has no desire for it, or will actually kill trying to stop it. This kind of unrelenting, selfless love "so" motivated God that He gave His only begotten Son to die for all people—"whoever." Such a plan of salvation exceeds rational explanation. Jesus Himself simply stated it without trying to justify it; instead, He kindly but emphatically asserted it.

In the face of this kind of love, both angels and men are "so" amazed they are left with awe and wonder, astonishment and delight (1 Pet. 1:12). The apostle John, who was also an evangelist, used similar exclamatory language in his first epistle:

> What marvelous love the Father has extended to us! Just look at it—we're called children of God! That's who we really are. But that's also why the world doesn't recognize us or take us seriously, because it has no idea who he is or what he's up to (1 John 3:1 MSG).

### The Gospel: Balancing the Attributes of God

Very serious errors occur when people claim the right to pick and choose between the character traits of God, instead of appreciating the blend of all aspects of God's nature.

> **Christian universalism, for example, makes this grievous error. Exalting only the love of God and concluding God's love could never permit eternal punishment is a huge, unwarranted conclusion. It can be reached only by picking and choosing between the scriptures.**
>
> **"Souls that leave this life on earth without significant spiritual growth will have other opportunities for learning after death," says the Christian Universalist Association Statement of Faith, Article Four. "No one will ever run out of chances to return home to their**

## Creator. Even the most evil beings who have ever lived can still be saved—and will be, in the fullness of time."

Without effort to be exhaustive, the following passages will show the danger of picking and choosing, which always misinterprets the character of God.

The greatest revelation of the character of God in the Old Testament came to Moses when God placed him in the cleft of the rock and proclaimed:

> ... His name, the LORD. And he passed in front of Moses, proclaiming, "The LORD, the LORD, the compassionate and gracious God, slow to anger, abounding in love and faithfulness, maintaining love to thousands, and forgiving wickedness, [forgiving] rebellion and [forgiving] sin. Yet he does not leave the guilty unpunished" (Exod. 34:5-7).

The distinctive values in the heart of God expressed in this reassuring list are framed by the love of God and the judgment of God, and these two character traits always operate in balance in the Godhead. Jesus gave a solemn warning, in fact, about changing a jot or a tittle of the scriptures (Matt. 5:18).

Jesus taught His followers whom they are to fear, and it is not those who can kill the body. Instead, believers are to fear the one who "has power to throw you into hell" (Luke 12:5).

The last book the Apostle John wrote was the Revelation. It catalogs the events that will wrap up time and usher in the eternal ages. After painting the picture of the Marriage Supper of the Lamb and Satan's doom in Revelation 20, John gives this telling description of the final judgment of the wicked, known as the Great White Throne Judgment:

> I saw the dead standing before the throne, and books were opened. Another book was opened, which is the book of life. The dead were judged according to what they had done as recorded in the books. ...
> If anyone's name was not written in the book of life, he was thrown into the lake of fire (Rev. 20:11-15).

1. Jesus came to a world populated with the walking dead—dead in trespasses and sins—with the curse of everlasting perdition already spoken over them. And if things could be any worse, without exception each individual lacked the knowledge and ability to rescue himself from eternal judgment.
2. With the human family in this desperate condition, the heavenly Father, being "so" motivated by His own selfless love (agape), sent His Son to redeem lost mankind. The result is all who repent and believe in Him will experience a second birth.

3. The cross of Jesus, therefore, defines both sin and the love of God. The crucifixion of Jesus defines sin because it shows the problem in man's heart to be "so" bad it took Jesus' unimaginable, cruel sacrifice to cure it. The death of Jesus also defines love because it reveals the heavenly Father loved us "so" much He was willing to send His only begotten Son to die voluntarily in our place, paying the full price sin demanded.

4. The people who are saved because of Jesus' sacrifice are those who believe God did in fact send Jesus, and His magnificently potent sacrifice accomplished its purpose in the new birth.

5. So what does it mean to have the divine attributes of God's love and God's justice in balance? Jesus gave the answer: "Whoever believes in him [love] will not perish [justice]." Instead, they receive the gift of "everlasting life" with all of the blessings associated with it, not the least of which is the status of sons in the family of God (Rom. 8:15; Gal. 4:6; I John 3:2). A person in his fallen state, however, is far from ready or fit for the glory of eternal life. He must be born again so that he can experience justifying grace that sets him apart and prepares him for the majesty of the kingdom of heaven.

The criteria is "believe in *him*" and no other (John 3:16). Faith in the atoning death and resurrection of Jesus is the gospel path to eternal life.

Religious pluralists dare to step into the requirements of all world religions and presume to impose a different path, actually rewriting the values of each religion. They seek to add, for example, the huge assumption that *people attain peace with God and eternal life if they are sincerely following the requirements of their religion.*

The disconnect here is huge. We are compelled to conclude:

- The gospel of Jesus offers no teaching that "all paths lead to God." So, by what authority is the change made that makes the message of the cross say something it does not teach? The presumption here to re-write the Bible is massive.
- Have no basis for asserting *sincere effort* as the benchmark requirement of the gospel to gain everlasting life. Indeed! How easy it is to be sincerely wrong.
- Cannot define *sincere* in such a way each person can know if he has met the benchmark.

**While indicting Jesus' followers for being dogmatic, pluralists are asserting a new dogmatism of their own.**

**We stand humbly under Jesus' cross that so reveals His love for all people. We maintain the plan of salvation for all people was settled when Jesus permitted three rugged nails to hold Him to two crude wooden beams until He died.**

Much of today's preaching and teaching latches on to the blessed truth of the "so" great love of God, but ignores that "perishing" was also in the Lord's message to Nicodemus. What a huge mistake! The whole purpose of Jesus' sacrifice is expressed in these seven words: "whoever believes in him shall not perish" (John 3:16).

No historian has ever dared to delete a sentence from Lincoln's Gettysburg Address. Why would anyone read the Lord's statement unveiling the antidote to the rebellion against God in every individual, and then try to rewrite what Jesus taught?

To ignore "perish" is to reject Jesus' teaching. Doing this is another form of rebellion against God that seeks to frame a new self-righteousness!

Christian universalism makes this error by denying the existence of hell and then asserting all people will ultimately be saved. The message of the Bible shows our own choices in this life determine if our eternal abode will be heaven or everlasting separation from God (e.g., Luke 16:22-31).

Jesus the Messiah is God's answer to the cry of the human soul for forgiveness and reconciliation with God, and there is no other path. To try to frame righteousness other than through Jesus Christ is to choose the path of self-righteousness. This is the spirit of Cain (Gen. 4:1-10). He presented "the fruit of the soil" to God instead of the sacrificial blood of a lamb (Gen. 4:3). Cain was the first recorded person in the Bible to reject a blood atonement and develop his own self-righteousness (See Heb. 9:22). From this ancient beginning, therefore, the self-righteous have been willing to kill their brothers, who vest their faith in the righteousness of God. Abel's death and Jesus' death are history's two prime examples.

## The One and Only Path to God

**17 For God did not send his Son into the world to condemn the world, but to save the world through him. [18] Whoever believes in him is not condemned, but whoever does not believe stands condemned already because he has not believed in the name of God's one and only Son.**

The sense of these verses is God did not send Jesus to continue what had been true with the prophets—pronounce condemnation on the world while offering only a temporary cure by making unending sacrifices of bulls and goats. Instead, the Apostle John recognized God's Son Jesus as the only path to enduring peace with God. Salvation comes "through him," faith is to be vested "in him," and condemnation comes to those who do not believe "in the name of God's one and only Son." Nicodemus did not miss the point that Jesus was claiming to be the Son of God, but he rejected the revelation.

It is the specific function of grace to help a person face his guilt. In fact, John teaches later in his Gospel it is in the job description of the Holy Spirit "to convict the world of guilt in regard to sin ... because men do not believe in [Jesus]" (John 16:8, 9).

While pointedly admitting the profound guilt in the heart of every man, Jesus' conversation with Nicodemus placed primary emphasis on the antidote. The Father has a plan to save the world through Jesus. This change marks a primary difference between the old and the new covenants. The Old Testament is highlighted by condemnation and unending sacrifices. The New Testament spotlights how grace offers a permanent cure in a new birth. "Whoever believes *in him*" will "live off his generous bounty, gift after gift after gift" (John 1:16 MSG).

The one and only path to restored fellowship with God is clear: "Whoever believes in [Jesus] is not condemned." Marvel of marvels! The new birth gives a person a new beginning, forgiven and free from the old condemnation, and with a clean slate as a son of God (See Rom. 8:1, 15). But rejecting the great love of God's one and only Son, and refusing to repent in the face of all the evidence is far and away the worst sin any person can commit. Nicodemus in his visit with Jesus that historic night committed just this sin (v. 18).

Abraham would have never made that mistake; neither would Moses! Rather, they wholeheartedly accepted the revelation when it came to them.

> Anyone who trusts in him is acquitted; anyone who refuses to trust him has long since been under the death sentence without knowing it. And why? Because of that person's failure to believe in the one-of-a-kind Son of God when introduced to him (John 3:18 MSG).

Use of the word "refuses" in verse 18, as The Message paraphrase renders it, conforms well to the Greek here. It is serious to deny God's Son and *refuse* to trust Him; the consequences are eternal. "What good would it do to get everything you want and lose you, the real *you*? What could you ever trade your soul for?" (Mark 8:36, 37 MSG).

All other sins are secondary to *refusing* to believe in the name of God's one and only Son (John 6:29; 16:9). How important to proclaim the gospel faithfully, always wrapping it in the great love of God revealed at Calvary, and delivering the message humbly, without haughtiness or condescension!

**This is the place where the rubber meets the road; where people say "Yes!" or "No!" to the absolutes Jesus expressed. Religious pluralists are among those who say "No!" and assert there are other equally valid paths to God. So do universalists, claiming all will ultimately be saved. Have you stood under Jesus' cross, felt the magnitude of His love, and made your choice?**

## The Offense of the Gospel

Some critics of the gospel level the charge that a father who sends his son to die on a cross cannot claim to be "loving." But Jesus acted as a volunteer and said as much Himself: "No one takes [my life] from me, but I lay it down of my own accord. I have authority to lay it down and authority to take it up again" (John 10:18).

The plan of redemption was developed in the counsels of the Godhead from eternity. The plan was for Jesus to come to earth voluntarily in an incarnation as the Lamb of God, and then be raised from the dead (1 Pet. 1:19, 20; Rev. 13:8).

If Jesus' Father had abandoned His Son to decay in the grave, the charge of "unloving" would be appropriate. But God did not surrender Jesus to corruption; instead, He raised His Son to immortal life. When Jesus' death and His resurrection are linked, they together become the ultimate demonstration of the Father's love, and it is "so" great that it exceeds the capacity of words to describe (John 3:35; 5:20). Jesus affirmed He received just this command "from His Father." The Lord said near the close of His ministry, "The reason my Father loves me is that I lay down my life—only to take it up again" (John 10:17).

While offering this explanation of the heavenly Father's love as expressed in Jesus' death and resurrection, let it also be underscored the cross of Jesus has always been offensive. Paul faced this squarely in his ministry and penned:

> We preach Christ crucified: a stumbling block to Jews and foolishness to Gentiles, but to those whom God has called, both Jews and Greeks, Christ the power of God and the wisdom of God. For the foolishness of God is wiser than man's wisdom, and the weakness of God is stronger than man's strength (1 Cor. 1:23-25).

It is also important to note that total comprehension of the heart of God will never fully be achieved in this life. The heavenly Father's classroom in eternity will be required to understand "the exceeding riches of his grace in his kindness toward us through Christ Jesus" (Eph. 2:7 KJV; Isa. 55:8, 9).

## The Judge's Verdict

**19 "This is the verdict: Light has come into the world, but men loved darkness instead of light because their deeds were evil. 20 Everyone who does evil hates the light, and will not come into the light for fear that his deeds will be exposed. 21 But whoever lives by the truth comes into the light, so that it may be seen plainly that what he has done has been done through God."**

"This is the verdict" (*krisis* — kree'-sis, meaning *a decision for or against; a judgment*). Jesus is speaking here as the ultimate decision maker in the eternal courts of heaven. (The KJV translates *krisis* as "condemnation.") People are lost for eternity because they hate the light. The result is they refuse to repent and accept Jesus Christ as God's Son. They reject the potent antidote of the new birth Jesus provided at Calvary, because it will bring them into the light and expose them. No other sin equals in its heinousness this deliberate rejection of Jesus as "the Lamb of God who takes away the sin of the world" (John 1:29-36; 6:29).

---

**I grew up on a farm in South Carolina and remember vividly the day electricity came to our rural area. With a flip of a switch the lights came on! The centuries' old custom of lighting lamps at dusk ended in our rural area of the country as brightness in abundance seemed to glow from those Edison bulbs and diffuse through the whole house.**

---

Jesus is the light. He is "the sun of righteousness" risen "with healing in His wings" (Mal. 4:2). He came to provide the specific medicine each soul needs. Jesus told Nicodemus, "You should not be surprised at my saying, 'You must be born again'" (John 3:7, 8).

No, Nicodemus should not have been, but he was.

What about you, dear reader; are you surprised?

## Those Who Hate the Light

The Apostle John was an honest writer. The gospel news about the heavenly Father's love is "so" good, it is hard to imagine anyone would reject this cure to the deadly venom identified as rebellion against God. John makes clear, however, there is a wicked and godless condition of the heart that does just this. Many people make the choice not to accept the gospel medicine that removes the chasm between man and God. Hence, they reject Jesus and the new birth He offers. They prefer darkness and despise the *Son*light of the gospel. Their hope is for the night to cover their sinful choices. In fact, they *hate* the name of Jesus and the light shining out of Him, because it exposes them.

Many religious people do good deeds. They will feed and clothe the naked, build beautiful churches, and provide private quality education for their children. They can even be faithful in their church attendance and their giving. They might also listen to the pastor's preaching, especially if it does not proclaim any real value in Jesus' death on the cross. Jezebel and Ahab had 400 prophets and liked them enough to underwrite them from the public treasury.

But when Jehoshaphat wanted to consult a prophet of God before going to war at Ramoth Gilead, Ahab told Jehoshaphat, "There is still one man through whom we can inquire of the LORD, but I hate him because he never prophesies anything good about me, but always bad" (1 Kings 22:7, 8).

Among those who despise the light are also people who recognize the importance of a form of religion in life, not realizing they are framing a new self-righteousness. They want part of Jesus, as long as their worship does not accept Jesus' claim, for example, to be the Son of God who holds the only path to God. And, for sure, they refuse to receive the diagnosis showing their own hearts to be so corrupt it took Jesus' death on the cross to make their personal redemption possible.

> **Ahab no doubt said exactly what he meant when he used the word "hate." Ahab has many followers today, people who feel contempt for Jesus Christ and disdain His teaching! Indeed! False messiahs never stir hate on the scale Jesus does.**

Proclaim to these self-righteous religious people all roads do not lead to God, and trouble will begin to brew. Then tell them the worst sin they can commit is to reject the love of God in the heart of Jesus Christ and refuse to confess Him ...

... as the one and only,

... as God's Son, and

... the singular Savior of the world, and

... the Messiah through whose sacrifice we are born again and have peace with God, and the pot will quickly come to a boil.

Then join rank with John the Baptist, who told Herod he had stolen his brother's wife and was living in adultery. Start naming their sins—doing it graciously and lovingly, with tears flowing from your broken heart—and the pot will nevertheless boil over (Matt. 14:3, 4; 1 Tim. 4:3, 4). Yet, the gospel of Jesus Christ draws a line in the sand, as the following three lists indicate:

1. **Jesus:** "Out of the heart come evil thoughts, murder, adultery, sexual immorality, theft, false testimony, slander. These are what make a man unclean" (Matt. 15:19, 20).

2. **The Apostle John:** "Blessed are those who wash their robes, that they may have the right to the tree of life and may go through the gates into the city. Outside are the dogs, those who practice magic arts, the sexually immoral, the murderers, the idolaters and everyone who loves and practices falsehood" (Rev. 22:14, 15).

3. **Paul:** "Ye do wrong, and defraud, and that your brethren. Know ye not that the unrighteous shall not inherit the kingdom of God? Be not deceived: neither fornicators, nor idolaters, nor adulterers, nor effeminate, nor abusers of themselves with mankind, Nor thieves, nor covetous, nor drunkards, nor revilers, nor extortioners, shall inherit the kingdom of God. And such were some of you: but ye are washed, but ye are sanctified, but ye are justified in the name of the Lord Jesus, and by the Spirit of our God" (1 Cor. 6:8-11 KJV).

## Those Who Accept the Light

A white lily of fragrant promise blossoms right in the middle of Paul's dark list: "And such were some of you: but ye are washed, but ye are sanctified, but ye are justified in the name of the Lord Jesus, and by the Spirit of our God" (1 Cor. 6:11). The marvelous message of Jesus Christ, empowered by the deeply felt love of God, can redeem those living in the deepest depths of sin.

> **The new birth is the grand solution to heal man's broken relationship with God, and forgiveness is its crown jewel.**

Many people, thank God, will hear the gospel and believe the good news, realizing they need help. "Whoever lives by the truth," Jesus taught Nicodemus, will choose to "come into the light" that shines down on the road named *Repentance*. Repentance means to turn around and go in the opposite direction; it's all about getting on the right road. Repentance brings our sins into the *Son*light that is Jesus Christ, where we receive forgiveness. Instead of receiving more condemnation, we are born again, becoming a new creation.

The result is what Jesus "has done, has been done through God" (John 3:21). Hence, "we should not be like cringing, fearful slaves, but we should behave like God's very own children, adopted into the bosom of his family, and calling to him, 'Father, Father'" (Rom. 8:15 TLB). Because this is true, "you are no longer a slave, but a son; and since you are a son, God has made you also an heir" (Gal. 4:6, 7).

How fundamentally important that all who follow Jesus comprehend the full standing they have as children of God and co-heirs with Christ (Gal. 3:26; Rom. 8:17; 1 John 3:1, 2).

## A NEW BIRTH CERTIFICATE

In August 2009, we got a rather amazing email from my wife's youngest brother, Jon. Six or seven years ago, when Jon and his wife, Lori, were working with a youth group in Nebraska, they met Amanda—a teenage girl the same age as their son, Wesley. Amanda came from a terribly abusive home and was eventually taken from her parents by the state. She has been part of Jon and Lori's family ever since.

After conferring with their two sons, Jon and Lori legally adopted Amanda. She is 22, and her name is now Amanda Foote. She even has a new birth certificate. Now Jon and Lori have three legal heirs, and Amanda has two new brothers. She no longer has any legal claim upon her former parents, who disowned her—nor they upon her. The process was relatively simple.

They had thought of Amanda as their daughter for a long time, but I asked if anything felt different after that day at the courthouse. Jon said, "Absolutely! When it was official there was a huge change in Lori and me—sort of like when you see your newborn for the first time. And for Amanda, there was a change in her, too. Now she knew she belonged. She knew we were her parents."

The beauty of it all made me offer a word of thanks to the way-clearing of our Elder Brother Jesus, God's Beloved Son. God has given us a new name (His), a new legal standing (we are His responsibility and His heirs), and a new family (brothers and sisters in Christ, with God as our true Father).

But God went even further. He gave us something that Jon and Lori can't give Amanda. God gave us his Holy Spirit. In some ways it's like God gives us His DNA. But even more than that, God implants in us His heart, His mind, His passion, His holiness—and people even look at us and say, "My, how you bear a striking resemblance to your Father!"

*Used by permission of the Foote family. Cited in PreachingToday.Com.*

The window this story opens up lets in powerful Sonlight. The Foote family extended to Lori the spirit of adoption before the adoption was legal and continued to show it after the legal process was final. Lori felt she had been accepted into the family as a daughter equal to the two sons.

Beautiful truth, this:

This resurrection life you received from God is not a timid, grave-tending life. It's adventurously expectant, greeting God with a childlike "What's next, Papa?" God's Spirit touches our spirits and confirms who we really are. We know who he is, and we know who we are: Father and children. And we know we are going to get what's coming to us—

an unbelievable inheritance! We go through exactly what Christ goes through. If we go through the hard times with him, then we're certainly going to go through the good times with him! (Rom. 8:15-17 MSG).

When man's relationship with God is restored, it always shows up in his associations with his fellow men. The wonderful reality is Jesus' death and resurrection, anchored in the love of God, launched this new beginning. When the new birth takes place, Sonlight pours into the soul, expelling all its darkness.

The new birth is real. It happens as a miracle of God's abundant grace and births a new creation. People who repent receive a new heart that produces a new affection toward God. The light of God's Son pours over it and enters into it. Anyone who approaches Christ by faith and in repentance will receive this spiritual heart transplant. The promise is backed by the guarantee of Jesus' sacrifice on the cross and sealed with His resurrection from the dead.

> **A pulpit that does not regularly, faithfully, and untiringly celebrate the death and resurrection of Jesus has effectively cut out the heart of the gospel and rejected Jesus as the Lamb of God who takes away the sin of the world.**

## Nicodemus: The Wrong Side of Salvation History

What a conversation Jesus had with Nicodemus! Although Nicodemus refused the divine antidote, little wonder this dialogue changed the course of history. Sadly, no Biblical record indicates Nicodemus, a member of the Jewish ruling council, accepted Jesus' teaching about the new birth and the agape love in the heart of the heavenly Father.

Nicodemus did have continuing sympathies and admiration for Jesus, however. He tried to defend the Lord before the Sanhedrin on one occasion by asking the question:

"Does our law condemn anyone without first hearing him to find out what he is doing?" They replied, "Are you from Galilee, too? Look into it, and you will find that a prophet does not come out of Galilee" (John 7:51, 52).

The final Biblical insight into Nicodemus' choices occurred after Jesus' death on the cross:

Joseph of Arimathea asked Pilate for the body of Jesus. Now Joseph was a disciple of Jesus, but secretly because he feared the Jews. With Pilate's permission, he came and took the body away. He was accompanied by Nicodemus, the man who earlier had visited Jesus at night. Nicodemus brought a mixture of myrrh and aloes, about seventy-five pounds. Taking Jesus' body, the two of them wrapped it with the spices, in strips of linen. This was in accordance with Jewish burial customs. At the place where Jesus was crucified, there was a garden, and in the garden a new tomb, in which no one had ever been laid. Because it was the Jewish day of Preparation and since the tomb was nearby, they laid Jesus there (John 19:38-42).

Nicodemus, the first person to hear the prophecy of the new birth, rejected it as good news for his own life. Following Jesus' crucifixion, however, he had enough respect for Jesus to help bury him. His sympathies for Jesus motivated him to pay the bill for the seventy-five pounds of spices he and Joseph of Arimathea used to embalm Jesus. As for Joseph, he was a secret disciple of Jesus "because he feared the Jews" (John 19:38).

The Apostle John wrote his Gospel perhaps some 40 years after the Lord's crucifixion and resurrection. If John had acquired credible information that Nicodemus had become a disciple when he helped bury Jesus, would John not have recorded it, as he did with Joseph?

Nicodemus went to Jesus that historic night sincerely wanting to talk and, at the same time, thinking he could befriend the Lord by helping Him get established with the Jewish religious authorities. When Jesus turned the tables and offered His gracious help to Nicodemus, Israel's teacher departed that evening refusing to accept Jesus' offer.

One is left to wonder what Nicodemus was thinking when he and Joseph embalmed Jesus. Could it have been: *It really is a shame to see it come to this. Jesus was such an intelligent man and had a close relationship with God, no doubt about it. He was an excellent teacher and wonderful miracle worker, and he had the potential to be one of the greatest in our history. If only he had been content with his teaching gift. I wanted to help him, but he would not let me. He was determined to get into left field with a Messiah complex. If Jesus had not gone Messianic, we wouldn't be burying him today. His dogmatism brought it on Himself. If only he hadn't gone Messianic and gotten into blasphemy!*

Many in the 21st century have a heart like Nicodemus', who liked some things about Jesus' character and reserved to himself the right to pick and choose. "Why can't we follow Jesus' ethical teachings and reject His death as our substitute? If only we could get rid of His cross!" But Jesus' death on the old, rugged cross is what demonstrates for all time that Jesus is the Lamb of God and the Son of God. Jesus' literal and bodily resurrection is the final and ultimate proof of His identity (Acts 17:31). We must never take the message of Jesus' death in our place out of the gospel. Never! The church of Jesus Christ is forever inseparably linked to the blood atonement of Jesus Christ.

Nicodemus was on the wrong side of salvation history. What he said to Jesus could be his epitaph: "I believed Jesus was 'a teacher come from God.'" He did not, however, accept Jesus as the Messiah and Son of God.

Nicodemus lives in the Biblical record as a classic example of what might have been. He rejected the invitation of the Holy Spirit, and he did it with his Messiah standing in front of him. If Nicodemus had only been willing to make a decision:

- Like Abraham when he left his homeland in Ur of the Chaldeans and ultimately separated from and surrendered his entire family in order to follow God (Gen. 12:1-5).
- Like Moses when he forsook Egypt and all it had to offer because he saw the invisible Messiah (Exod. 2:11-15; Heb. 11:27).
- Like Jesus, who left heaven to give His all at Calvary, and who calls on each of His followers to "deny himself and take up his cross daily and follow [Him]" (Luke 9:23-26).

Salvation does not come from the outside inward by our works of righteousness, and Nicodemus' participation in the Lord's burial further illustrates this fact. The new birth results when a person believes Jesus is the Son of God and wholeheartedly repents. Paying the bill for the spices and then helping to prepare Jesus' body for burial was certainly a noble deed. But it was not proof Nicodemus had a change of heart and believed he was holding in his arms the earthly body of his Messiah and God's Son. Hence, his kind deed was not acceptable to the heavenly Father as a substitute for faith in His beloved Son's supremely sacrificial death.

> **If Nicodemus was right and Jesus was merely "a teacher come from God," then religious pluralism might have a point—Christianity would be just another religion in the modern pantheon of gods, alongside Hinduism, Buddhism, Islam, etc. But Jesus always claimed to be the Son of God, and John's Gospel is all about Jesus' proofs of this claim.**

Nicodemus is venerated as a saint by the Roman Catholic and Eastern Orthodox churches, based on a tradition that he did become a follower after Jesus' resurrection. Many Protestants also feel special sympathy for Nicodemus and choose to believe he ultimately experienced the new birth. Indeed! All followers of the Lord who cherish the transforming power of the new birth fondly hope he did.

Luke records after Pentecost a revival occurred among the priests of Jerusalem so that "a great company of the priests were obedient to the faith" (Acts 6:7). Although Nicodemus was not a priest, a revival on the scale of "a great company" of converts among the priests could have directly influenced "Israel's teacher."

As Nicodemus is presented in the Sacred Canon, any interpretation of his feelings about Jesus Christ must take into account Jesus' compliment and indictment in John 3:10-12:

> *The compliment:* "You are Israel's teacher." *The indictment:* "and do you not understand these things? I tell you the truth, we speak of what we know, and we testify to what we have seen, but still *you people do not accept our testimony. I have spoken to you of earthly things and you do not believe; how then will you believe if I speak of heavenly things?"* (Emphasis mine).

Comprehending this indictment should be very humbling. How easy for all of us to hold to a self-righteousness that refuses the righteousness that comes by believing Jesus Christ. This can be true of the highly revered teachers in the land, as well as the common man in the streets of life.

## Self-righteousness cuts across all social and economic strata of society.

Another story in the life of the Lord had the same result. A ruler who was morally upright in many ways came asking Jesus the price—what he had to do to inherit eternal life. Jesus looked inside his heart and saw his covetousness. The Lord told him to sell everything he had, give it away to the poor, and then come follow Jesus. The man went away sorrowfully because he had great wealth (Luke 18:18-27). Could it be this rich man and Nicodemus shared a powerful influence—they both, in their own eyes, had too much to give up. But Moses did too; yet he chose to walk away from everything Egypt could offer (1 Cor. 1:26-31; Heb. 11:24-27).

Jesus let the wealthy man go. The Lord did not call him back and offer him a lower standard. In fact, Jesus has never lowered the standard for anyone. This conclusion leaves no room for haughtiness, however. Anyone who gains eternal life will do so solely because of the great grace of God. Hence, as with Nicodemus, we hope the rich man, too, came to Jesus in repentance and faith after the Lord's resurrection, experiencing the new birth.

## CONVICTED CEO'S GOOD WORKS
## DON'T COUNT

Bernard Ebbers stood before the judge and asked for mercy.

The former CEO of WorldCom had recently been indicted for orchestrating an $11 billion accounting fraud that shut down the telecommunications firm in 2002, yet he asked for mercy.

His company's collapse represented the largest bankruptcy in U.S. history and devastated the lives of thousands of people, yet he asked for mercy.

Speaking on behalf of his client, defense attorney Reid Weingarten cited 169 letters from Ebbers' supporters, detailing the 63-year-old's heart condition and numerous (often anonymous) charitable gifts.

"If you live 60-some-odd years," said Weingarten, "if you have an unblemished record, if you have endless numbers of people who attest to your goodness, doesn't that count? Doesn't that count particularly on this day?"

The judge said "No!" and sentenced Ebbers to 25 years in a federal penitentiary.

*"WorldCom's Ebbers Gets 25 Years in Prison,"* Newsmax.com (7-13-05); www.PreachingToday.com.

# "AFTER THIS"!
# John 3:22–36

### A Retreat With Jesus
**22 After this, Jesus and his disciples went out into the Judean countryside, where he spent some time with them, and baptized.**

Jesus walked away from His visit to Jerusalem and the Passover Feast feeling rejected. One can wonder if the disciples thought they needed to encourage Him, and tried. But Jesus knew well what He had taught David a millennium earlier, when David's years of running from Saul were almost over: "David encouraged himself in the Lord his God" (1 Sam. 30:6).

"After this"! What a transition statement. It comes after one of the most important conversations in human history, and assured millennia-old paradigms would rapidly start falling, such as:

- The 2,000 year tradition, from Abraham to Christ, of offering animal sacrifices to atone for sin.
- The priestly system perpetuating the sacrificial system.

- The Jewish temple on Mount Moriah, the architectural center of gravity for the system.
- The Law of Moses as the legal basis for "outside-in" salvation and the foundation of the system.

None of these made their way successfully into the new order in the Lord's church. The final nails in the coffins of these old paradigms were the spikes Roman soldiers drove into Jesus' hands and feet.

The center of gravity for the new order would be the hearts of Spirit-indwelt people in the Lord's church, and Jesus is its leader in the power of the Holy Spirit. Both the people and the church were purchased with Jesus' own blood (Eph. 5:25; 2 Pet. 2:1).

In this retreat after the Lord departed Jerusalem, "He spent some time with them." The disciples had Jesus' undivided attention. Wow! What a treasure—to be alone for a few days with the Master Teacher. One can wonder if Jesus spent some time discussing with His disciples the good news of the new birth.

### John's Faithful Testimony

**23 Now John also was baptizing at Aenon near Salim, because there was plenty of water, and people were constantly coming to be baptized. 24 (This was before John was put in prison.) 25 An argument developed between some of John's disciples and a certain Jew over the matter of ceremonial washing. 26 They came to John and said to him, "Rabbi, that man who was with you on the other side of the Jordan—the one you testified about—well, he is baptizing, and everyone is going to him."**

The Apostle John now turns his attention back to the ministry of John the Baptist, but the themes remain intertwined. Nicodemus rejected his Messiah's message, personally and graciously given to him in Jerusalem.

John records while the Baptist "was baptizing at Aenon near Salim ... an argument developed between some of John's disciples and a certain Jew." The specific reason for the argument is not stated, although it had to do with "the matter of ceremonial washing." The dispute could have centered around the claim "Jesus' baptism was best" (John 3:25 TLB). This conclusion finds at least some support in the statement: "the one you testified about—well, he is baptizing and everyone is going to him."

**Every pastor knows arguments can so easily develop in the church over minor things, and minor things can**

**quickly become major issues. One of the devil's most effective weapons is to move the agenda away from the message of the cross.**

What is interesting, and links directly to Jesus' visit to Jerusalem, is the way they presented the argument to John the Baptist: "Rabbi, *that man*." In this conversation Jesus is not recognized as the Lamb of God, or the Messiah, or the Son of God, or the Son of Man, but as "that man"! And "that man"—the one who was with you on the other side of the Jordan, the one you testified about, "well, he is baptizing, and everyone is going to him."

The Apostle John in this chapter, therefore, contrasts the unbelief of Nicodemus with the faithful testimony of John the Baptist. The Baptizer did not flinch in his testimony at Aenon about Jesus, the Messiah and Son of God.

## 27 To this John replied, "A man can receive only what is given him from heaven."

Recognizing Jesus as Messiah always comes by revelation, and we then choose what we are willing to do with the revelation (see Matt. 16:17). The implication seems to be John's disciples might have been doubting Jesus was in fact who John announced Him to be. This would explain John's statement affirming he could only share what he had received from heaven. Even Nicodemus came close to the gospel when he said, "We know you are a teacher come from God" (John 3:2). But to come close is to fall woefully short!

So many people through the centuries have been born again when the revelation of Jesus as Savior has been met with faith. Others get the revelation, and like Joseph of Arimathea, are only willing to become secret disciples. Still others, like Nicodemus, are very willing to meet with Jesus and offer to help bring Him into their religious establishment and get Him accepted. After all, He could become one of the greatest of teachers! But when the tables are turned and the revelation of Jesus as the Son of Man unfolds right in front of their faces, they make the choice to walk away. These people turn their backs knowing, as Nicodemus did, "No man could do the things you are doing if God were not with him." Each of these responses indicates it is the work of the Holy Spirit to make Jesus known as the Messiah and Son of God, but the Holy Spirit does not compel obedience.

Although Nicodemus said "No" and John's disciples doubted, the Baptizer did not. His testimony was bold and clear. John followed a simple belief system, as verse 27 shows: *I know what I heard from heaven!* And water baptism, to Him, was a public testimony of heartfelt repentance, in anticipation of Messiah's pending appearance.

This great prophet lived with the incredibly exciting daily expectation, "This could be the time when it will all happen. I might meet Israel's long-awaited Messiah today!"

The day arrived! John met Him at Jordan River.

## Do you live with the hope any day now, perhaps today, could be the day-of-days for the Lord's second coming?

God broke into an ordinary day to fulfill exactly what the Holy Spirit foretold regarding His first appearing. The Father, His Son Jesus, and the Holy Spirit showed up at the Jordan River and transformed the day into one of the most extraordinary in human history. Mark recorded the sky was "torn open" (Mark 1:10). Whatever the phenomena as the event unfolded, it must have been an exhilarating moment for John the Baptist. The great Baptizer followed it up by pronouncing Jesus as the "Lamb of God" and the "Son of God" (John 1:29, 34).

Even when it goes against all conventional wisdom and political correctness, the first decision is to believe what Jesus says. Accept implicitly what He says and does. As your trust grows, you will also start living out the meaning of His teaching.

### The Ministry of the Best Man

**28 "You yourselves can testify that I said, 'I am not the Christ but am sent ahead of him.' 29 The bride belongs to the bridegroom. The friend who attends the bridegroom waits and listens for him, and is full of joy when he hears the bridegroom's voice. That joy is mine, and it is now complete. 30 He must become greater; I must become less."**

The analogy of a best man at a wedding is an apt illustration of John's role. The great joy of the best man is to bring the groom and the bride together and then stand back and delight in their overflowing joy. John the Baptist fulfilled this friend-of-the-bridegroom function by announcing Jesus to the world as the "Lamb of God."

> John replied, "God in heaven appoints each man's work. My work is to prepare the way for that man so that everyone will go to him ... and I am filled with joy at his success. He must become greater and greater, and I must become less and less" (John 3:27-30 TLB).

John's work as the "friend of the bridegroom" was winding down, and the Bridegroom's star was beginning to rise. John was not jealous; instead, he was at peace with his role. This word picture of groom and bride seems to be the closest John came to comprehending that Messiah's bride would be a pure and holy church (Eph. 5:27).

**31 "The one who comes from above is above all; the one who is from the earth belongs to the earth, and speaks as one from the earth. The one who comes from heaven is above all. 32 He testifies to what he has seen and heard, but no one accepts his testimony. 33 The man who has accepted it has certified that God is truthful. 34 For the one whom God has sent speaks the words of God, for God gives the Spirit without limit. 35 The Father loves the Son and has placed everything in his hands. 36 Whoever believes in the Son has eternal life, but whoever rejects the Son will not see life, for God's wrath remains on him."**

John the Baptist himself had received a powerful revelation from heaven telling him how to recognize the Messiah. Based on this understanding, John gave a marvelous summary of the basic elements of "the gospel of God" (Rom. 1:1).

1.  "The one who comes from above is above all." This is how John viewed the Messiah. Since He came from God, He is superior over all. As for John, he saw himself as having come "from the earth"; therefore, John understood himself as belonging to the earth. To make sure the point was not missed, John restated it: The Messiah came from heaven and "is above all" (See Eph. 1:21; 4:26; Col. 2:9, 10).
2.  The great tragedy regarding this highly distinguished visitor from heaven, John said, was "no one accepts his testimony." The rejection of the Messiah whom John introduced must have been very painful to the Baptizer, as it surely was to Jesus.

> **One of the great lessons in the life of the Lord is how marvelously the gospel advanced amid the pain of conflict and rejection. It still does!**

3.  "The man who has accepted it has certified that God is truthful." John knew he had bonded to Messiah's teaching and was fully prepared to say it. The opposite also was true: many Israelites rejected their Messiah and His teachings. To walk away from Jesus is also to forfeit His gift of eternal life.
4.  The capstone in John's reasoning, as a man of great faith, was "the one whom God has sent speaks the words of God." Jesus' ministry as the voice of God, who came speaking *heaven talk*, began with Jesus' baptism in Jordan River. This great Trinitarian moment marked Jesus' inauguration as Messiah.

The Father spoke from heaven at the grand event and affirmed He was "well pleased" with His Son (Matt. 3:13-17). In that moment His Father poured the Holy Spirit without measure into Jesus (John 3:34).

The Baptizer knew what it had meant to his life to have the Holy Spirit with him from his earliest childhood memories—from his mother's womb. John could not have done his work without this anointing (Luke 1:15). But he also knew what he received was measured and focused for a particular mission: to announce the Messiah.

Each of the Old Testament prophets served in the power of the Spirit, and degrees of anointing can be seen in each of them. This is not to say one prophet was better than another, or more important than another. Each was faithful in his call from God and each looked forward to Messiah's appearing. Their prophecies culminated with the greatest prophet, John the Baptist, who was given the mission to introduce God's Son.

None of these prophets in the routine of their lives manifested all of the gifts of the Spirit as expressed in the ministry of Jesus, the ultimate prophet. He set the standard in His own ministry for what would become the gifts of the Spirit in the church. Jesus Christ is the fountainhead of these ministry gifts, and the ultimate illustration of what it means to be *multi-gifted*. All the Spirit does in the church flows out of the ministry of Jesus, the Christ. He was and is "the One and Only," who is "the head of the church" (Eph. 1:10, 22; 4:15; 5:23; Col. 1:8).

5.  Then follows another of John's marvelous insights into the nature of the Trinity that he could have comprehended only by revelation. The heavenly Father loves His Son, so much, in fact, He "has placed everything in his hands." *Everything* in this instance is universally applicable, but it also focuses here on one primary idea: "everything" about the plan of redemption has been "placed in His hands."

6.  The Baptizer also understood Jesus as the Messiah and knew the Lamb of God would be successful. Therefore, John could reassuringly say, "Whoever believes in the Son has eternal life." The flip side of John's reasoning is also true: "Whoever rejects the Son will not see life, for God's wrath remains on him." This statement is about as clear as the gospel gets. It balances grace (the love in the heart of God that forgives and does favors) and truth (the justice in the heart of God that judges and applies consequences).

Said another way, the heavenly Father loved the world so much He gave His only begotten Son to take our sins to the cross and die in our place. In the face of such an overwhelmingly generous gift, if people exercise their free will and say "No!" to God's Son—what is left but judgment? Is not the justice of God fully justified in judging sin?

> **John the Baptist's message was straightforward, offering no apology to anyone. John *knew* he had heard from God and that Jesus Christ is the one and only road to heaven and eternal life. The Baptizer never watered down this message for anybody.**

John 3 is unquestionably one of the most important chapters in the New Testament. It is a portrait of Jesus' diagnosis of the human dilemma and the antidote He provided at Calvary. It is also a chapter that shows Jesus being rejected in Jerusalem (especially by Nicodemus), as well as at Aenon, a long way from Jerusalem. In fact, no one publicly confesses faith in Jesus as the Son of God for the first time in Chapter 3.

But John the Baptist remained faithful.

To willfully reject God's Son is also to reject the Son's heavenly Father. While this is offensive to the Father, the bottom line is we are judged by the choices we make. Our own words convict us when we reject His Son, and the wrath of the Father must follow. If the Father does not judge, then He also loses His right to love. This is true because love is not love if it refuses to judge evil. All the evidence needed to demonstrate this conclusion can be obtained by asking a father or mother who is lovingly rearing a child. For the good of the child, a parent will make judgments and enforce them when the child errs. A dad (or mom) who does not do this does not love his child (John 16:9; Heb. 12:5-11).

If Chapter 3 is a record of people rejecting Jesus' offer of the new birth that came to them from the Son of God and Savior of the world, then Chapter 4 is refreshingly the opposite. The Apostle John next weaves a winsome story about Jesus being enthusiastically accepted as the Messiah and Savior of the world by a woman who was a Samaritan.

# CHAPTER 4

## JESUS: THE SOULWINNER
### The New Birth Illustrated

*The Samaritan woman whom Jesus met at Jacob's Well shows the fruit of the new birth. To win her and her village, Jesus demonstrated what would become a five-fold ministry gift-mix in the church: apostle, prophet, evangelist, pastor and teacher. Jesus' discussion with this woman marks the third of the major discourses John records. In stepping across centuries-old boundaries to reach out to ethnically diverse peoples, Jesus demonstrated just how attractive the gospel would be after His death and resurrection. In this chapter Jesus also finds acceptance in Galilee and performs at Cana His second of the seven miracles John records.*

### DISPUTING WATER BAPTISM
### John 4:1-3
**1 The Pharisees heard that Jesus was gaining and baptizing more disciples than John, 2 although in fact it was not Jesus who baptized, but his disciples. 3 When the Lord learned of this, he left Judea and went back once more to Galilee.**

The Apostle John was emphatic here: "... in fact it was not Jesus who baptized, but his disciples." The reason Jesus did not baptize anyone may have been He knew the tendencies in the hearts of people. If the snake on a pole over time could become an idol, then the meaning of water baptism could expand beyond the original intent as well. It would not be long before every generation of the Lord's church would connect water baptism with salvation. But baptismal regeneration is not a doctrine taught by Jesus or His apostles. Water baptism must be viewed as a public testimony to the inward, redemptive work of the Holy Spirit in the heart of a believer that results in a new birth. Water baptism offers no redeeming grace; the salvation Jesus provides always works from the inside out.

The satement "When the Lord learned of this ..." shows insight into the true humanity of Jesus. One way Jesus learned was by talking to people. At other times, Jesus received information directly from His Father as His life was guided by the Holy Spirit. John will give more insight into how this latter process worked in Jesus' life in Chapter 5.

Obviously, Jesus wanted to avoid unnecessary tension regarding the size of His crowds compared to His forerunner's smaller following. In addition, Jesus chose not to be part of the "counters"—those who were collecting the numbers of how many people were being baptized by Jesus' disciples and by the Baptizer. Consequently, Jesus "left Judea and went back once more to Galilee."

# TWO DAYS WITH JESUS IN SAMARIA
## John 4:4–42
### 4 Now he had to go through Samaria.

When the Lord told His disciples His intent, they had no idea what was ahead in their next 48 hours, but they could feel His strong determination. They would have to get the explanation for going through Samaria as events unfolded amid those very life-changing two days.

> **This "had to go" is an expression of necessity; no other options were available. Have you ever felt compelled by the Holy Spirit?**

Chapter 3 records the Lord in dialogue with one person, and so does Chapter 4. This time Jesus stepped out of His Jewish comfort zone to reach out to a woman in a different subculture, although they both spoke the same language. This is a picture, therefore, of Jesus as the first fruits of apostolic missionaries, who regularly cross cultures and languages to reach people groups who have never heard the gospel story.

One of the subthemes of the ministry of Jesus is how He gave honor and dignity to women in a male-dominated culture, thus elevating their social status. The traditions of the day held women to a status not much better than a slave—but not Jesus. This story of the Samaritan woman ends with her becoming an evangelist to her own people, literally bringing them to meet Jesus.

## Animosities of the Centuries: Jews vs. Samaritans

The ancient city of Sychar is about 35 driving miles north of Jerusalem. Three roads could have taken Jesus back to Galilee: the western coastal road along the Mediterranean Sea, the road east of the Jordan that went north through Perea, and the road straight north through Samaria. Jesus chose the latter, the middle road. "He had to go through Samaria." After He arrived at Sychar, His goal became clear: He wanted to open up a forgotten people group to the gospel. This was an apostolic act.

The Samaritans intermarried with the pagan population the Assyrian government imported into northern Israel after the Assyrian conquest of the northern ten tribes of Israel in 732 B.C. (see 2 Kings 17). For this reason, Jews did not recognize Samaritans as true sons of Abraham, and they regularly used the derogatory term "half-breeds" to describe them. The Samaritans responded to the rejection with construction of their own temple on Mount Gerizim. They also developed their own version of the Torah. The chasm between the Samaritans and the Jews at the time of Jesus' ministry had become so enormous, the Jews and Samaritans had effectively cut off any social interaction. But business dealings were acceptable!

> **Prejudice is very deceitful. The disciples could go into town to buy bread (John 4:8), but they could not evangelize the Samaritans.**

### Jesus, the Apostle Sent From God

As the Apostle sent by God, Jesus did not consider Himself bound by these ancient rivalries (Heb. 3:1). Instead, Israel's Messiah showed special interest and love to the discarded Samaritans. Jesus blazed a new trail that cut through the centuries of religious bigotry. To Jesus, there are no half-breeds; all people can become sons of God. No ethnic group is beyond hope in Jesus' eyes, for anyone is a son of Abraham who chooses to share Abraham's faith in God (Matt. 3:9; Luke 3:8; John 8:39-58; Gal. 3:6-9).

### Jesus as an Evangelist

Chapter 4 unveils Jesus as a winner of souls, putting into practice what He had taught Nicodemus about the new birth (see Prov. 11:30).

> **Religious pluralists in the first-century Roman Empire would have seen no need to try to bring Nicodemus or this woman to a new birth. Their reasoning would say the Jewish road to God was already adequate, and the Samaritan path too. In fact, why did Jesus need to establish Christianity at all if the other roads were adequate to get to heaven?**
>
> **This kind of erroneous thinking portrays Jesus' death on the cross as totally unnecessary and even stupid (1 Cor. 3:19).**

Nicodemus, the morally upright national leader whom Jesus recognized as "Israel's teacher," definitely needed a Messiah, and this immoral Samaritan woman with her reputation in shatters did too. Nicodemus rejected his opportunity, but the Samaritan woman quickly opened up to the gospel.

Most people of her time would not have viewed her as a likely prospect for restoration to a new life. In fact, the Jewish people would not talk to her—she suffered from great rejection. The Samaritans who were her neighbors had also written her off. After all, she had been married five times and was living with a man out of wedlock. No one, in fact, could offer her any hope. Instead, the men she had known had been all too willing to take advantage of her.

Prejudice ran rampant between Jews and Samaritans. Pharisees, who believed in the resurrection, were known to pray that Samaritans would not be raised from the dead. On one occasion, the Lord's critics used the term *Samaritan* as an epithet to insult Jesus (John 8:48).

Samaritans were equally prejudiced toward Jews. Luke records an episode in which the people in a Samaritan village would not extend to Jesus a welcome that showed even basic hospitality. Their sole reason was "because he was heading to Jerusalem" (Luke 9:53)! These could have been Jesus' Samaritan critics who remembered this first visit when He did not affirm their own brand of religion.

Jesus, however, the Son of Man from Galilee, knew this woman was crying out in her heart for help. She wanted to escape the life she was living. In going to her, Jesus shows how people who have lost all hope and are excluded by society are, in fact, prime candidates for the gospel. The Samaritans were proud and haughty, as were the Jews. Both believed they were right. This story shows how easy it is to be *sincerely* wrong! Sincerity alone does not prove truth.

Jesus knew the Jews and the Samaritans needed redemption, as was true for all people worldwide (John 3:16, 17). The Apostle Paul, following in the Lord's footsteps, presented this need as universal too (Rom. 1:18–3:20). Every person, no matter his ethnicity or status in life, deserves a good chance to hear the gospel.

To Jesus, she alone was worth His trip through Samaria. A primary principle of the gospel is do not write anyone off!

### "I WANT THAT WATER!"

Philip Yancey wrote in Christianity Today of an encouraging truth he heard from a young man named Mike who worked among the homeless:

"Mike told me that homeless people, having hit bottom, don't waste time building up an image or trying to conform. And they pray without pretense, a refreshing contrast to what he found in some churches.

"I asked for an example.

"He said: 'My friend and I were playing guitars and singing *As the Deer Panteth for the Water*, when David, a homeless man we knew, started weeping. "That's what I want, man," he said. "I want that water. I'm an alcoholic and I want to be healed." ' "

*Philip Yancey, "The Word on the Street," Christianity Today (January 2006), p. 80.*

**5 So he came to a town in Samaria called Sychar, near the plot of ground Jacob had given to his son Joseph. ⁶ Jacob's well was there, and Jesus, tired as he was from the journey, sat down by the well. It was about the sixth hour.**

The town of Sychar is the setting for this story. The place was historic. Its Old Testament name was Shechem, first mentioned in the Bible as a site of Abraham's wanderings (Gen. 12:6). Abraham's grandson, Jacob, dug a well there, known in history as Jacob's Well. It remains to this day a source of lifegiving water. Jacob bequeathed the land "to his son Joseph" (Gen. 33:18, 19; 34:2; 48:21, 22). The connection to Jacob and Joseph helps to explain why the Samaritans later valued highly the five books of Moses, also known as the Torah. The city is the site where Joseph was buried (Josh. 24:32). The West Bank city of Nablus (its Arabic name) has developed in the modern era in the area of Sychar. It has a population of 130,000.

In a book dedicated to presenting Jesus as the Son of God, John shows Him again in His true humanity. John did it with the statement: "Jesus, tired as he was by the journey, sat down by the well." This was John's way of saying the Son of Man lived with the limitations of physical frailty, one of which was demonstrated here: He was exhausted "from the journey."

Jesus' sole motivational tool for reaching this woman was the agape love of God. The Lord's model as an evangelist was to invite only in love; He never compelled her or anyone else with a dagger or a spear. We admit, however, there was a time in salvation history when people in the name of Jesus used the sword to compel conversions; e.g., the medieval crusades. (The term *crusade* derives from a French word that means "taking up the cross." Roman Catholics from all over Europe between 1095 and 1291 fought a series of wars to rid Palestine from the "infidel Muslims" and take back the Holy sites in Israel. The earliest wars had some success; ultimately, the crusaders were not able to hold the Palestinian territory they conquered.)

The Apostle John would have been revolted by the crusades. He would not have recognized the crusaders as faithful followers of the Lord whom He listened to, saw, and "touched with his own hands" (1 John 1:1 TLB). The Savior who gave the new commandment taught, "Love one another as I have loved you" (John 13:34; 15:12, 17). In contrast, when measured by the standard of the love of God demonstrated on the cross, the crusades were decidedly unchristian.

**This sad chapter in church history does not justify, however, carving the Great Commission out of the gospel by adopting the mindset of Christian universalism: *If all people will ultimately be saved anyway, what is the need for evangelists?***

**When the progress of the gospel is powered humbly by the "great love wherewith he loved us" (Eph. 2:4 KJV), Jesus' message of transforming love is such good news, it always advances.**

**7 When a Samaritan woman came to draw water, Jesus said to her, "Will you give me a drink?" 8 (His disciples had gone into the town to buy food.)**

In the Jewish way of counting time, the sixth hour would typically be about noon. Samaritan women usually went to the well early in the morning when the day was cool. But not this very rejected woman. She went about noon, in the heat of the day.

One can easily picture Jesus sitting at the well, waiting on the woman to arrive whom He already knew in the Spirit was coming. How long He waited, we are not told. She had a noon appointment with the Savior of the world, but did not know it.

It is easy to imagine what she would have missed, as well as her whole town, if she had not kept the appointment she did not know she had. People in every generation for 2,000 years of gospel preaching would have also lost a story offering them great hope and encouragement if she had not shown up.

The woman who approached the well walked slowly. No bounce was in her step and all sparkle was gone from her eyes. She was lonely and downcast, and kept looking at the ground. She just wanted to be left alone. Her whole demeanor said, "Don't bother me; my life is miserable and I'd fix it if I could, but I can't. So please, just leave me alone!"

**Perhaps Jesus has sat at your "well," too, waiting for you to show up. What a tragedy to miss an appointment with the God of the universe!**

As she neared the well she looked up, and what did she see?
A man was sitting on the well.
But not just a man
Worse, a Jew.
"Oh no! How in the world will I handle this?"
Then she might have reasoned, "Since he is a Jew, maybe I can draw my water fast and leave, and he won't say anything; and I certainly won't speak to him."
The separating prejudices of both the Jews and the Samaritans are demonstrated vividly in this scene. They would not carry on a conversation with each other (other than to do business!). These verses show how Jesus firmly refused to live by those

prejudices. Based on the conventional standards of what she expected from a Jew, Jesus the evangelist was very forward with her. He engaged her in conversation, touching an area of instant mutual need: "May I please have a drink of your water?"

> **All effective evangelism begins at this point. Acting out of sincere concern for another human being, establish common ground.**

## 9 The Samaritan woman said to him, "You are a Jew and I am a Samaritan woman. How can you ask me for a drink?" (For Jews do not associate with Samaritans.)

Her answer blurted out of her mouth. She was taken aback by Jesus talking to her at all, and certainly His request must have come through as incredible. Her response portrays the depth and breadth of the ugly racism of the day: Jews and Samaritans "do not associate." A Jewish man could not ask a Samaritan woman for even a drink of water!

Without question, Jesus the Evangelist had thrown out the hook, and the woman had taken the bait. "What is going on?" she must have thought. "Why is this man asking *me* for a drink of water?" Curiosity took its hold.

### Jesus, the Master Teacher

Jesus at this point became her teacher and responded to her question, but not as she expected. Instead, He further whetted her appetite.

## 10 Jesus answered her, "If you knew the gift of God and who it is that asks you for a drink, you would have asked him and he would have given you living water."

Jesus was leading this woman to discover three vitally important facts: who He was, the gift he had to offer, and how she could receive it. In achieving these, He did not enter into a discussion with her about the cruel racial divides separating Samaritans and Jews. Instead, He deflected that subject to teach her He had a gift far better than anything she had ever imagined. It was superior to the abundant water supply from Jacob's Well that had sustained the lifestyle of the area for some 1,700 years.

Jesus already knew she carried deep in her heart the hope that Messiah would one day come and straighten everything out. He also knew she realized she was trapped in a destructive lifestyle and yearned to break free, but did not know how. She desperately needed the aid of the Master Teacher to lead her to freedom.

The Lord's instruction in this discourse shows salvation is a "gift of God." It is never earned because no one can do enough good deeds in life to be worthy of it. This discourse also demonstrates the mission of gospel preaching is not to debate the existence of God. Jesus did not say to the woman, "If you knew God is real." Jesus assumed she already knew God exists and spoke to her accordingly: "If you knew the gift of God."

Gospel preaching takes for granted people know God exists and they are not living up to the light they have about God (Rom. 1:18-21). The image of God in the soul of every unbeliever is shattered, dead in trespasses and sins. But the Holy Spirit has the power to resurrect that image and convince people Jesus is their Messiah. In fact, doing this is basic to the job description of the Holy Spirit (Eph. 2:1 KJV; John 16:8). The primary mission of all preaching, therefore, is to offer people the "gift of God," and Jesus Christ in His own person is this gift.

The word picture Jesus chose to communicate this good news came from her natural surroundings. The Samaritan Woman had walked to Jacob's Well to draw water, so the Master Teacher made the well His classroom and the water His object lesson. God's Son (also Jacob's son and Jacob's God) was sitting on the well. Jesus taught this hurting woman with His own gentle demeanor and His kind and accepting voice. He was also generous with His grace. In fact, Jesus had a special gift for her—yes, for her. This lesson was all the more exciting to her because all of the men in her life had been *takers*; and what they wanted most was to use her body for their own selfish pleasure.

The Jew at Jacob's Well spoke in a way she had never heard. He approached her as a person worthy to receive a gracious gift; He was offering her "*living water*"—for free!

She had never met a man in her life so genuinely concerned about her. "Surely there is a catch!" she must have thought.

But Jesus' concern for her was genuine and free, and without deceit. Jesus was a true pastor/shepherd to her.

## PASTORS: AGENTS OF CHRIST'S COMPASSION

Around 7 p.m. on the evening of Friday, May 31, 1985, an F3-magnitude tornado swept through Beaver County, Pennsylvania, just north of Pittsburgh. We were at church for a meeting, and when we got word of the storm, we had no idea how bad it had been. When our meeting came to an end, we headed to the home of some friends just as we had planned on doing.

My friend is a surgeon, and when we arrived at his home, one of his colleagues was already at the door. All the physicians in the area were being summoned to the medical center. My surgeon friend, Roy, ran to his car and left immediately. We stood there wondering what we could do. I thought, *"I'm a pastor. Maybe I should go to the Medical Center, too."* But I did not want to go. I was frightened. *"I'd probably be in the way,"* I reasoned. *"What could I possibly do? They've already got people lined up for these things."*

You may think pastors enter their line of work to help people, but that night I wanted no part of it! Finally, with God's sharp finger in the middle of my back, I reluctantly drove to the hospital.

The devastation was worse than we'd imagined. Phone lines were down. Traffic was at a standstill. Kids were driving around, and their parents had no idea where they were. It turned out that the hospital was the only place where worried people could think to go. Many had been injured and three people were dead. The lady in charge of the emergency room—a woman from our church—would call out from time to time: "Is there anyone from the Jack Smith family here?" Otherwise, folks sat and worried.

Having no better idea of what to do, I just started walking up to clusters of people. I would say, "I'm a pastor, and I wonder if you'd like me to pray for you and your family."

"Yes, please," they said. "That would be great."

No one asked me what church I served, and no one—not one person—even hesitated to accept my prayers. I think I was the only one at the hospital that evening praying for people.

It hit me later that night that I am an agent of Christ's compassion in this world, and that means going where people are "harassed and helpless, like sheep without a shepherd." I do this not because I'm a pastor, but because I am a Christian. When others retreat from heartache and sorrow, we step in because we walk with Jesus.

Lee Eclov, Vernon Hills, Illinois. Cited in PreachingToday.Com.

What Jesus taught the woman at the well shows a masterful balance of grace and truth. Jesus' goal was to correct her and not punish her. Without being judgmental, Jesus led her to face truthfully the many choices in her past that had ended with such terrible life consequences. He also opened up to her a gracious promise showing *she* could discover the fountain of "living water." Jesus did it without any desire to manipulate or use her, and His grace did not have a price tag.

When Jesus' identity as the Son of God and the Lamb of God dawns in the awareness of people, they become candidates for what He does perfectly. Jesus always balances grace and truth in every offer of the new birth. The Apostle Paul later penned a classic summary of this stunningly good news:

**TRUTH:** "It wasn't so long ago that you were mired in that old stagnant life of sin. You let the world, which doesn't know the first thing about living, tell you how to live. You filled your lungs with polluted unbelief, and then exhaled disobedience. We all did it, all of us doing what we felt like doing, when we felt like doing it, all of us in the same boat. It's a wonder God didn't lose his temper and do away with the whole lot of us.

**GRACE:** "Instead, immense in mercy and with an incredible love, he embraced us. He took our sin-dead lives and made us alive in Christ. He did all this on his own, with no help from us! Then he picked us up and set us down in highest heaven in company with Jesus, our Messiah" (Eph. 2:1-6 MSG).

The word picture for grace Jesus offered Nicodemus was a second birth; with the woman at the well, it was living water. Both communicate the same message: the radical change that produces a new creation must take place in a person's heart, the innermost sanctum of life (2 Cor. 5:17; Gal. 6:15).

The prophets understood repentance was a requirement for the rebellion against God to be cured in the DNA of all people:

Repent! Turn away from all your offenses; then sin will not be your downfall. Rid yourselves of all the offenses you have committed, and get a new heart and a new spirit. Why will you die, O house of Israel? For I take no pleasure in the death of anyone, declares the Sovereign LORD. Repent and live! (Ezek. 18:30-32; 36:26; see also Jer. 31:31-33).

How is "a new heart and a new spirit" to be achieved? The prophets gave a clear diagnosis of the problem, but they were powerless to offer the antidote. Only Jesus the Messiah was able to make the sacrifice guaranteeing this cure.

It is easy to see why the ministry of Jesus as the Master Teacher set the stage for *teaching* to be one of the gifts of the Spirit in the Lord's church.

**11 "Sir," the woman said, "you have nothing to draw with and the well is deep. Where can you get this living water? 12 Are you greater than our father Jacob, who gave us the well and drank from it himself, as did also his sons and his flocks and herds?"**

This woman may have never seen the Mediterranean Sea or the Sea of Galilee. Quite possibly the only water she understood was what she had pulled thousands of times out of Jacob's well. Her ancestors had been going back to this same water supply for some 17 centuries; it had been the lifeline of her people. Yes, the well was deep and Jesus had no jar to draw the water up to the surface. So, she asked Him, "Where can you get this living water? Are you greater than our father Jacob?"

Except for her deep seriousness in asking it, this would have been an amusing question to Jesus—"Are you greater?" Yes, Jesus was both greater than Jacob and greater than the well Jacob dug. The water Jesus was talking about is greater, too, because it is eternal.

In His gentle reply to her humorous question ...

**13 Jesus answered, "Everyone who drinks this water will be thirsty again, ¹⁴ but whoever drinks the water I give him will never thirst. Indeed, the water I give him will become in him a spring of water welling up to eternal life."**

She certainly understood the statement about thirst. Since she was a little girl walking with her mother, she had made the daily trip to the well to draw water. Before she was even close to being strong enough to carry a jar of water on her head, the habit had been established in her to go to the well early in the morning. Her ancestors had done the same thing with their daughters, day after day, century after century.

It is a compliment to the authority of Jesus that the woman began to catch the figure of speech Jesus was using and the rich meaning behind it. She did not think He was joking. His offer to her was genuine. This water would end the dehydration of her soul. She would "never thirst" again. Jesus' sincerity came through to her as the Holy Spirit communicated Jesus really could deliver on His promise.

**Jesus not only spoke the vocabulary of heaven; He said it with the weight and force of heaven. He always does!**

**15 The woman said to him, "Sir, give me this water so that I won't get thirsty and have to keep coming here to draw water."**

She made her request. Her statement summarizes the cry in the heart of unsaved people worldwide. All live with a restless fear of coming judgment (Acts 17:31; Ps. 96:13; Heb. 9:27). People want a new life, but don't know how to find it. How desperately they need someone to tell them how to discover the living water to end all thirst! The result is the experience of a new birth, and it offers a fresh start in their relationship with God. If only Nicodemus had opened his heart like she did—but Nicodemus did not think he needed Jesus' help.

## SPIRITUAL DEHYDRATION

An Algerian named Lag Lag and his companion's truck broke down while crossing the Sahara desert.

They nearly died of thirst during the three weeks they waited before being rescued. As their bodies dehydrated, they became willing to drink anything in hopes of quenching their terrible thirst. The sun forced them into the shade under the truck, where they dug a shallow trench. Day after day they lay there. They had food, but did not eat, fearing it would magnify their thirst. Dehydration, not starvation, kills wanderers in the desert, and thirst is the most terrible of all human sufferings.

Physiologists use Greek-based words to describe stages of human thirst. For example, the Sahara is *dipsogenic*, meaning "thirst provoking." In Lag Lag's case, they might say he progressed from *eudipsia*, "ordinary thirst," through bouts of *hyperdipsia*, meaning "temporary intense thirst," to *polydipsia*, "sustained excessive thirst." Polydipsia means the kind of thirst that drives one to drink anything.

For word enthusiasts, this is heady stuff. Nevertheless, the lexicon has not kept up with technology. I have tried, and cannot coin a suitable word for drinking rusty radiator water. That's what Lag Lag and his assistant started into when good drinking water was gone. In order to survive, they were willing to drink, in effect, poison.

Many people do something similar in the spiritual realm. They depend on things like money, sex, and power to quench spiritual thirst. Unfortunately, such "thirst quenchers" are in reality spiritual poison, a dangerous substitute for the "living water" Jesus promised and gives freely, attaching no price tag (Isa. 55:1).

*William Langewiesche, Sahara Unveiled (Vintage, 1997). Cited from PreachingToday.Com.*

### Jesus as Prophet

What follows is a classic display of the role of prophecy in evangelism.

**16 He told her, "Go, call your husband and come back." 17 "I have no husband," she replied. Jesus said to her, "You are right when you say you have no husband. 18 The fact is,**

**you have had five husbands, and the man you now have is not your husband. What you have just said is quite true."**

This is prophecy woven into Jesus' special gift as an evangelist—the gift-mix of prophetic evangelism. Jesus discerned a series of facts about her He could not have known except by the gift of God. He also had the anointing to speak them prophetically to her.

1. *"You are right ..."*—Jesus agreed she spoke truthfully. He knew her life so well He could immediately compliment her for telling the truth.
2. *"... when you say you have no husband."* Of the five men who had been in her life with the title of husband, it is quite possible not one of them had been a true husband to her. It really is heartrending to hear her admit she was living with a sixth man, but most probably neither did he treat her as his treasured partner and helper, and the pearl of great price in his life. Instead, he most probably saw little value in her either, except for what he could get. We are only left to wonder how many times men had cursed and physically beaten her, always with the goal to use her, and no one had ever come to her rescue.
3. *"The fact is you have had five husbands."*—Only the spirit of prophecy working in Jesus could have discerned this and revealed it to Him.
4. *"The man you now have is not your husband. What you have just said is quite true."*

> **Her self-estimate must have been zilch. The important people in her life routinely treated her as worthless. How many times she had cried out from the depth of her soul, "Will anybody ever treat me as somebody?"**

Wow! When a prophet in the contemporary church speaks one important fact about a person's life he had no way to know except by the revelation of the Holy Spirit, it is amazing to watch how people positively respond. Prophecy is a powerful compliment to an evangelist's ministry. It routinely penetrates the hardest hearts, opening them up to Jesus, the Lamb of God, as the antidote for their rebellion against God. If Jesus had said, "You have had four husbands, and the man you are living with now is not your husband," she would have rejected Him as a prophet and the conversation would have been over.

One of the functions of prophecy is to penetrate the dark inner strongholds that keep people from seeing and accepting the truth. The Apostle John in his first epistle identified this blinding effect of sin, so that people live with a shroud over their spiritual ability to see. "The person who hates his brother is in the dark—yes, he is walking in the dark, and he doesn't know where he is going, because the darkness has blinded his eyes" (1 John 2:11 CJB).

The Apostle Paul also explained this spiritual blindness: "The god of this age has blinded the minds of unbelievers, so that they cannot see the light of the gospel of the glory of Christ, who is the image of God" (2 Cor. 4:4, 5).

All soul winning efforts must face this spiritual blindness and trust the Holy Spirit to enable the soul winner to discern the stronghold keeping people in spiritual darkness. Jesus set the example with perfect accuracy in the life of this Samaritan woman.

### 19 "Sir," the woman said, "I can see that you are a prophet."

This woman knew enough about the scriptures to understand the fundamentals of the role of prophets. Prophets predict the future, discern people's hearts, and call them to renewed commitment to the foundational principles of the gospel.

This woman immediately recognized Jesus' prophetic ability. But Jesus was getting too close to the most painful things in her past by identifying her multiple marriages and her current live-in arrangement. Hence, she went into self-preservation mode, trying to escape from where the conversation had gone. With five failed relationships over the years, she had tried time and again to be her own physician and heal herself. She could make the decision to forget and move on, but she never could quite achieve it; the noose called sin held her too tightly. She was a trapped woman. So, to avoid facing the pain, she turned to a technique she had used so many times—change the subject when people got too close to the shambles in her past.

---

**A congregation that does not give place to prophetic ministry is spiritually anemic. It will most likely never reach people like this woman—even though they are crying out for help! Instead, they most likely will write her kind off as beyond help. To try to do the work of the Great Commission while neglecting the gifts of the Spirit routinely leads to futility!**

---

### 20 "Our fathers worshiped on this mountain, but you Jews claim that the place where we must worship is in Jerusalem."

The Samaritan woman's memorable effort at diverting attention was to start a theological argument. It had worked for her so many times. But it was not good enough to break the focus of the Son of God who had "nailed" her inner core. No doubt she was thinking: *Please! No more discussion about my personal life because I am a failure and of no value anyway. Let's talk about things of importance to the world like, "… tell me, why is it that you Jews insist Jerusalem is the only place of worship, while we Samaritans claim it is here [at Mount Gerizim], where our ancestors worshiped?"* (John 4:20 TLB.)

Jesus did not take the bait. Her soul to Him was priceless. In fact, He had walked until He was bone tired just to arrive on time to meet her. She was far more important to Jesus than the stones and precious metals in either temple. Jesus was focused on healing *her*, not the great estrangement between Jews and Samaritans. His solution for that chasm would come later.

Jesus wanted to fill the far deeper hole in her heart that had developed between her and her God.

**21 Jesus declared, "Believe me, woman, a time is coming when you will worship the Father neither on this mountain nor in Jerusalem. ²² You Samaritans worship what you do not know; we worship what we do know, for salvation is from the Jews. ²³ Yet a time is coming and has now come when the true worshipers will worship the Father in spirit and truth, for they are the kind of worshipers the Father seeks. ²⁴ God is spirit, and his worshipers must worship in spirit and in truth."**

Jesus planned to offer healing to Jews and Samaritans alike. But it would not be done by settling the dispute between temple worship on Mount Moriah or Mount Gerizim. To both the Samaritans and the Jews, worship was centered on a *place*; it had been so for centuries—first in the Tabernacle, then in Solomon's temple, then in the competing temples on Gerizim and Moriah. This "place" paradigm was about to end with the death and resurrection of Jesus and the destruction of the temple some 40 years later. A new order would be birthed and it would replace both Moriah and Gerizim (See John 2:19-21; Acts 7:48-50).

The Jews themselves helped to bring about the change, for "salvation is from the Jews." Jesus Christ, Himself a Jew, is the purest essence of the temple; the ultimate fulfillment of His Father's "House." He spoke of His own body as a temple (John 2:19). Jews became the apostles who took the message of the New Covenant to the nations and wrote the New Testament.

The day was at hand when the most superior form of worship ever devised was about to be launched. The new paradigm would center on the heart, and its primary focus would be on the *who* and the *how* of worship. Yes, the paradigm was changing and the *where* of worship would become "anywhere" and "everywhere."

Jesus replied, "The time is coming, ma'am, when we will no longer be concerned about whether to worship the Father here or in Jerusalem. For it's not where we worship that counts, but how we worship—is our worship spiritual and real? Do we have the Holy Spirit's help? For God is Spirit, and we must have his help to worship as we should. The Father wants this kind of worship from us" (John 4:21 TLB).

This new worship paradigm is superior because the true temple is in the heart. Jehovah crafted man in Eden to worship God "in spirit and in truth." The New Covenant set the emphasis not on *place* but on a *relationship* with Jesus Christ and His Father. The worshippers God is seeking can be filled with the Holy Spirit and honor and adore God wherever they are, anywhere in the world (See Jer. 31:31-34). The new model is crafted for meaningful worship to take place when even two or three gather together (Matt. 18:20). In fact, wherever Spirit-filled followers of Jesus journey the temple goes with them, because *they* personify the temple (1 Cor. 6:19).

If Jesus had not made this paradigm shift from *place* to *heart relationship* with God, the gospel would have never been able to go around the world. And this new paradigm makes choosing between Moriah and Gerizim nonsensical.

Jesus Christ is history's greatest changer of old paradigms and builder of new ones.

**In John 1-4 alone, Jesus introduced four new paradigms: a new sacrifice (John 1:29), a new temple (John 2:19-21; 4:20-24), a new birth (John 3:1-7), and new, living water (John 4:11).**

**25 The woman said, "I know that Messiah" (called Christ) "is coming. When he comes, he will explain everything to us."**

This woman, whom both the social and religious establishments at Sychar had cast aside as beyond help, had a deeply felt hope her Messiah would one day come. "When he arrives," she reasoned, "we'll get the whole story" (John 4:25 MSG). Her lifestyle did not show this yearning for God, but it was in her. Jesus discerned it and spoke prophetically to it. (The Apostle Paul later listed discerning of spirits as a manifestation gift of the Holy Spirit [1 Cor. 12:10].)

The people associated with this woman had always seemed to misread and abuse her; they saw the tragic results of her choices and not the yearnings of her heart. But she did not like her life. She was not proud of her past choices or her present situation; instead, she earnestly wanted a new life. All too often we fail to discern the stronghold keeping people in their blindness, and write off souls like her. But not the Messiah; He gave focused and undivided time to her and brought her to healing and salvation. Yes, prophecy and discernment are closely connected.

## Has Jesus ever surprised you with the people He wins?

The statement "explain everything to us" applies to more people than the Samaritans. The "us" is prophetic and embraces all people trapped in the dark like her, worldwide. She believed Messiah would straighten out everything, including her life. What she spoke in verse 25 might have been her first prophecy.

Sometimes in giving appropriate attention to the grand scheme of the church, we become so focused on God's *eternal objectives*, we lose sight of His *present purposes*. We can also easily get caught up in what is of *lesser importance* and miss what is *most important*. When this happens, we usually also forget the gospel primarily focuses on leading one more individual, one more *Samaritan woman*, to Christ. It is also about planting one more church in which new believers can grow and mature in Christ-likeness.

When we get trapped in the rut of what is of *lesser importance*, we always seem to lose sight of people—hungry, hurting, trapped people who need to experience a new birth that will give them eternal life. Instead, we want to find the grand solution for situations akin to the big problem between the Samaritans and the Jews: after all, we conclude there can be only two choices, Gerizim or Moriah.

The truth is there was a third option. With Jesus, the *place* of worship was not a priority. Moses discovered, for example, he could worship God on the back side of the desert at a burning bush. Elijah worshipped by a brook. Just to ask the question of place is to take the road of *lesser importance*. Instead, the highest priority is finding the next *Samaritan woman* whose heart is screaming out a desperate plea for the redemption only her Messiah can give. When we lose sight of *her*, we also fail to see why Jesus died on the cursed cross. We also fail to appreciate that if she is won to the Lord, she might become an evangelist who can bring her whole village to Christ.

With Jesus, the only *place* of importance was her heart! This was the temple that counted. And Jesus was the Messiah who was beginning, as they talked, to make the great paradigm change from the *temple* to the *heart*.

Moisture in the ground combines with the sunlight and opens an orchid so that it reveals its gorgeous petals. As this nameless Samaritan woman over the noon hour began to drink the living water Jesus had to offer, she began to blossom from the inside out in the new inner beauty of Godly character. She had found the key that unlocked her imprisoned soul: simply believe Jesus; accept Him and His teaching. This alone swings open the door to eternal life.

## 26 Then Jesus declared, "I who speak to you am he."

I wish I could have been on the scene to get the reactions on people's faces when the Lord did His mighty works. If only a movie camera had been available to capture the woman's face and especially her eyes when Jesus told her, "I … am he!" She did not have to "wait any longer or look any further" for her Messiah (John 4:26 MSG).

Whatever her reaction, to her eternal credit, she as a daughter of Abraham had a heart like his. She believed her Messiah and did not reject Jesus as a braggart with a Messiah complex. She had finally found Him and she knew it. Her Messiah believed in her and wanted to transform her. He accepted her without manipulating and using her.

> **Jesus made her realize she had great value. It was a brand new emotion for her!**

Something huge was happening in her life. In those few moments of conversation the Christ had "explained everything" she needed to hear. Jesus gave her an inner awareness that each of her very sinful choices was forgiven. She had drunk her very first glass of refreshing *living water*, and the red rose inside her was already springing up unto eternal life. In fact, for the first time since her youth she felt clean, like she had become a morally pure woman again.

Ah! Living water. She was reborn and felt brand-new. Now she had a story to tell her world and was more than willing to share it!

How does a person receive this living water? The answer is *believe Jesus; accept Him and His teaching* (Acts 16:31). This alone opens the door to eternal life.

Some 20 years later, Paul and Silas were beaten at Philippi in northern Greece and thrown into the inner cell of the jail because of their testimony for Jesus Christ. In the exchange with the jailer, after an earthquake had freed them, the trembling jailer:

> [T]ook Paul and Silas outside and asked, "Sirs, what do I have to do to be saved?" They answered, "Believe in the Lord Jesus, and you and your family will be saved." They spoke the Lord's word to the jailer and everyone in his home (Acts 16:29-32 GW).

Access to this living water that refreshes the soul has always been just this simple—"Believe in the Lord Jesus."

The human and the divine had merged truly into one in Jesus. At the root of the mystery of Godliness is this man, Jesus of Nazareth. Mary's son, who was also the Son of Man, is the person who was sitting on the stones wrapping Jacob's

Well. It is also true the Son of God, the Lamb of God, the God-Man and Israel's Messiah sat on the well. This Messiah, the Christ, in the power of the Spirit broke open the stronghold in this woman while doing the work of the ultimate Evangelist at Sychar. Jesus is the soul winner; we are but His messengers.

Jesus led this Samaritan woman in the conversation to the point He revealed Himself to her as her long-awaited Messiah. "The Father who sent me ... draws people to me," Jesus said to the critical Jews in Galilee. "That's the only way you'll ever come" (John 6:44 MSG).

This story of the Samaritan Woman at Jacob's Well also shows the importance of witnessing to one person. She was worth Jesus' focused time and effort. One broken woman at Sychar could receive attention from Jesus as quickly as did Nicodemus, a ruler of the Jews in Jerusalem.

### The Samaritan Woman as an Evangelist
**27 Just then his disciples returned and were surprised to find him talking with a woman. But no one asked, "What do you want?" or "Why are you talking with her?" 28 Then, leaving her water jar, the woman went back to the town and said to the people, 29 "Come, see a man who told me everything I ever did. Could this be the Christ?"**

### The water jar left sitting by the well said it all.

The woman whom everyone had written off had become a new creation. By giving her living water, Jesus the apostle, prophet, evangelist and teacher had transformed her life. She was brand new—clean and chaste again—and genuinely thrilled about it. She was so liberated she felt no shame about sharing her experience with her neighbors in Sychar.

When the Messiah revealed Himself to this Samaritan woman, He took away her disgrace. In its place, He gave her a restored sense of dignity. She was no longer trapped in the inner prison of immorality; she had finally escaped that old prison (Eph. 2:1-4). In her excitement and her newly found sense of self-worth, she could face people she had tried to avoid for years. Now she could approach them and look them in the eye! "Come with me, and meet a man who told me everything I've ever done. Could he be the Messiah?" (John 4:29, 30 GW). The sense of her statement was this: *"I am convinced he is the Messiah and I think He will convince you too!"* (See verses 39, 40, and 42 to discover her testimony showing she accepted Jesus as her Messiah.)

Jesus unveiled everything of importance to her about her most painful life choices. How could he be anything less, she reasoned, than the Messiah?

Her neighbors listened to her because they saw the change in her. The brand-new sparkle in her eyes was so evident the townsfolk could only marvel. Her voice was different—it had enthusiasm in it. She was exhilarated and could talk with the men and women of Sychar face-to-face, looking them in the eye.

"What in the world is going on?" the villagers must have thought.

Samaritans who would not be seen walking across the street with her—not with *her*—actually began to follow her to meet the man at the well! Wow! How the tables had turned.

**30 They came out of the town and made their way toward him.**

## SOMEONE ALWAYS COMES

An evangelist is a person with a special gift and a special calling from the Holy Spirit to announce the good news of the gospel. You're an announcer, a proclaimer, an ambassador. And it's a gift from God. You can't manufacture it, you can't organize it, you can't manipulate it.

I study and read and prepare all the time, but my gift seems to be from the Lord in giving an appeal to get people to make a decision for Christ. Something happens I cannot explain. I have never given an invitation in my whole life when no one came.

We are not saved by our view of the Bible. We are saved by our view of Jesus Christ and our acceptance or rejection of him and the life we live after we come to Christ.

*Billy Graham from "A Prophet With Honor" (Morrow). Christian Reader, Vol. 32, no. 2.; Cited from PreachingToday.Com.*

What a testament to Jesus the Evangelist, when "The people left the city and went to meet [Him]" (John 4:30 GW)!

What a testament to this Samaritan woman, who discovered the gift of evangelism at work in her own heart!

What an eye-bulging sight to the disciples when they saw the whole town following her, especially *her*, as she led them to their Messiah sitting on Jacob's Well!

What this Samaritan did defines the gift of evangelist. It is telling people in the power of the Holy Spirit what Jesus has done for you and inviting them to drink the living water too.

Yes, Jesus knew the importance of winning people one by one. In fact, even in the dynamic ministry of mass evangelism, every person who comes to Christ does so one by one. Even in our generation, when the numbers of people who believe Jesus is the Son of God are so great and diverse they cannot be counted, the Holy Spirit makes Jesus known individually to each of His followers. God has no stepchildren and no grandchildren—only sons and daughters.

The Apostle John's objective in sharing back-to-back the story of Nicodemus and the Woman at the well is to contrast the two responses to Jesus Christ. Nicodemus was viewed by Jewish society as an upstanding and moral, spiritual leader, but when "Israel's teacher" met his Messiah, Nicodemus rejected Him and the second birth He offered. This Samaritan woman, whose character was in shreds, met the same Messiah and believed Him. She drank deeply the living water that springs up to eternal life.

Her story was meant for more people than her Samaritan village. Wherever the gospel has gone, her experience has been celebrated around the world. Only heaven can reveal how many have come to Christ because of her witness.

To this day, her testimony continues to give hope to people who feel like outcasts.

> **The gospel truly does liberate to this extent. Yet, some church groups have bought in to the thinking of religious pluralism and Christian universalism and have rejected all missionary ministry that has a goal to convert people to Christ. The reasoning goes, since they are already on a valid path to God, and because they will have another chance in the afterlife to get right with God, why try to lift people out of their paganism by bringing them to Jesus?**
>
> **This kind of thinking focuses the job description of missionaries away from evangelism to social improvement: such interests as hygiene techniques, better farming methods, AIDS prevention, etc.**
>
> **It also means the people like this Samaritan woman will never hear the liberating gospel of God's great love that can give them a new beginning. Instead, they will be left to die in their sins (John 8:24).**

**31 Meanwhile his disciples urged him, "Rabbi, eat something." 32 But he said to them, "I have food to eat that you know nothing about." 33 Then his disciples said to each other, "Could someone have brought him food?" 34 "My food," said Jesus, "is to do the will of him who sent me and to finish his work."**

Jesus' ability to put *spirit* above *flesh* is one of the dominant themes of His ministry. Most of us are ruled by our flesh; Jesus was ruled by His spirit. Food and drink, to Him, were primarily a compliment to His spirit. Jesus ate to live; He did not live to eat.

This dynamic stood out very clearly in the Lord's wilderness temptation. It was also very apparent at His trial, and especially on His Cross. "My nourishment," Jesus said, "comes from doing the will of God who sent me, and from finishing his work" (John 4:34 TLB). Jesus knew the will of His Father was the choicest food.

> **Jesus made the trip to Jacob's Well for the sole purpose to give this Samaritan woman spiritual water, a new birth that gives eternal life.**

The disciples went into town to buy food. While there, they probably did not talk with a single person about their own experiences with Jesus the Messiah, who was waiting at Jacob's Well. The Samaritan woman went to the well to draw water, and in the process, discovered living water. She went back into her village and did what the disciples did not do—she told her story, which is the heart of the spiritual gift of evangelist (Eph. 4:11).

Which is more important to us? Stomach food or soul food? Or, do you have the two in balance in your life?

**35 "Do you not say, 'Four months more and then the harvest'? I tell you, open your eyes and look at the fields! They are ripe for harvest."**

The disciples were looking for their lunch! Jesus' lunch was the harvest, ripe and at hand at that very moment, and not later down the road. "The food that keeps me going," Jesus said, "is that I do the will of the One who sent me, finishing the work he started" (John 4:34 MSG).

> **Christian universalism has a strong tendency to take the sense of immediacy out of the gospel. But Jesus said, "The harvest" is ready now; four months later will be too late. "Open your eyes and look at the fields! They are ripe." Jesus was in their village and the people were ready to receive Him! That is the essence of harvest time!**
>
> **Universalism says you have plenty of time, including time after death. This kind of thinking rejects the compelling determination Jesus felt in Samaria. The harvest there was so pressing, Jesus stayed with them two days!**

The encounter with the Samaritan woman also demonstrated to the disciples that the people hurting the most will typically respond to Jesus and His message the quickest. In this sense, the woman was both a life worth saving and a symbol of things to come. One of the great conclusions to be learned at Sychar is that feeding the soul is a far higher priority than feeding the stomach. Another is that no one should ever diminish the urgency of the moment in winning one person to Christ.

### Jesus as an Apostolic Pastor

**36 "Even now the reaper draws his wages, even now he harvests the crop for eternal life, so that the sower and the reaper may be glad together. 37 Thus the saying 'One sows and another reaps' is true. 38 I sent you to reap what you have not worked for. Others have done the hard work, and you have reaped the benefits of their labor."**

The pressing motivation Jesus felt to minister in Sychar is underscored by the phrase *"Even now."* In this phase of the story, Jesus the apostle opened the door to reach a new subculture that had been cut off from the Jewish family. As Jesus did so, He also served as a pastor to the Samaritan woman and to the villagers in the town. A pastor is a shepherd who tends the sheep; pastors care for people. Her conversation with Jesus might not have consumed more than 10 minutes. But it was life-changing. Following that encounter, she needed a pastor.

It was harvest time. Sychar was the field and the Samaritans were the crop. The blessing of God's grace was the gift of living water that yielded eternal life. Jesus Christ was the harvester and this woman was his helper; His evangelist. The disciples stood aside and watched. They were witnessing a miracle as Jesus showed genuine love for what they thought were these mixed-blood Samaritans.

It must have been mind-boggling to them when it began to soak in, the Samaritans were not half-breeds in Jesus' eyes. In time, they would assimilate the distinct blessing of being harvesters in fields they did not plant; where others did all of the hard work. Yes, harvesting is always the more rewarding labor.

**39 Many of the Samaritans from that town believed in him because of the woman's testimony, "He told me everything I ever did."**

The Samaritan woman was convincing; amazingly, they believed her testimony. Jesus had told her everything she deemed important, and anyone who could turn this woman around and give her a clean, new life was an instant celebrity to the townsfolk.

**40 So when the Samaritans came to him, they urged him to stay with them, and he stayed two days. ⁴¹ And because of his words many more became believers.**

For two full days they had the undivided attention of Jesus of Nazareth—the Son of God and the Lamb of God, their long-awaited Messiah. He was in their town as an apostolic pastor, eating with them, laughing and socializing and enjoying their company, sleeping among them, and showing them what their heavenly Father is really like. For those dynamic 48 hours, He talked the language of heaven to them and led them to the green pastures of New Covenant faith. It all started with one very hungry woman. During this time, the Master Teacher introduced harvest principles to His disciples, including the laws of planting and sowing, as well as harvesting and reaping.

Two days with Jesus! And their excitement was such, they did not want Him to depart.

It would later become clear after Jesus went back to heaven, He was still with His followers. It is the role of the Holy Spirit to make Jesus just this personal; hence, Jesus is always amid His children. "I will never leave you nor forsake you," He promised (Heb. 13:5; Deut. 31:6).

**42 They said to the woman, "We no longer believe just because of what you said; now we have heard for ourselves, and we know that this man really is the Savior of the world."**

The villagers were first drawn to Jesus because of the witness of the woman. Then they moved past her testimony to "We're no longer taking this on your say-so. We've heard it for ourselves and know it for sure" (MSG). It is striking that these Samaritans did not acknowledge Jesus as merely the Savior of *all Samaritans*, or of *all Jews*, but as "the Savior of the world" (John 4:42).

This confession was prophetic; a bold demonstration of the work of the Spirit in the lives of these new converts. It would have been a huge step of faith if they had concluded Jesus only had the answer for Samaritans and Jews. Instead, their leap of faith was quantum: they affirmed the Lord's universal mission. At this point the Biblical record does not show the *disciples* had caught the international, missionary vision of Jesus, but these Samaritans did. This woman and her neighbors had the faith of Abraham.

This Samaritan village with these new converts also foreshadowed the importance of the Lord's church yet to be born. These Samaritans needed opportunity to grow and develop in their new faith after Jesus' two-day visit ended. Jesus expressed in prophecy His intention to meet just this need at Caesarea Philippi: "I will build my church ..." (Matt. 16:18). It was one of the most important prophecies of His ministry. One of the reasons Jesus went to the cross was to accomplish this vital component of His international vision (Eph. 5:25).

## THE BEST ADVERTISING

When John Grisham wrote a book called *A Time to Kill*, it sold just 5,000 copies in hardcover. I don't think it was advertised, ever made a list, or was reviewed by anybody that I know of. It was sort of a flop.

Then he wrote *The Firm*, and it wasn't advertised either. It was hardly reviewed, and the reviews it got weren't very good. But people read it and liked it and told other people they liked it. *The Firm* sold 7 million copies.

John Grisham has written several other books, and today the No. I paperback best-seller in the United States is by John Grisham, as are No. 2 and No. 3. And the No. I hardcover best-seller is by John Grisham. That has never happened before in history, and it's not because of advertising, not because of the publisher's clever marketing plan, but because somebody liked the book.

I guess a lot of people liked the book and told other people, until millions of these books have been sold.

*Leith Anderson, "Making More Disciples," Preaching Today, Tape No. 165.*

## The Ladder of Faith

The Samaritan woman during the encounter at the well climbed up the ladder of faith as her awareness of Jesus' true identity blossomed:

- She first recognized Jesus as "a Jew" (vv. 7-10).
- She next progressed to the level of a Jew "greater than Jacob" (vv. 11-15).
- Then she advanced to "a prophet" (vv. 16-24).
- Her final step up the ladder of faith was to the Messiah, the Christ (vv. 25-30).

John's account shows Jesus, the Son of God, ministering in Jerusalem (John 2:23). Then he went north in the Roman province of Judea (John 3:22). From Judea, He went to Sychar in Samaria (John 4:4). After the conversion of the Samaritan woman and Jesus' two days as an apostolic pastor among the people, they made the prophetic statement, "We know [Jesus] really is the Savior of the world."

Interestingly, when this tracking of Jesus' movements is compared to His commission of His apostles (Acts 1:8), the progression is the same. "You will receive power when the Holy Spirit comes on you; and you will be my witnesses in Jerusalem, and in all Judea and Samaria, and to the ends of the earth." The Apostle John shows Jesus modeled what would later become after Pentecost the "Acts 1:8 Formula." This paradigm became the pattern for the advance of His church around the world.

## Philip the Evangelist: After the Resurrection

Jesus' visit to Sychar also laid the groundwork for a revival led by a deacon named Philip after the Lord's crucifixion and resurrection. Philip went down to Samaria and preached Christ to them (Acts 8:5-26). When the apostles heard about the revival they sent Peter and John, who took the revival to another level.

As soon as they arrived, they began praying for these new Christians to receive the Holy Spirit, for as yet he had not come upon any of them. For they had only been baptized in the name of the Lord Jesus. Then Peter and John laid their hands upon these believers, and they received the Holy Spirit (Acts 8:15-17 TLB).

So much changed with the death and resurrection of Jesus. For one example, the centuries-old dispute between Mount Moriah and Mount Gerizim rapidly faded as an issue. The bright light of the gospel draws all men—Jews and Samaritans, Greeks, Romans and pagans—to the foot of Jesus' cross (2 Cor. 4:6). Jesus' prophecy continues to be fulfilled even today. The Father is looking for those who will worship Him in spirit and in truth (John 4:24).

## The Critical Need: The Gifts of the Spirit in Action

It remains to be expressed in this study that Jesus did all of His ministry in the power of the Holy Spirit. The Lord Jesus, the God-man:

   ... worked with human hands,
     ... acted with a human will,
       ... thought with a human mind, and
         ... loved with a human heart.

The methods of ministry Jesus demonstrated became the ministry gifts of the Holy Spirit in the Lord's church. The Apostle Paul expressed them:

He gave some, apostles; and some, prophets; and some, evangelists; and some, pastors and teachers; For the perfecting of the saints, for the work of the ministry, for the edifying of the body of Christ: Till we all come in the unity of the faith, and of the knowledge of the Son of God, unto a perfect man, unto the measure of the stature of the fullness of Christ (Eph. 4:11-13 KJV).

Since these were all present in the Lord's ministry to the Samaritan woman, does it not follow that without each of them, neither she nor her village would have ever tasted the "living water"? Merely a casual reading of the story demonstrates that of the five, prophetic ministry was the big key to her transformation.

We conclude, therefore, the Lord's church suffers today from a lack of these gifts of the Spirit manifest in the church, as well as in believers out in the streets of life. Many more people would come to Jesus if the body of Christ understood the place of spiritual gifts in breaking up the hard soil of the soul, making it ready for the new birth.

Should we not prayerfully believe God for a mix of these same gifts for ministry in our own lives?

- Surely there is a place for apostolic pastors, for example, and apostolic prophets, and apostolic teachers, and apostolic evangelists.
- What about pastors who are also prophetic evangelists?
- Or pastors who are prophetic teachers?
- Or teachers who are also prophetic evangelists?
- The options are multiple.

Our Lord demonstrated them all, and when the church was birthed on the Day of Pentecost, the Holy Spirit placed these gifts and gift-mixes in the church to multiply its ministry. The Gospel of John, therefore, in presenting Jesus Christ as the Son of God, also lays the foundation for the Holy Spirit to carry out ministry in the church following the Lord's pattern. Not to follow His blueprint is to raise up, at best, an anemic church.

---

**With all earnestness I call on the church to hunger for the baptism in the Holy Spirit. This blessing releases the gift-mixes that result in a whole new level of effective ministry to reach and redeem even the outcasts and the misfits of society.**

---

## JESUS' MINISTRY IN GALILEE
## John 4:43–45

**43 After the two days he left for Galilee. 44 (Now Jesus himself had pointed out that a prophet has no honor in his own country.) 45 When he arrived in Galilee, the Galileans welcomed him. They had seen all that he had done in Jerusalem at the Passover Feast, for they also had been there.**

Israel's Messiah and the Lamb of God was not welcomed when He visited the temple at the Passover Feast in Jerusalem (John 2). Because He was rejected in His Father's house, on this visit He moved into the streets of Jerusalem to do the work His Father sent Him to do. Life-changing anointing from the Holy Spirit flowed out of Him in Jerusalem into the lives of the people. Heaven came down to earth at this Passover feast because the Messiah was in their streets, talking the language of God and doing the mighty works of God. Most of the people viewed Him, however, like Nicodemus did, at best as merely "a teacher sent from God."

Some of Abraham's descendants, however, were beginning to open their hearts to believe Israel's extended wait for her Messiah was over. In the journey of faith, it really is a long way from "a teacher come from God" to the "Son of God" and the "Lamb of God who takes away the sin of the world."

When He arrived back home in Galilee, "the Galileans welcomed him" because those who were at the Feast remembered "all he had done in Jerusalem at the Passover Feast." Jesus did many more mighty acts than are recorded by John or any other of the Gospel writers (See John 2:23).

---

**No one confessed Jesus as the Son of God in His first Jerusalem visit after His baptism. But they certainly began to do so outside the capitol, in Sychar and in Galilee.**

---

## Snippets of Honor

Thus far in Jesus' ministry, Israel's Messiah had received morsels of honor and affirmation, but it was not anything close to a national affirmation. One must remember, the religious system would no doubt have made a place for Jesus, like Nicodemus did, if He had been content "as a Teacher come from God." Jesus was always willing to accept this kind of affirmation from people as the first level and the starting place, but not as the sum total of His identity.

To welcome Jesus of Nazareth because of His miracles is not the same as accepting Him for who He said He is: Israel's Messiah, the Son of God, the Lamb of God, and the Son of Man. Not to accept Him as God's-Son-in-the-flesh, thereby opening up our hearts and minds to His equality with God, was fundamentally to reject Him completely. It was at this level "He came to his own, but his own received him not" (John 1:11).

In Chapter 3, a nationally recognized leader in Israel refused the New Birth. In Chapter 4, a very lonely woman in Sychar reached out for Jesus' offer of the love of God and eternal water. Also in Chapter 4, a needy family in Capernaum opened up to Jesus like a springtime tulip.

# JESUS' SECOND MIRACLE: THE NOBLEMAN'S SON
## John 4:46–54

### Jesus Returns to Cana
**46 Once more he visited Cana in Galilee, where he had turned the water into wine. And there was a certain royal official whose son lay sick at Capernaum.**

John states Jesus saw it as necessary to go through Samaria, where He visited Sychar. He then went on north into Galilee. John gives no specific reason why He went back to Cana of Galilee, the site of His first miracle. But the purpose soon became obvious.

Jesus' first miracle at Cana followed a request from His mother. The second of the seven miracles John records took place because of a dad's plea for his son. Jesus was equally willing to receive the plea of this father as He was to honor the request of His mother. No, our prayers do not need to be routed through Mary to motivate the Lord to intervene.

The man is described as a "royal official" who lived in Capernaum. The Greek word for "royal official" is *basilikos*, and it carries the idea of a king or a nobleman, or it could have been a person associated with royalty.

Herod Antipas was the ruler of Galilee at the time, and two of his servants are named in scripture: Chuza, in Luke 8:3; and Manaen, in Acts 13:1. John offers no hint of this official's identity, and thereby places the focus not on the particular man, but on the magnitude of the miracle itself. This miracle, too, has had the power through the centuries to bring many people to faith in the Deity of Jesus.

**47 When this man heard that Jesus had arrived in Galilee from Judea, he went to him and begged him to come and heal his son, who was close to death.**

It was a hard day's journey of 16 miles on horseback from Capernaum to Cana, and there were no telephones or iPads with which to send instantaneous messages. Instead, this nobleman had to put significant effort into making his plea for help. In doing so, he demonstrated His faith in Jesus as the last hope for his son. The family was in a crisis so great, this father could do nothing himself to save the lad. Neither could the physicians and religious leaders in Capernaum. Further, his association with Herod Antipas offered him no help.

Jesus was this father's last resort.

The child was dying and his dad knew it. When he arrived in Cana and located Jesus there, he "begged him to come and heal his son, who was close to death." This term "begged" (*eeroóta*) carries such depth of emotion and feeling, it is akin to earnest "praying." What was happening at Cana in those moments was much stronger than a polite request. The crisis was real and this father was desperate.

How many dads over the centuries of the church have been in the same situation and have gone to the Lord in prayer—begging, beseeching, and earnestly asking for a child to be restored to health.

## THE ONLY THING THAT MATTERED

Bully was a gentle man who got his nickname from his days of barking orders at construction sites. Wayne Cordeiro noticed one day the scars on Bully's hands and asked him, "Bully, how'd you get so many cuts?"

Bully told a gripping story about a tsunami that hit the Hawaiian Islands in May 1960.

"I was working above the bay that our home overlooked in the Hawaiian Islands," he began. "One morning, the tide receded so much that the children ran out to catch fish in the tide pools left behind. We'd never witnessed the tide so low before, and it gave the kids a special opportunity to play and romp through the reefs that now protruded above the waterline like newly formed islands in the ocean. But what we didn't know was the ocean was preparing to unleash the largest tsunami our sleepy little town had ever experienced.

"Within minutes, a 35-foot wave charged our unsuspecting town with a force we'd never seen before. The hungry waters rushed inland. Like bony fingers, the waters scratched and pulled homes, cars, possessions, and people into a watery grave. The devastating power of that wave left in its wake twisted buildings, shattered windows, splintered homes, and broken dreams.

"I ran as fast as I could to our home and found my wife sobbing uncontrollably. 'Robby is missing,' she shouted. 'I can't find Robby!'

"Robby was our 6-month-old child who was asleep in the house when the ocean raged against our helpless village. I was frantic as I looked over the shore strewn with the remains of the frail stick houses that were now piled in heaps along the sands.

"Realizing that another wave may soon be following, I began running on top of the wooden structures, tearing up pieces of twisted corrugated roofs that were ripped like discarded remains of a demolition project. I tore up one piece after another running over boards and broken beams until I heard the whimpering of a child under one of the mattresses that had gotten lodged beneath an overturned car.

"I reached under and pulled up my little son, Robby. I tucked him under my arm like a football player running for the end zone. Then I sprinted back over the debris until I reached my wife. We ran for higher ground, hugging our child and one another, and thanking God for his mercy.

"Just then, my wife said, 'Bully, your feet and your hands. You're covered in blood!'

"I had been wearing tennis shoes, and I didn't realize that as I ran over the wreckage, I was stepping on protruding nails and screws that had been exposed in the rubble. And as I pulled back the torn corrugated roofing looking for Robby, the sharp edges tore into my hand .... I was so intent on finding my boy nothing else mattered."
*Wayne Cordeiro, Sifted (Zondervan, 2012), pp. 205-208.*

Getting help for his dying son was all this father from Capernaum was thinking about too. This dad knew only Jesus could help him. Does it not follow that offering help for the lost condition of our sons and daughters, friends and relatives is what the gospel is all about too?

## 48 "Unless you people see miraculous signs and wonders," Jesus told him, "you will never believe."

Jesus' first response was to put him off, obviously testing his faith. But this nobleman believed Jesus could heal his son. What he had not figured out was Jesus did not have to be physically present to do it. He only had to speak the word, because the authority of what Jesus said was not limited by distance. So Jesus said to him, "Unless you people are dazzled by a miracle, you refuse to believe" (John 4:48 MSG).

## 49 The royal official said, "Sir, come down before my child dies."

The man would not be put off. "Please go with me!" he pled, "It's life or death for my son" (MSG). His need was urgent and his faith was genuine, although misguided. This meant he underestimated who Jesus was and what He could do. He, too, had not yet progressed on the ladder of faith to acknowledge Jesus as Israel's Messiah and God's Son. But he did believe Jesus could heal his child, and that is a very good starting place in the journey of faith.

## 50 Jesus replied, "You may go. Your son will live." The man took Jesus at his word and departed.

This dad expressed the core of all faith, doing what Abraham did: "Abraham believed the LORD ..." (Gen. 15:6). He took Jesus at face value and accepted what He said. This is all Jesus asks of any of His followers. The nobleman knew by the time he arrived back at Capernaum, two days would have passed; he was racing the clock with his son's life. This father's faith is worthy of high commendation. He did not know how it would happen or what he would find when he arrived home, but at a minimum, he expected to see his child on the road to recovery. His journey home had a new expectation that made traveling the dirt road far easier.

A big surprise was ahead for him!

> **The stories of Chapter 3 and 4 have as their overarching theme the blessing of the new birth. Nicodemus did not believe and act upon the Lord's word, but the Samaritan woman did, and so did this nobleman. How important to take Jesus at His word instead of trying to add to or explain away what He said. In fact, it is a lesson all followers of Christ should re-learn.**

> **51 While he was still on the way, his servants met him with the news that his boy was living. 52 When he inquired as to the time when his son got better, they said to him, "The fever left him yesterday at the seventh hour." 53 Then the father realized that this was the exact time at which Jesus had said to him, "Your son will live." So he and all his household believed.**

Jesus had said to this father, "Your son will live." This authoritative word did not specifically promise an instantaneous miracle, nor did it specify a gradual recovery. What he discovered from the servants' reports was the miracle had been immediate and full. Jesus spoke the authoritative word in Cana, a day's journey from Capernaum. "The fever left" the child at that exact time in an instantaneous miracle in Capernaum. No, Jesus did not need to make the trip and place his hands on the child to heal him.

This nobleman could not text his wife to learn His son's condition. He had to wait and travel in faith the long hours required until the servants could come to meet him with the wonderful news.

> **Jesus' word was adequate, and neither distance nor geography was a barrier!**

"That clinched it. Not only this father but his entire household believed. This was now the second sign Jesus gave after having come from Judea into Galilee" (MSG). This official and His whole family took the final step up the ladder of faith because of this confirming miracle. They all accepted Jesus as their Messiah, believing He came from God.

With the Samaritan woman, prophecy was the final trigger in her progression of faith: "[Y]ou have had five husbands, and the man you are living with now is not your husband." With the nobleman, the path to faith was the realization that Jesus' spoken word was authoritative; distance or space was not a barrier to Him. His son was fever-free, out of bed, playing, and eating with a child's voracious appetite.

This father started with crisis faith; he and his family ended with a confident faith in Jesus as his Messiah.

We today can easily believe the data for a computer can be stored in the cloud; should we not also be able to believe the word of Jesus spans all distances? How many thousands of people around the world since then, in their own life crises, have believed the word of the Lord like this nobleman did, and discovered the same results? The miracle power of God is inherent in the word of Jesus. When the word of God is spoken, distance is not a barrier at all. Jesus is Lord over space or distance.

We are left to ask, "Would this nobleman and his entire family have discovered Jesus as their Messiah without the miracle?" The story demands a negative answer. This miracle shows the close bond, therefore, that exists between the gift of evangelism and miracles of healing in bringing people to faith in Christ.

**When the ministry of the church does not combine faith for salvation with faith for miracles, the numbers of people who come to Christ and experience the new birth will be significantly diminished.**

How desperately the church needs all of the gifts of the Spirit operating in the lives of believers, both in the assembled church and in the church scattered in the streets of life!

### 54 This was the second miraculous sign that Jesus performed, having come from Judea to Galilee.

The first sign was turning water into wine. It demonstrated Jesus' Lordship over time and seasons, and the processes of nature. The second was healing this royal official's son; it showed the authority of the spoken Word of God over the limits of distance and geography. Both of these miracles had the power to motivate people to recognize only God could do what they had witnessed. The result was to birth faith in His disciples as well as the people of Israel that Jesus was their Messiah; God had become a man and was living among them. "[The nobleman] and all his household believed."

This is what the message of the new birth is all about: believe Jesus in repentance and take Him at His word.

Yes, miracles in ministry help people take the big step of faith.

This miracle was also a sign of things to come from the hand of the Son of God. Jesus was always about the business of demonstrating Himself as Israel's Messiah and the Lamb of God who reconciles God to man (2 Cor. 5:17-21). He then grants to His followers the high status of sons of God, making them joint heirs with Christ (Rom. 8:17).

> **In this chapter the Son of God, who holds life itself in His hands, used the village's water well as the setting to give the Samaritan woman a new beginning. And when Jesus gave the nobleman's dying son new health, Jesus was not in a synagogue.**
>
> **Many followers of Jesus do all of their worship and ministry inside their churches. But Jesus did not limit His ministry to the synagogues of Israel, and neither should we.**
>
> **Who can believe the Lord who gave the Great Commission would agree to be restricted in the modern era to inside the four walls of churches?**
>
> **Neither should His followers submit to that restriction.**

In Chapter 5 the Apostle John shows Jesus pulling back the curtains and showing the closed hearts of the religious establishment in Jerusalem. John also contrasts in this chapter the openness of God the Father and His Son. But Jesus' solution was met with utter hardness in the face of all the evidence. The result was the religious leaders made their choice and refused to accept Jesus as Israel's Messiah and God's Son.

Yes, Jesus was headed to a cruel cross.

# CHAPTER 5

## JESUS: THE GREAT PHYSICIAN
### Unveiling the Heart of God

*The Apostle John did not identify the feast focused in this chapter, and Bible scholars have reached no consensus as to its identity. What Jesus did and taught at the feast, however, is certain. One of His greatest miracles occurred at this celebration, and the fourth of the Lord's seven discourses permits John's readers to gaze on the great love in the heart of God. While this chapter contains doctrinal truths about Jesus Christ, Christology at its finest, it also shows the total rejection of Jesus as the Son of God by Israel's ruling elders.*

## THE MIRACLE AT THE POOL OF BETHESDA
### John 5:1–15

**1 Some time later, Jesus went up to Jerusalem for a feast of the Jews. ² Now there is in Jerusalem near the Sheep Gate a pool, which in Aramaic is called Bethesda and which is surrounded by five covered colonnades. ³/⁴ Here a great number of disabled people used to lie — the blind, the lame, the paralyzed.**

Is there any help in the gospel for these kinds of people? Yes, there is. Jesus gave special attention to the blind, the crippled and the paralyzed. This story of the man at the Pool of Bethesda shows how deeply the Lord feels about desperate people for whom there is no help, except from Him. The miracle is the third of the seven John records.

**5 One who was there had been an invalid for thirty-eight years. ⁶ When Jesus saw him lying there and learned that he had been in this condition for a long time, he asked him, "Do you want to get well?"**

Jesus "saw him lying there" and felt special compassion for him. He asked the bystanders at the pool how long the man had been unable to walk. Jesus "learned," John records, "he had been in that condition for a long time"— almost 40 years. This is another statement that shows John balancing Jesus' humanity and His divinity as he presents Jesus as the Son of God.

## WHAT DO YOU SEE?

Russell Moore recounts a memorable conversation with the evangelical theologian Carl F. H. Henry. As Moore and some of his friends were lamenting the miserable shape of the church, they asked Dr. Henry if he saw any hope in the coming generation of evangelicals.

Dr. Henry replied: "Of course, there is hope for the next generation of evangelicals. But the leaders of the next generation might not be coming from the current evangelical establishment. They are probably still pagans. Who knew Saul of Tarsus was to be the great apostle to the Gentiles? Who knew God would raise up a C. S. Lewis or a Charles Colson? They were unbelievers who, once saved by the grace of God, were mighty warriors for the faith."

Russell Moore added: "The next Jonathan Edwards might be the man driving in front of you with the Darwin Fish bumper decal. The next Charles Wesley might be a misogynistic, profanity-spewing hip-hop artist. The next Billy Graham might be passed out drunk in a fraternity house. The next Charles Spurgeon might be making posters for a Gay Pride March. The next Mother Teresa might be managing an abortion clinic right now."

*Russell Moore, "The Next Billy Graham Might Be Drunk Right Now," Moore to the Point blog (1-2-12). Cited in PreachingToday.Com.*

John possessed keen insight into the true humanity of the Lord because he lived with Jesus every day for almost three years. With the woman at the well, Jesus' prophetic knowledge of her marriages could have come only from the Holy Spirit. The Pool of Bethesda story shows Jesus "learning" about the health of this crippled man. Someone told Jesus the lame man's sad story.

### Spiritual Gifts

What would later be understood in the church as the manifestation gifts of *knowledge* and *wisdom* flowed out of Jesus in this encounter (1 Cor. 12:8). Jesus knew the man's problem included attitude issues. Hence, he showed wisdom in asking a question to penetrate the stronghold in the man's attitude and help him acknowledge it. "Do you want to get well?"

People sometimes make peace with their infirmities and would need to make dramatic changes if they recovered fully. A few grow so accustomed to their illnesses, in fact, they come to prefer sickness to getting well. In this context, Jesus showed himself as the "wonderful counselor" (Isa. 9:6). Any professionally trained therapist understands physical and mental health can often have a link to attitude. The large majority of people, however, really do want to be free from sickness, disease and pain.

The lists of the gifts of the Spirit in the New Testament epistles should not be considered exhaustive, so that no other gifts can be added from the Old Testament (See Rom. 12:6-8; 1 Cor. 12:4-11, 28-31; Eph. 4:11-13; 1 Pet. 4:9-11). Spiritual gifts must anchor in the ministry of Jesus, but should be as expansive as the whole of scripture. Isaiah prophesied, for example, the Lord would carry the name "wonderful counselor," and this story shows the gift in action.

**7 "Sir," the invalid replied, "I have no one to help me into the pool when the water is stirred. While I am trying to get in, someone else goes down ahead of me."**

The sense of this heartbreaking testimonial seems to be, "I do want to get well, but I have no one to help me into the pool." This answer served as a mirror into his soul. It showed he had given up on trying, given up on life. He was a *lame man*; it had become his badge of identity. He expected to live out his life without ever walking again. In asking him this attitude question, Jesus demonstrated Himself as the wise and "wonderful counselor."

The only help the man could imagine was what he had come to believe was a futile hope—he needed someone to put him into the healing waters. The man did not yet realize the wonderful counselor whom Isaiah foretold was standing right in front of him and was fully prepared to help him. Jesus in His own person is the pure essence of healing water!

===
**This man's Messiah is the answer to all people who have given up on life and stopped trying.**
===

**8 Then Jesus said to him, "Get up! Pick up your mat and walk." 9 At once the man was cured; he picked up his mat and walked. The day on which this took place was a Sabbath, 10 and so the Jews said to the man who had been healed, "It is the Sabbath; the law forbids you to carry your mat."**

This miracle shows how the Holy Spirit was with Jesus in His ministry. Jesus asked the bystanders for information about the man's condition. Then He demonstrated perfect knowledge of the man's attitude and possessed the wisdom to apply the knowledge. Jesus served the man as counselor before He served him as miracle worker.

"Get up!" Jesus said to him. "Pick up your mat and walk." With those words, Jesus released a creative miracle into this man's crippled body. It launched him on the exciting journey of a new life.

Because the crippled man had been an invalid for 38 years, the muscles in his legs had atrophied years earlier. He had no capability to stand up and walk. Yet, he responded to Jesus' command and stood up. Jesus' order to the man was a creative command. In the moment of His speaking, the miracle happened. To the man's utter amazement, strong, fully developed muscles, nerves and blood vessels in a flash appeared on his supernaturally strengthened bones. He did what he had not done in 38 long years—he walked!

The God who spoke in the creation, "Let there be light," is the same Lord who spoke this man's fully developed legs into being. "Instantly, the man was healed! He rolled up the mat and began walking!" (John 5:9 TLB). A man who had been paralyzed for 38 years would need to be taught how to balance himself in order to walk. But not this man. His muscles were strong and his balance was perfect.

**This is another of Jesus' miracles demonstrating His creative power. When people face the enormity of the miracle, it motivates them to believe the scriptures establishing Jesus as the creator of all things. This story also shows the gospel is not merely one of many paths to God. No other founder of a world religion created wine out of water in the flash of a second, or gave a man muscles, blood vessels, nerves, and perfect balance in a creative moment.**

**Jesus Christ is indeed the one and only who has no equal.**

Jesus healed this man on the Sabbath. But the Jews had a law saying no work could be done on the Sabbath. They also reasoned they had the right to define what laboring on the Sabbath meant. By their definition, Jesus was working when He performed this miracle. Obviously, they cared far more for their interpretation of the Law than they did for the destitute and defeated man who had been in this condition 38 years.

### "JUST LET ME TRY!"

During World War II, Agnes Sanford volunteered as a Grey Lady in the Red Cross, working in Tilton Army Hospital at Fort Dix, New Jersey. There, amid wounded soldiers sent home from the battlefields, she was given "a two-level cart filled with cigarettes, comic books and adventure magazines, candy, cookies, and sometimes flowers or fruit. Pushing this before us, we were to cover a certain section of wards, greeting each soldier with a cheery word and offering him his choice from our wagon."

As a Christian, Agnes would silently pray for the men. On Ward 17, she met Frederick, who lay in a private room because he was about to die.

He was so gaunt and shriveled that he looked like a wizened old monkey. His skin was yellow, the ribs protruded, and the skin fluttered between them as he breathed. There were tubes in both nostrils and attached to both wrists. And usually there was a doctor or nurse with him.

"You look like you're about washed up," I said. (I had found that the men liked this direct, unvarnished approach.)

"Yep," he said.

"What's the trouble?" I asked; I could see no wounds, nor could I smell any osteomyelitis.

"Blood clots," he replied, unilluminatingly.

*This,* thought I, *should not be too difficult to heal.* Therefore, I told him of the power that might help him get well. He was not interested. In fact, he shut his eyes, a clear dismissal. ...

"Listen," I said at last, causing him by my forceful tone to open his eyes. "If you'll just let me try the way I told you, I promise I'll never mention the matter again, win or lose. Now how about it?"

"Okay," he said wearily, and with a definite lack of enthusiasm. Whereupon he drew back the sheet, and I saw to my horror that his abdomen looked like a pool of dark blood, barely covered by a thin membrane. "Guts torn out," he said, noting my dismay. "They didn't want to carry me in from the battlefield, but I told them they had to." ...

[Frederick] had been kept alive for months by intravenous feeding, drugs, and stimulants. If I had seen his abdomen at first, without stomach or any other digestive organ as far as I could tell, I would not have spoken the word of faith. But there it was, and I could not retract it. So I laid my hands on the two sides of this red gaping pool of blood and visioned a stomach and all other organs perfect and called upon the Lord to bring this about.

When I reached home, I telephoned every powerful prayer group that I knew and called for help. ... And I myself prayed for a miracle to take place in Frederick. This would require an out-and-out miracle. This was no speeding up of normal healing processes. Nothing could do this except the direct work of God through Jesus Christ.

The next week I passed his room with fear and trembling, but he was asleep and I did not go in. A week later, two weeks after our prayer, I again passed his room. It was empty. He was not in his bed. But the bed was rumpled, his things were scattered about, and his name was still on the door. I went on to the common room at the end of the ward where men sat about in wheelchairs, but I did not see him.

Then across the room my eyes fell upon a young, good-looking, ruddy-faced man who bore not the slightest resemblance to the wizened old monkey for whom I had prayed in the cell.

The young man gazed at me with a twinkle in his eyes and a knowing grin, and presently I noticed that there was a tiny shade of resemblance.

Agnes Sanford, *Sealed Orders* (Logos International, 1972), pp. 178-9, 185-7; cited in *Preaching Today.Com*.

## How the Miracle Angered the Jews

The centerpiece of the story is the creative miracle Jesus performed at the Pool of Bethesda that restored the man. The miracle also gave Jesus the opportunity to deal with the Jews' anger at Him for doing it on the Sabbath. As the Apostle sent from God, Jesus took the opportunity in the discussion that followed to challenge the Pharisees' hearts and their rules, and in the process showed how God thinks. While doing this, Jesus reached out to open their minds with marvelous insights into the awesome ways of God.

The miracle established Jesus had a higher right to interpret the Law of Moses than did the religious leaders, who could not help the man. Jesus, and not them, was the creator of the cycle built into nature's days and weeks in the rhythm of life. It was God Himself who decreed one of those days as a time of rest (Gen. 2:2, 3; Exod. 16:26). This meant, of course, Jesus had the sovereign right to choose the time and place to do good in the power of agape love.

**The Messiah who is Lord over time and space demonstrated He was also Lord over vanished hopes and dreams.**

"The Judeans said to the man who had been healed, 'It's Shabbat! It's against Torah for you to carry your mat!'" (John 5:10-11 CJB). In their thinking, the man was doing lawbreaking work on the Sabbath because he had rolled up his mat and was carrying it.

It was clear what keeping the Sabbath holy meant to the Pharisees: man was made for the Sabbath (Mark 2:27). Israelites were responsible, therefore, to perpetuate the Sabbath as a major symbol of preserving the Law of Moses. In their minds, one of the reasons this poor man—indeed, all people—was created was to preserve the Sabbath as a holy day (Matt. 12:8, 12; Mark 2:27). This applied even to "helping people"; therefore, "doing good" could not become an excuse for "breaking the Law."

As for the unfortunate invalid, the religious system had no help to offer him. Because they could not come to his aid, they wrote people like him off as not worth helping (see John 7:49). This kind of callous thinking enabled these

Jewish leaders to claim the final authority to interpret what kind of doing good on the Sabbath would be allowed—and Jesus' miracle was not on their list.

Their thinking and God's values were poles apart!

Jesus showed with this miracle just how far these leaders actually were from the heart of God. Jesus was Lord of the Sabbath because he was the Creator of the Sabbath. To Jesus, the purpose of the Sabbath was to benefit man (Mark 2:27). This meant Jesus, the apostle sent from God, had the lawful right to do good on the Sabbath (Mark 3:4).

Jesus' message to the religious leaders was they should not think it strange that God, the Creator of the Sabbath, reserves the right to define what work on the Sabbath is, and what rest is. The Lord is greater than the Sabbath He created. This meant Jesus, the Son of God incarnate in flesh and blood, could do good and help people on the Sabbath, and He was not in violation of the third commandment when He did it (Exod. 20:9, 10; Mark 3:4). It also meant people have the right to do good on the Sabbath.

Exposing the total inability of these Pharisees to feel for the needs of hurting people was obviously one of the Lord's motivations for healing the man. It was in Jesus' power to help him, and He did. This miracle, then, was a marvelous illustration of what keeping the Sabbath holy meant to God.

God's Son knew the Law of Moses perfectly and had been there when Moses received the Ten Commandments. In His incarnation, the Son also had the same perfect knowledge of the Old Testament—the Pentateuch and the poetic books, as well as the historical volumes and the prophetic books. His furious detractors did not stand a chance in debate against His knowledge of the Old Testament.

By performing this miracle, Jesus cut the foundation out from under their thinking and left them looking weak and exposed. This meant their authority over the people was challenged. These leaders had one way of dealing with people who crossed that line—eliminate them. Yes, the cross was becoming more inevitable with each passing day.

---

**This poor man's story demonstrates religion can lose all ability to feel for people.**

**We must exercise caution, however. When the gift of miracles is not operating in the Lord's church, we too will explain away the "desperate people" among us as "beyond help." The end result for us will be the same as it was with these Pharisees. The result will be the influence of the church to change the culture will be diminished and will lose its authority to impact the society (Acts 2:22; Rom. 15:19; 1 Cor. 12:28, 29; Heb. 2:4).**

## Embarrassment: A Reason for the Crucifixion

These critics felt increasingly shamed before the anointing of the Spirit in Jesus' ministry. In short, Jesus threatened them and their way of life. Taken from this perspective, their defense of the Law was but the mirage; their embarrassment before the people was probably a deeper root cause for their despising the Lord. If Jesus' influence kept growing, they would lose their power and positions.

Yes, the cross was drawing ever closer. "He came to his own, but his own received him not."

Jesus was acting in the power of God and speaking heaven talk, saying the thoughts of God. An anointing and power was in His ministry that the Jewish leaders knew nothing about. They lived with their system of do's and don'ts; Jesus lived in relationship with His Father. Their system could control people with their rules and regulations, but could not help them find freedom from their sicknesses, diseases, and sinful bondages. Ah! But Jesus could. In His relationship with His Father Jesus kept the spirit of the Law, but did not feel bound by their twisted interpretations of the letter of the Law. Jesus had deep love for people—all people—and had awesome power to help them. He was able and willing to release them from their burdens and restore their quality of life.

> **Why did these Pharisees pour such derision on Jesus? One reason was the miracles of Jesus were embarrassing them—showing them up as powerless to help people.**

**11 But he replied, "The man who made me well said to me, 'Pick up your mat and walk.'"**

It made perfectly good sense to the man who had been crippled for so long to do what Jesus said. After all, Jesus had just done in a moment what no one else in Israel had done for him in 38 years. This "no one to help him" included these same critics of Jesus (John 5:7).

**12 So they asked him, "Who is this fellow who told you to pick it up and walk?" 13 The man who was healed had no idea who it was, for Jesus had slipped away into the crowd that was there.**

Jesus performed this creative miracle and gave the man the use of his limbs without the man knowing His name! The miracle was a quantum act of grace. As for Jesus, He knew a firestorm was about to erupt, so He chose for the moment to fade into the crowd.

**14 Later Jesus found him at the temple and said to him, "See, you are well again. Stop sinning or something worse may happen to you."**

Sin has consequences. This man's sinful choices, including the choice of his attitude, had produced an invalid of 38 years. And worse would follow unless he made a change of heart. He deeply needed a new birth.

The prophet Isaiah perceived the Messiah would be a counselor. Both Moses and Isaiah made the link between sin, sickness and disease and how a person thinks: "Let the wicked forsake his way, and the evil man his thoughts. Let him turn to the LORD, and he will have mercy on him, and to our God, for he will freely pardon" (Isa. 55:7; Exod. 23:25; see also Prov. 18:4; Eph. 4:23).

> **For repentance to be genuine and total healing to follow, a person must come to the place before God he realizes and admits, "I chose my way of living and it has cost me dearly."**

Only then can he make a new choice to forsake his way and turn to the Lord. But it is not enough for a person to forsake "his way." He must also forsake the *thinking* or attitude(s) that go with the road he has chosen. Paul's insight adds an additional dimension. A person must be "transformed by the renewing of his mind," and this includes giving his body to God (See Rom. 12:1, 2). Worship itself is an attitude of the heart that embraces an attitude toward the body. Both the new birth and sanctifying grace of necessity must work their way out of the heart of a person into his flesh. His hands, feet, eyes, ears, nose, mouth, stomach, pocketbook, sexuality, daydreams—each of these and more must become participants in worshipping the sovereign Son of God.

**15 The man went away and told the Jews that it was Jesus who had made him well.**

The story of this man, to whom the Lord had been so generous, ends with the man witnessing to the Jews about what Jesus had done for him.

The man in John 5 found no help in first-century Judaism. But Jesus had the capability to meet his deepest need, and did it! In fact, Jesus gave him a mind-boggling, creative miracle.

# THE MIRACLE: A TEACHING OPPORTUNITY
## John 5:16–47

Jesus follows up on this miracle by throwing open the door to heaven in this fourth of John's seven discourses. The Lord reveals marvelous insights about

His person and work. This is Christology at its best—the study of the nature, character and work of Jesus. The great miracle of Jesus healing the man at the Pool of Bethesda is the backdrop. It makes abundantly clear Jesus has authority to heal on the Sabbath.

**No serious student of the life and ministry of Jesus can neglect the insights into the heart of God flowing out of the great miracle at the Pool of Bethesda.**

**1. God is at work around the clock, 24/7, including the Sabbath!**
**16 So, because Jesus was doing these things on the Sabbath, the Jews persecuted him. 17 Jesus said to them, "My Father is always at his work to this very day, and I, too, am working."**

The writer of Hebrews summarized the intense persecutions Jesus faced, and showed it was ongoing and unrelenting:

Consider him that endured such contradiction of sinners against himself, lest ye be wearied and faint in your minds. Ye have not yet resisted unto blood, striving against sin (Heb. 12:3, 4 KJV).

No one enjoys being contradicted. But Jesus faced it routinely.

**Contradiction was one of the hounds of hell that never left Jesus' trail. Are you like your Lord? How well you handle contradiction is one good measuring stick.**

God is omnipresent; He is everywhere; there is no place where He is not. God is omnipotent; He is all-powerful everywhere that He is, all the time. At the same time, He is not everywhere equally active. At the point of this exchange, Israel's Messiah, God in the flesh, was standing in front of His own people in Jerusalem on the Sabbath, actively teaching them to expect God to show up for good in their lives any day of the week. God is Spirit, and He works around the clock, 24/7. Jesus was the Son of God who revealed the Father. This meant He chose the time and place to do the works of God. In verse 18, therefore, Jesus makes a clear claim to being Diety, so clear his accusers could not miss it. To make this explicit for his readers, in fact, the Apostle John interpreted the claim in verse 18 as meaning just that.

## 2. Jesus' equality with God.
**18 For this reason the Jews tried all the harder to kill him; not only was he breaking the Sabbath, but he was even calling God his own Father, making himself equal with God.**

The Jews' antenna did not pick up on the continuing gracious concern God in Christ has for His children, day and night. But they clearly heard Jesus when He made Himself equal with God. This made them so angry "the Jewish leaders were all the more eager to kill him" (TLB). In making the claim, however, Jesus was merely telling the truth. But they had no intention to receive that kind of truth. In the eyes of the religious leaders and the majority of the people, Jesus was a mere man, an imposter, who falsely claimed the prerogatives of Deity.

## 3. How Jesus received guidance from His Father.
**19 Jesus gave them this answer: "I tell you the truth, the Son can do nothing by himself; he can do only what he sees his Father doing, because whatever the Father does the Son also does. 20 For the Father loves the Son and shows him all he does. Yes, to your amazement he will show him even greater things than these."**

Jesus continued His defense by inviting these Jews to step inside the heart of God to discover how the God of their own patriarchs thinks and functions. It was a grand invitation; a golden opportunity of a lifetime to discover how the Father supported His Son in His incarnation. These verses show how this worked out in His ministry.

In one moment, Jesus talked with the local people at the Pool of Bethesda and learned the lame man had been an invalid 38 years. But in the next breath, He received guidance from His Father through the Holy Spirit regarding how to penetrate the man's attitude. The root question in the lame man's approach to life was, "Do you want to get well?"

Jesus, the Messiah who was equal with God, depended in His true humanity on the guidance and instruction of His Father and the Holy Spirit:

> I'm telling you this straight. The Son can't independently do a thing, only what he sees the Father doing. What the Father does, the Son does. The Father loves the Son and includes him in everything he is doing (John 5:19, 20 MSG).

The bond of trust between Jesus and His Father was implicit, and it held throughout all of the trials and tests of His ministry. "Independence" is not even a concept in the operations of the Trinity.

In the book *Our Awesome Lord: A Pentecostal Christology* (Creation House, 2008), the author devotes the first two chapters to developing how God became flesh and lived truly as a man, but without compromising His Deity (Phil. 2:5-13; Acts 10:38). Jesus was very God and perfect man, two natures in one person.

Suffice it to be said here that Jesus the Son of Man, Mary's Son, did all of His mighty works and gave all of His profound teachings while guided by His Father, and acting in the power of the Holy Spirit (Matt. 26:65; Mark 14:63; see also Dan. 7:13).

We should not be surprised Jesus lived His life watching and listening to His Father, saying what He heard and doing what He saw. In his Pentecost sermon, Peter quoted King David, for example, who claimed a similar relationship with God: "I saw the Lord always before me. Because he is at my right hand, I will not be shaken" (Acts 2:25; Ps. 16:8; Gal. 5:16, 25 GW). Jesus was the first fruits of Spirit-filled men, who lived in His incarnation with total loyalty to His Father. Jesus observed His Father and then did what He heard and saw.

The Holy Spirit continues to this day to be about the business of showing people the Father through Jesus Christ. This, in fact, is what walking in the Spirit is all about.

How important for people to be baptized with the Holy Spirit and anchored in the Word of God! Then they can develop sensitive hearts to see and hear what God is saying and doing, and with implicit trust do what they see and hear.

### 4. Like His Father, Jesus holds life itself in His hands.
21 "For just as the Father raises the dead and gives them life, even so the Son gives life to whom he is pleased to give it."

This is another claim to Deity. The heavenly Father is sovereign over death and has given the same authority to His Son. The Son of God, the eminent Person who raises the dead and gives life, was standing in front of His Jewish detractors, who were angry enough to kill Him, yet He continued to lay out His true identity. "In the same way that the Father brings back the dead and gives them life, the Son gives life to anyone he chooses" (John 5:21 GW).

The miracle of the crippled man at the pool should have shown that Jesus held life in His hands, making Him infinitely superior to the prophets. Elijah and Elisha raised the dead, for example, but did so as men of prayer who interceded before God (1 Kings 17:22; 2 Kings 4:32-35). The same was true with Peter and Paul, both of whom were apostles and raised the dead in the power of the name *Jesus* (Acts 9:40; 20:7-12).

Neither Elijah, Elisha, Peter, nor Paul, however, claimed *inherent* power in their own person to resurrect a person. With each of them, raising the dead was an authority derived from God. But Jesus held inherent authority as a member of the Trinity. He *is* the resurrection, and the *life* that follows resurrection (John 11:25). Jesus demonstrated this authority throughout His ministry. He gave *new life* to the man at the Pool of Bethesda. Jesus also raised Jairus' daughter from the dead (Mark 5:35-42), the widow's son at Nain (Luke 7:11-15), and Lazarus of Bethany (John 11:14-44).

### 5. Jesus' authority to judge.
### 22 "Moreover, the Father judges no one, but has entrusted all judgment to the Son, ²³ that all may honor the Son just as they honor the Father. He who does not honor the Son does not honor the Father, who sent him."

Jesus continues His confrontation to explain His role in the Trinity. He makes the claim His Father has placed judgment in the hands of His Son. This alone should motivate people to give Him honor. The Apostle Paul wrote that God "has set a day when he will judge the world with justice by the man he has appointed. He has given proof of this to all men by raising him from the dead" (Acts 17:31; see also Acts 10:42; Heb. 9:27).

### 6. Dishonoring the Son Rejects the Father.

The Jews chose to believe they could worship God and at the same time refuse to admit the Father had a Son. Many people today try to do the same thing. They will pray to the Father, for example, while bypassing the revelation that God has a Son, who is of the same essence as the Father. It deeply dishonors "the God and Father of our Lord Jesus Christ" when people refuse to recognize His only begotten Son (2 Cor. 1:3; 1 Pet. 1:3). Why would anyone in his right mind dishonor his own judge or the father of his judge?

### 7. The path to everlasting life.

### 24 "I tell you the truth, whoever hears my word and believes him who sent me has eternal life and will not be condemned; he has crossed over from death to life."

This verse can be viewed as one of the first creedal, summary statements of the Christian era. It outlines in simple language the road to eternal life, and it is all about *hearing* and *believing*. This and this alone is the path to life eternal. This edict comes from the voice of the Judge of the universe, and only fools disregard it. Salvation and eternal life result from hearing the voice of Jesus and trusting the Father who sent Him. This is the basis of the new birth that gives a person a new heart and delivers him from condemnation. "I can guarantee this truth," Jesus said. "Those who listen to what I say and believe in the one who sent me will have eternal life. They won't be judged because they have already passed from death to life" (John 5:24 GW). The sense of the phrase "They won't be judged" is their sins have already been judged at the Lord's cross. They will not face the judgment to come.

> **How much better to repent before the Lord today and receive His forgiveness! It is dangerous to trust the false promise of Christian universalism and have to face Jesus in eternity as Judge, when it will be too late! (Matt. 7:21-23).**

The miracles of the Lord and His teaching—saying things human ears had never heard and demonstrating divine power never seen—showed these Jews had plenty of reasons to open their hearts to Jesus. But the self-righteousness they had built presupposed they would respond to Jesus with hateful and obstinate unbelief.

The Apostle Paul later described their spiritual blindness:

> Brothers, my heart's desire and prayer to God for the Israelites is that they may be saved. For I can testify about them that they are zealous for God, but their zeal is not based on knowledge. Since they did not know the righteousness that comes from God and sought to establish their own, they did not submit to God's righteousness. Christ is the end of the law so that there may be righteousness for everyone who believes (Rom. 10:1-4).

Jesus required them to make a choice between their own "righteousness" based on performance and His that comes solely by faith. When Jesus appeared as the Son of Man, doing the mighty works of God, their sense of what was right had already predetermined they would despise Him. Even with the evidence right in front of their faces on the scale of the lame man at the Pool of Bethesda, their commitment to their own righteousness held. Instead of accepting the obvious, their stubborn loyalty to their own perception of what was right and best for themselves and the nation pointed straight to one great conclusion—they had to kill Jesus to protect themselves.

This "righteousness" to which they held so tenaciously, some four decades later forced them to rise in rebellion against Rome, and when they did, their defeat marked the end of the land of Israel as their homeland for 2,000 years. Jesus saw it coming and gave the warning, but to no avail (Matt. 24:2; Luke 14:34, 35; 23:28).

## 8. A prophecy Jesus will raise the dead.
**25 "I tell you the truth, a time is coming and has now come when the dead will hear the voice of the Son of God and those who hear will live."**

The Bible recognizes two kinds of death. The first is spiritual death. This is what occurred simultaneously with Adam's and Eve's first sins in the Garden of Eden (Gen. 3:16-19, 22-24). All of their descendants since then have been born in trespasses and sins and live in this spiritual death—the walking dead. The iron grip of sin on all of Adam's progeny ultimately meant the rejection of Jesus as Messiah. The Apostle Paul described this reality of spiritual death when he wrote to the church in Ephesus: "[Y]ou ... were dead in trespasses and sins" (Eph. 2:1 KJV). Physical death, when the soul departs the body and physical man goes back to dust, is the direct result of this spiritual death. The final chapter of spiritual death, also identified as the "second death," is eternal death in the lake of fire—hell itself (Rev. 20:14, 15).

> **Christian universalists feel compelled to try to explain away the Apostle John's statement, "If anyone's name was not found recorded in the Book of Life, he was thrown into the lake of fire" (Rev. 20:15).**

The gospel, however, is all about the plan of redemption Jesus accomplished in His ministry, and it includes the wonderful news of resurrection. In verse 25 Jesus was back in prophetic mode, and it relates to what He said in verses 20 and 21: "... the Son will do far more awesome miracles than this man's healing. He will even raise from the dead anyone he wants to, just as the Father does" (John 5:20, 21 TLB). Jesus brought this great hope to the human family for all who repent and believe in Him. In fact, as Jesus spoke, the time for resurrection to begin to unfold was already at hand.

## 26 "For as the Father has life in himself, so he has granted the Son to have life in himself."

Verse 26 also links to verses 21, 24 and 25, but takes the revelation of Jesus' Deity a step further. It shows Jesus reaffirming that His heavenly Father inherently holds universal authority over life itself, and has "granted" to His Son to hold life in His hands. Many rulers hold the power to kill, or to take life. But Jesus' authority is far superior. The Lord holds the authority to give life, including resurrection life. He does so in His own person as a member of the Triunity of God. It is another bold reaffirmation of Jesus' Deity.

### 9. The Son of Man as the Chief Judge.
**27 "And he has given him authority to judge because he is the Son of Man."**

While this statement builds on verse 22, it also carries a new dimension of the power and authority of Jesus. Jesus did not say His Father gave Him the right to judge because He was the Son of God. Instead, His authority to judge is based on His being the *Son of Man*. This is classic incarnational thinking. The fact that Jesus willingly became a man qualifies Him to judge men. He became man to die on the cross to save all who repent. This Chief Judge, who in His incarnation became one of us, is "touched with the feelings of our infirmities" (Heb. 4:15; 5:1, 2).

### 10. Prophecy of a Universal Resurrection and Ultimate Rewards.
**28 "Do not be amazed at this, for a time is coming when all who are in their graves will hear his voice ²⁹ and come out—those who have done good will rise to live, and those who have done evil will rise to be condemned."**

Jesus continued as a prophet here, announcing the judgment to come. He asserts those whose bodies are in their graves are still very much alive in spirit; fully capable to hear His voice and respond to it—and they will hear His voice.

Verses 28 and 29 give a clear teaching on rewards and punishments. *All* who are in the grave will hear the voice of the Son of God, including the righteous and the wicked. Both will come out of their graves to receive their rewards. The resurrection of the righteous dead who have departed this life will include all believers who have died in the faith. (See 1 Thess. 4:13-18 for Paul's rendering of the resurrection to come.) These people will be those who have believed in Jesus as the Son of God and responded to Him in genuine repentance. They will rise to eternal life. But those who have rejected the Son of God will rise "to be condemned."

> **No reward can be greater than the gift of eternal life. This teaching drives a strong spike into the coffin of Christian universalism: "... those who have continued in evil, to judgment" (John 5:29 TLB).**

It specifically should be underscored that nothing in any of these passages suggests the Roman Catholic doctrine of purgatory, or the teaching of Christian universalists that a person can be cleansed from sin after his death, so as to complete his preparation for heaven.

## 11. Jesus never acted solo.
**30 "By myself I can do nothing; I judge only as I hear, and my judgment is just, for I seek not to please myself but him who sent me."**

This verse connects with verse 19 and reaffirms the divine interaction between the Heavenly Father and His Son, Jesus.

Jesus' method in His incarnation was to limit His choices and decisions to what He saw and heard from His Father. Jesus knew there was safety in looking and waiting for guidance from the Holy Spirit (see vv. 19, 20). The devil never succeeded one time in pushing Jesus to act alone. Instead, Jesus judged by what He heard from His Father. King Saul is an example of the tragic results of not waiting on the guidance of the Lord. Israel's first king did not wait on the prophet Samuel to give him the word of the Lord. He presumed to take the priestly role and offered the sacrifice himself when Samuel was delayed. That solo act cost Saul his throne (1 Sam. 13:9-14).

## 12. Jesus' guiding motivation.

Jesus was bonded stronger than steel to implicit obedience of His Father. This meant the Son always listened to His Father. No Satanic effort in Jesus' ministry successfully penetrated this Trinitarian bond, not even the horror of the cross. Satan tried repeatedly, but was unable to isolate Jesus from His support system in the Godhead. Jesus never could be maneuvered into a situation to make Him believe He had a self-interest that overrode His Father's interest. Instead, Jesus always acted to please His Father and the Holy Spirit. This ability to commit to His Father's interests is the Golden Rule displayed to perfection. Jesus knew if He acted in His Father's best interest, His Father would also act in His best interest.

> **The Golden Rule has always been golden, first and foremost, because it describes the heart of God.**

How many times do we make decisions that are not based on the Golden Rule? Instead, we believe we do have self-interests and act to protect them without listening to the Father or to the Spirit. Jesus lived with a heart to hear His Father, and it enabled Him to get it right every time He judged. The Trinitarian Godhead has always operated from this principle: the Father, the Son and the

Holy Spirit, one in essence or substance, have been committed from eternity to the interests of each other. The concept of self-interest does not exist in the Triunity of God.

Since the fall in Eden, it has been man's nature to protect his rights and defend his turf. Jesus never did it, not a single time. Without question, the fact that Jesus was willing to reject personal interests for His Father's interests was a strong protection that enabled Him to complete successfully His march to the cross.

### 13. Validating Jesus.
**31 "If I testify about myself, my testimony is not valid. ³² There is another who testifies in my favor, and I know that his testimony about me is valid. ³³ You have sent to John and he has testified to the truth. ³⁴ Not that I accept human testimony; but I mention it that you may be saved."**

Verses 31-40 give five sources of testimony for the character and person of Jesus as the Son of God.

a. The sense of verse 31 is this: "I have the right to give testimony on my own behalf, although I know you will say my testimony must be validated. Moses' Law required two or three witnesses to settle a matter, but I can be one of them" (Deut. 19:15).
b. Then Jesus proceeded to say He had a second witness: John the Baptist. The Baptizer spoke in Jesus' favor, and Jesus asserted He knew John "testified to the truth."

**What a compliment to John the Baptist! Oh! Dear reader, will Jesus on the judgment day be able to say about you and me, "He testified to the truth"?**

The Baptizer was Jesus' witness. John's testimony to the identity and character of Jesus should have been adequate to settle the matter of testimony. After all, the people believed John was a prophet (Matt. 21:26).

### 35 "John was a lamp that burned and gave light, and you chose for a time to enjoy his light."

Another compliment for John! But the statement is also a sad indictment of the religious establishment: "[Y]ou chose *for a time* to enjoy his light." The religious leaders knew John was a prophet of God, but ultimately spurned John too!

**36 "I have testimony weightier than that of John. For the very work that the Father has given me to finish, and which I am doing, testifies that the Father has sent me."**

Jesus acknowledged the testimony of the Baptizer that validated Him, but He also appealed to a higher testimony.

c.  The fruit of Jesus' miracles spoke for him. Consider the evidence:

*   *The water that turned into wine in an instant.* Does it not establish Jesus' creative Lordship over time and seasons, and the processes of nature?
*   *Healing the Capernaum nobleman's son.* Does it not show Jesus' Lordship over distance and space?
*   *Healing the poor man at the Pool of Bethesda who had been lame for 38 years.* Does it not show Jesus' creative power? This was a miracle that called into being what did not exist. Muscles and nerves and blood vessels appeared on this man's legs in a flash of time, so that the man astonishingly stood up and walked without needing to learn to balance on his two miracle legs.

The statement, "The very work the Father has given me to finish," speaks to Jesus' march to Calvary to die for the sins of all people who repent. He was the Lamb of God, and He intended to finish the work His Father gave Him to do.

**37 "And the Father who sent me has himself testified concerning me. You have never heard his voice nor seen his form, [38] nor does his word dwell in you, for you do not believe the one he sent."**

d.  Jesus' Father was His witness, and Jesus regarded His testimony as primary. First, the Father audibly and joyfully validated Jesus' identity at Jordan River when He claimed Jesus as His "beloved Son." This was before Jesus had preached a single sermon or performed one miracle. In doing so, the Father's witness affirmed the trustworthiness of Jesus' character and commitment to His mission (Matt. 3:17).

Jesus' testimony and His Father's testimony unite to declare Jesus in His incarnation was both the Son of Man and the Son of God. The Father audibly reaffirmed His Son again on the Mount of Transfiguration, and a third time in the shadow of His cross when a group of Greeks came asking to meet Jesus (Matt. 17:2; Mark 9:2; John 12:21). These, Jesus claimed, were more than double His two witnesses the Law of Moses required (Deut. 17:6; 19:15).

Consider: the heavenly Father as a character witness—it does not get better than this! But the Father's testimony went right over the heads of these leaders and certainly escaped their hearts. It is possible to memorize the Torah word for word, for example, without ever hearing the voice of God speaking to you out of the Scriptures.

The Father is always present and continually active, encouraging people to listen to His Son, and Jesus' role is to reveal His Father (John 5:17). Yet, it is probable none of these religious leaders had ever heard God's voice even once. And when they did hear it from the lips of the Son of Man, it was a foreign language to them, so they rejected it. "Nothing [was] left in [their] memory of his Message because [they did] not take his Messenger seriously" (John 5:38 MSG).

Sadly, the self-righteousness these leaders and their fathers had framed provided no categories to expect to hear the voice of God giving compelling testimony. *Hearing God*, to them, was reading the Torah, and they did that avidly, looking through the lens of the narrow bifocals their righteousness had framed. The Lord's indictment was penetrating: "His word does not dwell in you." Reading the Scriptures without experiencing the Presence of the Lord of the Scriptures will always produce legalism accompanied by self-serving license that actually ends up breaking the Law.

Caiaphas, Israel's high priest, was a Sadducee who did not believe in miracles or the resurrection. He and the other leaders like him would have felt totally out of place if they had been in the first Temple when Solomon dedicated it. The priests of the first Temple were eyewitnesses to the miracle when the Cloud representing the Presence filled the Temple so that the priests could not do their work. Caiaphas and his associates most probably tried to explain away this part of Israel's history. If they had been there, they would not have understood what was happening.

Solomon's high priest, Zadok, did know how to recognize the Presence and believed strongly in the miracle power of God. Zadok never would have permitted Caiaphas and his kind to become priests in the worship he led, and he would have been revolted at the condition of the high priesthood in Messiah's day (1 Kings 1:39; 4:2; 1 Chron. 6:6-8). Tragedy of tragedies that Israel's Messiah, the anointed One sent by God, had to bypass the whole Temple system of worship. He did it to ensure His message would go around the world in the power of the Holy Spirit.

## 14. Manifestation of the "voice" and the "form."

The God who is invisible spirit is demonstrated in the Person and ministry of the Holy Spirit. The Spirit is the essence of the cloud and the Presence in the Lord's church. This *Presence* is a manifestation of God, expressed in the New Covenant in the baptism with the Holy Spirit. God the Holy Spirit can be experienced as present and active, indwelling the people of God. The Holy Spirit speaks and gives guidance to those He indwells. His primary role is to make Jesus known (John 1:33, 34). This anointing gives a clear sense someone special and powerful, the Presence, has come into their lives to make all the difference in their future. The Holy Spirit also manifests by coming into a room or sanctuary in a way that is evident that God has entered the sanctuary. In these experiences, people routinely receive special guidance and encouragement from the Lord. This *form* of God I have experienced many times over the years. But one day, oh the blessed day! We will experience not merely God's Presence, but will see "His face, and His name will be on [our] foreheads" (Rev. 22:4, 5).

While we affirm this manifestation of the Spirit, at the same time in the worship of the church we exalt the written Word of God over all prophecies and manifestations of the Spirit. The Apostle John taught: "just because someone says it is a message from God, test it first to see if it really is. For there are many false teachers around" (1 John 4:1 TLB).

How many thousands of people yearn to hear the voice of God as John the Baptist did (John 1:33; Luke 3:22)? In the case of these first-century Israelites, Messiah was standing among them, demonstrating in His own Person the Shekinah presence. He was speaking with them in their language. Yet, they were unwilling to open their hearts to God's Messenger. Instead, they made the calculated choice to reject Him. This meant they also rejected His message, His miracles, and His Father, although He was doing before their eyes miraculous things only God could do. Is it any wonder Jesus indicted His critics for missing the revelation offered to them?

### 15. Messiah, the theme of the Old Testament scriptures. 39 "You diligently study the Scriptures because you think that by them you possess eternal life. These are the Scriptures that testify about me, 40 yet you refuse to come to me to have life."

e.  Jesus' fifth witness came from the Old Testament scriptures. Amazingly, their rejection of Jesus was happening while they were faithfully reading the scriptures and continually memorizing them. The Old Testament pointed straight to Jesus as Israel's Messiah, who was doing the work of God right under their noses.

The Lord Jesus was bluntly honest with them: if you do not accept the Father's Son who is living among you as the Word of the Father, then it is abundantly clear you do not have God's Word living in your hearts. This is true no matter how much you study the Scriptures, and no matter how much scripture you can quote. It is highly probable, in fact, that not only Nicodemus, but every member of the Sanhedrin had memorized the Torah word for word.

Yet, the religious establishment kept searching, telling themselves their earnest quest was adequate to earn them eternal life (See 2 Tim. 3:7). Although they knew the Scriptures promised Israel her Messiah would come, their knowledge of the Biblical *facts* did them no good. Their idea of "righteousness" was to expect a militaristic Messiah "who could restore the kingdom again to Israel," not a miracle worker for sick people (Acts 1:6). They simply refused to accept that Israel's Messiah would come to them meek and lowly, riding on a donkey, and a colt, the foal of a donkey (Zech. 9:9; Matt. 21:5). The uniqueness of His incarnation itself became a stumbling stone (Isa. 8:14; Rom. 11:9; 1 Pet. 2:8; 1 John 2:10).

## 16. Jesus, the rejected Messiah.

These leaders made a choice to dismiss Jesus, even in the face of these five credible and persuasive witnesses, and Jesus knew it was their decision. The Messianic scriptures, for example, were well known to them. All the signs were present, but they *refused* to come to Jesus for eternal life.

What an indictment!

How well our Lord Jesus Christ knew the pain of rejection. "Even in his own land and among his own Jewish people, he was not accepted" (John 1:11 TLB).

## UTTER REJECTION, TOTAL ACCEPTANCE

Shortly after the Korean War, an American soldier had an affair with a Korean woman and became pregnant. He came back to the United States, and she never saw him again. She gave birth to a little girl, but the little child looked different than the other Korean children. She had light-colored, curly hair. In that culture, children of mixed race were ostracized by the community. In fact, many women would kill their children because they didn't want them to face such rejection.

This woman didn't do that. For seven years she tried to raise her little girl as best she could, until the rejection was too much. She did something that probably nobody in this room could imagine ever doing. She abandoned her little girl to the streets.

This child was ruthlessly taunted by people. They called her the ugliest word in the Korean language, *tooki*, "alien devil." It didn't take long for this youngster to draw conclusions about herself based on the way people treated her.

For two years she survived on the streets, until finally she was accepted in an orphanage.

One day, word came that a couple from America was going to adopt a little boy. All the children in the orphanage got excited, because at least one little boy was going to have hope. He would have a family. So, this little girl spent the day cleaning up the little boys, giving them baths, and combing their hair, and wondering which one would be adopted. The next day the couple came, and this is what the girl recalled: "It was like Goliath had come back to life. I saw the man with his huge hands lift up each and every baby. I knew he loved every one of them as if they were his own. I saw tears running down his face, and I knew if they could, they would have taken the whole lot home with them.

"He saw me out of the corner of his eye. Now let me tell you. I was 9 years old, but I didn't even weigh 30 pounds. I was a scrawny thing. I had worms in my body. I had lice in my hair. I had boils all over me. I was full of scars. I was not a pretty sight.

"But the man came over to me, and began rattling away something in English. All I could do was look up at him. Then he took this huge hand and laid it on my face.

"What was he saying?

"He was saying, 'I want this child. This is the child for me.'"

*Lee Strobel, "Meet the Jesus I Know," Preaching Today Audio #211. Cited from PreachingToday.Com.*

Jesus visited the temple that was dedicated to Him, for example, but walked around in it unrecognized. Think about it: Jesus was merely a visitor, a stranger in His own sanctuary. He acknowledged the temple as His Father's house, but in the hearts of the religious establishment Mammon was the god to whom the temple belonged. Jesus understood they were also equally rejecting His Father, who wanted to be their own heavenly Father too. In short, they literally despised their own Savior.

The rebellion was uglier than all of the sedition combined of their Fathers in the wilderness. This time, Israel was insubordinate to her *Messiah* living among them—the ultimate revolt. The denunciation must have been acutely heartbreaking for the Lord!

The pride in the human heart is the breeding ground of the self-righteousness that births such mutiny. This arrogance says man can build righteousness better than the revelation of God's righteousness. A revolution always blossoms when the effort begins to construct self-righteousness. This is all the more striking when one understands they did it while being avid students of the Old Testament scriptures, and very committed to memorization of its texts.

Jesus was innocent; yet He was brutally beaten and then crucified. But His Father raised Him from the dead. Then, "because of the great love wherewith he loved us," Jesus proceeded to adopt into the family of God all who repent and come to Him in faith. He was even willing to receive the very people who rejected Him with such cruelty (Eph. 2:4).

---

**Please be careful, dear reader, very careful. This might fit you as well, as it has me. I, too, have read the books of the Bible in a quest for knowledge, but in the process missed fellowship with the Lord of the Book who is the living Word. Hence, I had no anointing to offer people the good news in the Bible.**

---

### 17. Jesus' Motivation.
### 41 "I do not accept praise from men ..."

Most of us *do* accept praise from people, although we know much of it is flattery. Jesus understood this fatal flaw inherent in man's praise. The classic illustration came at the end of His life. Many of the same people who welcomed Him into Jerusalem on Palm Sunday no doubt yelled, "Crucify him," a scant few days later (Matt. 21:9; Mark 11:9; 14:1; John 12:13).

This ability not to accept praise from people is a part of Jesus' character that positioned Him head and shoulders above His fellows. Praise from people did not motivate Jesus, and the primary reason was He focused only on the praise of His Father. This firm source of honor released Him from the need for praise from people (John 2:25; 5:41-44; 12:43).

The righteousness the religious leaders constructed was dependent *on* and satisfied *with* the praise of men. The result was they had no concept it was appropriate to seek God's praise. While the affirmation of God was not one of their expectations, it clearly was the primary expectation with Jesus. In fact, He was wholly reliant on His Father's guidance. As for them, they made "no effort to obtain the praise that comes from the only God."

### 18. What Jesus Knows About Our Hearts.
### 42 " ... but I know you. I know that you do not have the love of God in your hearts."

The statement is compelling: "I know you." The writer of Hebrews expressed this full and total knowledge of God when he penned: "God's word judges a person's thoughts and intentions. No creature can hide from God. Everything is uncovered and exposed for him to see. We must answer to him" (Heb. 4:12, 13 GW).

With this kind of broad knowledge, Jesus specifically judged the deadly flaw in the lives of these spiritual leaders: "I *know* that love, especially God's love, is not on your working agenda (John 5:42 MSG). This was the fatal error of their "righteousness." They understood rules and regulations and how to enforce the letter of the law as they interpreted the Law, but they lacked "the love of God" in their hearts. In fact, they believed their future as a people was dependent on keeping their interpretation of the Law of Moses. Only this would protect them from the ravages of Greek and Roman polytheism and the idolatrous way of life it produced. And they were absolutely certain *agape love* would never end the occupation of the brutal Roman military machine! For Israel to overcome, Roman military strength must be met by superior might. So they needed another David. A Messiah who came showing compassion for lame people, even if He was of the seed of David, was what they were *not* looking for. Why, Jesus did not even own a sword! But the hindsight of history shows just such a Messiah was exactly what Israel truly did need.

## 19. The Love That Conquers.

Jesus' method of conquest, therefore, was their opposite. He intended to win solely with the love of God (agape) because it transforms the hearts of men. This alone, and not a single sword, was His weapon of choice. Israel's leaders, however, saw no place for a Messiah who offered the inner transformation of a new birth. Instead, they were guilty of deliberately casting Jesus aside, although He was the purest essence and manifestation of the love of God.

The indictment is Jesus *knew* they despised Him and *chose* not to cultivate God's love in their hearts. They could not show in their relationships what they did not have inside them.

For this indictment to be truthful, however, they had to have the knowledge *agape* love was possible for them. Then, they had to choose to respond to their circumstances by saying in their unique situation God's love did not apply to them and would not work in their culture as an occupied country dominated by the world's strongest foreign power.

In this regard, Moses' words [that they could quote] came back to haunt them:

Listen, Isra'el, and take care to obey, so that things will go well with you, and so that you will increase greatly, as ADONAI, the God of your ancestors, promised you by giving you a land flowing with milk and honey. Hear, Isra'el! ADONAI our God, ADONAI is one; and *you are to love ADONAI your God with all your heart, all your being and all your resources.* These words, which I am ordering you today, are to be on your heart; and you are to teach them carefully to your children. You are to talk about them when you sit at home, when you are traveling on the road, when you lie down and when you get up. Tie them on your hand as a sign, put them at the front of a headband around your forehead, and write them on the door-frames of your house and on your gates (Deut. 6:3-9 CJB). "*Love your neighbor as yourself.* I am ADONAI" (Lev. 19:18 CJB).

## SON'S KILLER BECOMES MOTHER'S SON

Regine came to Christ while reading her sister's Bible during the genocide that ravaged her homeland of Rwanda. When she fled to Canada for refuge, she met her husband, Gordon. They decided to return to Rwanda to show the love of Christ to the people who had once been her enemies.

Regine related to Mark Buchanan this story of *agape* love that unfolded:

Regine's only son was killed. She was consumed with grief and hate and bitterness. "God," she prayed, "reveal my son's killer."

One night she dreamed she was going to heaven. But there was a complication: in order to get to heaven she had to pass through a certain house. She had to walk down the street, enter the house through the front door, go through its rooms, up the stairs, and exit through the back door.

She asked God whose house this was.

"It's the house," He told her, "of your son's killer."

The road to heaven passed through the house of her enemy.

Two nights later, there was a knock at her door. She opened it, and there stood a young man. He was about her son's age.

"Yes?"

He hesitated. Then he said, "I am the one who killed your son. Since that day, I have had no life. No peace. So here I am. I am placing my life in your hands. Kill me. I am dead already. Throw me in jail. I am in prison already. Torture me. I am in torment already. Do with me as you wish."

The woman had prayed for this day. Now it had arrived, and she didn't know what to do. She found, to her own surprise, that she did not want to kill him. Or throw him in jail. Or torture him. In that moment of reckoning, she discovered she only wanted one thing: a son.

"I ask this of you," she said to the obviously contrite young man. "Come into my home and live with me. Eat the food I would have prepared for my son. Wear the clothes I would have made for my son. Become the son I lost."

And so he did.

Agape lovers do what God himself has done, making sons and

daughters out of bitter enemies, feeding and clothing them, blazing a trail to heaven straight through their redeemed hearts.
*Mark Buchanan, Hidden in Plain Sight (Thomas Nelson, 2007), pp. 187-189; Cited from PreachingToday.Com.*

The leaders of Israel, however, made the decision that agape love would not work in a world dominated by Roman power and Greek culture. As for the Romans, they were masters at using the brutal power of the sword to dominate the very soul of conquered peoples, and their rule held an iron sway over the Israelites' life and culture. It was in this context the Jewish people proceeded to frame their own righteousness, choosing to believe they could not fight Rome with agape love. It was a proud and haughty, self-righteous choice.

They could quote Moses' command to love God and their neighbors, but did not make the connection. Who could even think, for example, of vile, pagan Romans as neighbors. The way they could love God best, they believed, was to preserve the Law of Moses and drive the occupiers out of their land. It was unthinkable to them that the job could be done without warfare.

The result was they formulated their own system that demanded as much subservience in its own way as the Romans did with their legions (Rom. 10:3). Yes, religious subjugation demands total loyalty too. In the case of these leaders, the requirements went right down to every one of their rules and interpretations of the Law.

**Even today, when people reject Jesus as the Son of God, they underestimate Him, making a massive miscalculation.**

Jesus' plan to win the world was their polar opposite. Little wonder the Lord responded after Peter severed Malchus' ear in the Garden of Gethsemane: "Put your sword back in its place, for all who draw the sword will die by the sword" (Matt. 26:52). Jesus added, if He had wanted to forsake agape love, He could fight the world's way, calling twelve legions of angels to His defense. But Messiah was committed to win with the swordless power of divine love.

The Pharisees were correct about the threat from Greek and Roman culture, but were very wrong about the solution. In fact, it was the agape love of God unleashed by Jesus at Golgotha that ultimately conquered and transformed the Roman Empire.

God's love *is agape*—this love will do good for you and bless you even when you do not merit or deserve it, and have no idea it is coming. The invalid at the Pool of Bethesda, for example, did not even know the name of the man who healed him, but received his miracle anyway! The Lord sends his rain on the righteous and the unrighteous, and this included Israel's Greek and Roman oppressors (Matt. 5:45). In fact, Jesus would love a pagan Greek or Roman as quickly as He would a Jewish son of Abraham.

These ruling Pharisees diagnosed the Roman occupation and its aftereffects as the core of their problem, including such things as its backbreaking taxation policies and its decadent lifestyle. If they only had a king who would lead them in throwing Rome out of Israel and restoring King David's throne! Then their problems would be solved.

> **People are absolutely convinced society has become ruthlessly competitive ("dog eat dog"). They reason Jesus' kind of love just will not work: *"If you do not look after yourself, no one else will!"***

Jesus diagnosed the human condition very differently. He said man's core problem is all about the rebellion against God in man's heart. He also said His diagnosis applied to Jews and Gentiles alike, and it included all pagans—worldwide. Expelling the occupiers out of Israel, therefore, would not even come close to the solution for a proud heart in rebellion against God.

In Jesus' diagnosis, the field was level. This was true not because all people have the same knowledge about God. Instead, Jews and Gentiles alike, everybody lives in rebellion against the knowledge of God they do have. The Apostle Paul would later say the Jews "knew God" and still rejected Him (Rom. 1:21). Jews would steal, and commit adultery, and rob temples too (Rom. 2:17-24). The only solution, therefore, was "circumcision of the heart, by the Spirit" (Rom. 2:28, 29).

Taken in this context, the incarnation of Jesus shows the unimaginable effort to which God went to provide the real *solution* for man's rebellion against his own Creator. The cure demanded nothing less than the life of the sinless Son of God. His job description to save the world meant He would sacrifice His own life, as the Lamb of God, and do it impaled on three crude nails. Jesus showed just this kind of love. It was not based on what He could *get* but what He could *give*, and Jesus gave freely and unsolicited. Isaiah foretold Messiah's method of dealing with people would not include yelling and screaming commands at them: "He will not shout or cry out, or raise his voice in the streets ... till he establishes justice on the earth" (Isa. 42:1-4).

Like these ancient religious leaders, most sons of Adam today, by their choice, do not pursue the God kind of love. But Jesus said, "The man who loves his life will lose it, while the man who hates his life in this world will keep it for eternal life" (John 12:25, 26). This indictment was correct regarding these Jews and left them with "no excuse" (Rom. 2:1).

What they wanted was power, influence and control. They loved you if they controlled you. This meant the whole you, and especially your belief system and your pocketbook. They were clearly opposites to the love of God. These leaders claimed to be righteous, but the truth was they were under the control of the same major heart problems as all Greeks, Romans and pagans. They had deliberately rejected the revelation of the love of God given to Moses and substituted in its place a righteousness they crafted. "Since they did not know the righteousness that comes from God and sought to establish their own," Paul wrote, "they did not submit to God's righteousness" (see Rom. 10:1-4).

Jesus said to them, "I know you," and indeed He did; He knows what is in man's heart without anyone telling Him (John 2:25). Paul summarized the matter when he wrote: "Christ gives to those who trust in him everything they are trying to get by keeping his laws. He ends all of that" (Rom. 10:4 TLB).

> **Their self-righteousness meant when the Lord came guided by the love of God, they despised and spurned him.**
> **The conclusion was self-evident: Jesus was headed to a brutal but triumphant cross, and Israel was headed to a military catastrophe.**
> **The cross came first; the tragedy unfolded about 40 years later.**

This discussion opens up a very important conclusion: man has a free will and in his pride can choose to rebel even against God. People can actually say "No!" to their Creator—but there are consequences (Num. 32:23; Rom. 3:19-23; 6:23).

### 20. Acceptance, a Universal Need.
**43 "I have come in my Father's name, and you do not accept me; but if someone else comes in his own name, you will accept him."**

All people yearn for affirmation by the significant people in their lives. Of course, Jesus wanted to be accepted by His own people, but also knew when He came He would not get it. Instead of celebrating Jesus, the religious leaders rebuffed Him. They were actually known to turn their backs on Him when He walked by so they would not have to look at Him (Isa. 53:3 TLB). In their value system, Jesus was not Israel's Messiah. They calculated His solution based on agape love, and wielding no sword was a path no king would choose as his method to break the yoke of Rome.

Jesus' final proof showing He had the power to redeem the world came at Golgotha when He stayed on the cross.

The religious leaders made the conscious decision, however, to spurn both Jesus' diagnosis of man's condition and His cure. Spiritual blindness is how Paul described their malady. In fact, Israel is blind to this day to the message of the cross (Rom. 11:25; 1 Cor. 1:23 KJV). Yet, God is long-suffering and Israel remains the chosen people of God (see Rom. 9-11).

Jesus was not at all on the Sanhedrin's wavelength, including their system of belief and way of doing things. He deeply loved His own people and wanted them to accept Him. But He came in His Father's name and required no commendation from the Sanhedrin to conduct His ministry. Jesus needed only the favor of His Father; therefore, He claimed His Father's testimony was His ultimate validation. The very nature of this claim sailed past the Sanhedrin like ships silently passing in the night.

Jesus was fully aware if these leaders did not accept His Father's affirmation of Him, neither would they accept Him as the Son of God. Jesus had only two options: stay the course with total loyalty to His Father, or come under the thumb of the Sanhedrin (Matt. 4:8-10), and the latter He would not do. Jesus could not afford for a moment to bow to their false interpretations of the Old Testament and serve under their authority, and it soon became obvious they would not come under His.

The Sanhedrin might well have affirmed Him if he had gone to them in only His own name (but not His Father's) and asked them to sponsor him as a scribe, teacher, or perhaps a doctor of the law. In their minds, the path to greatness as a spiritual leader in Israel included enrolling in their classes and submitting to their rules, including their interpretation of Moses. But to do this would have admitted to them God was not His Father, and He would never, not for a moment, deny He was the Son of God sent from the Father to redeem the world. Jesus had made this decision from eternity and reaffirmed it in the wilderness of temptation:

> The Devil took [Jesus] on the peak of a huge mountain. He gestured expansively, pointing out all the earth's kingdoms, how glorious they all were. Then he said, "They're yours—lock, stock, and barrel. Just go down on your knees and worship me, and they're yours." Jesus' refusal was curt: "Beat it, Satan!" He backed his rebuke with a third quotation from Deuteronomy: "Worship the Lord your God, and only him. Serve him with absolute single-heartedness" (Matt. 4:8-10 MSG).

**In the final analysis, we all live before an audience of One. So, "whether you eat or drink or whatever you do, do it all for the glory of God" (1 Cor. 10:31; see also 2 Cor. 5:20, 21).**

## 21. The danger of serving in your own name.

So many through the centuries have come in their own name and have gone to the various perceived power people to win their acceptance and support, building a power base for their mission. But not Jesus! He never curried favor with people, asking them to validate Him or give Him permission to carry out His agenda. Instead, He was Israel's King and Messiah, the Son of God, and Son of Man. His intent was to serve their deepest needs so completely, they would ultimately choose to acknowledge Him voluntarily as their Savior and Lord.

Let it be established clearly: Jesus came to save the world. This meant as the Servant of His Father, He loved even the Pharisees who accused Him— loved them too much to submit to them, as it would have meant rejecting the authority of His heavenly Father (Luke 23:34). The result would have been He could never give eternal life to "whosoever will" worldwide, an offer that included these same Pharisees who wanted Him dead. So the plan was initiated early in His ministry that would unfold its last straw on the Hill of the Skull.

> **How is your ministry validated? As you look into your heart, do you serve because you are submitted to Jesus Christ and the authority of His Word, as guided by the Holy Spirit?**

**44 "How can you believe if you accept praise from one another, yet make no effort to obtain the praise that comes from the only God?"**

Jesus recognized they would never come to faith in Him as God's Son and heir to David's throne on the path they were walking. Their commitment was to gain praise from each other in their religious system. This meant, in their concept of God, they did not believe Jehovah even gave personal affirmation; thus, they did not feel a need to seek praise from God. Their religious system was proudly and solely responsible, in their understanding, either to affirm or reject Jesus' claim as the Son of God.

Jesus knew his validation came from His Father and from the fruit of His ministry that was so miraculous. It was obvious God was on the scene. The Lord Jesus intentionally presented Himself to the nation, asking them to put their faith in Him as Israel's Messiah and King on the basis of His Father's validation and His miraculous works.

## 22. Believing Moses Selectively.
**45 "But do not think I will accuse you before the Father. Your accuser is Moses, on whom your hopes are set. ⁴⁶ If you believed Moses, you would believe me, for he wrote about me. ⁴⁷ But since you do not believe what he wrote, how are you going to believe what I say?"**

The Lord Jesus knew the most important prophecy Moses ever spoke foretold Jesus as the Messianic Prophet (Deut. 18:15-19). Jesus showed, therefore, the Pharisees believed Moses only selectively; they rejected His prophecies about Messiah. Hence, Jesus' statement, "[Moses] wrote about *me*."

It was a heavy indictment: Moses was but a prop for their brand of self-righteousness. They accepted Moses only as He fitted their schema. If they had believed Moses, they would have recognized Moses "wrote about me," Jesus said. "Since you do not believe what he wrote, how are you going to believe what I say?"

Their own words accused them before the heavenly Father, because they were committed to preserving the Law of Moses at all costs, as they chose to interpret it. It was their way of preserving Jewish life and culture. It did not seem to occur to them they were following Moses only very selectively.

Jesus' objective was to correct the religious leaders' misinterpretations of Moses, and at the same time, give Moses the high honor he was due. An important part of affirming Moses in Messianic focus goes to the way Jesus authenticated the great emancipator and lawgiver as a writer of the Old Testament. Verse 47 makes the point: "… since you do not believe what he wrote, how are you going to believe what I say?"

This affirmation shows Israel's Messiah and the Son of God complimenting Moses as an Old Testament writer. Moses is commonly accepted as the writer of the Pentateuch, the first five books of the Bible.

Jesus' only choice, as the apostle sent from God, was to blaze a whole new path. Jesus' road, in fact, totally bypassed the religious establishment operating out of Herod's temple.

Choosing between His Father and the Sanhedrin was not a temptation to Jesus. Instead, in Jesus' eyes, the possibility the Sanhedrin might have been willing to visit with Him showed the Father's plan for Jesus to become the Lamb of God was working. It meant, when He chose His Father's authority and not theirs, the Sanhedrin would categorically reject and kill Him, making Him the sacrifice to save the world.

**Yes, Jesus cast His lot with His Father's plan and set his face with determination to walk the winding road toward the Hill of the Skull (Isa. 50:7; Matt. 16:23).**

Is the validation of your ministry anchored at Jesus' cross?

## 23. How Jesus Handled Shame.

This understanding in verse 45 raises the question of the shame Isaiah prophesied in the third of his four Messianic Songs of the Servant: "Because the Sovereign LORD helps me, I will not be disgraced. Therefore have I set my face like flint, and I know I will not be put to shame. He who vindicates me is near" (Isa. 50:7-9).

Jesus underwent great humiliation. The writer of Hebrews wrote that "He endured the cross," all the while despising its shame (Heb. 12:2). Just to be nailed to a cross embraced a curse and great disgrace (Deut. 21:13; Gal. 3:13). But He was also quite possibly crucified without a loincloth to give Him even a modicum of dignity.

Isaiah's prophecy means Jesus would not be put to ultimate or lasting shame. Jesus took upon Himself all of the humiliation heaped on Him at Calvary, none of which He deserved. He became the sacrifice to cover with His blood the shame of every lost soul.

> **Jesus carried on Himself your humiliation and mine, and triumphed over it all at the cross.**

Jesus' glorious resurrection followed His swallowing the bitter dregs of embarrassment, and established Him as the victor over it. At the Lord's empty tomb, shame turned into jubilation. This paved the way for Jesus to take His seat in triumph "at the right hand of God" (Heb. 12:2; Isa. 51:17, 22). As a result, "I will not be put to shame" applies in this ultimate and final sense.

### SHAME – PAINFUL BUT GOOD

When I was a teenager, I stole a hat. What is worse, I arrived at the store with a wad of cash in my pocket. Staring at the price tag, I thought, *Hey, why should I spend my money on that hat? I can get it for nothing by pinching it; then save my money for something else.*

As I headed for the door, the store manager stopped me. I [suddenly] wished I were dead. The manager saw I was not yet a hardened criminal and sent me home with instructions to have my parents call him back with the news or he would call the police. I went home to take my lumps. To this day, I remember what my 18-year-old sister said when she overheard me confessing: "How totally embarrassing. I've got a brother who's a thief!"

She called me a thief.

Feeling ashamed of what we are as a result of what we do is a good thing and a necessary part of getting real about guilt. If you commit adultery, you are an adulterer. If you lie, you become a liar. I stole, and I had become a thief. It led me to my room weeping and ashamed of myself.

But that was good!

Painful, but good.

*Adapted from John Ensor's The Great Work of the Gospel (Crossway, 2006). Cited in PreachingToday.Com.*

Shame can be a friend when we are guilty by helping us face the truth. But what do you do when you are accused falsely and have to bear shame for something you did not do? This is what Jesus faced. He carried the shame for your sins and mine to His cross and triumphed over it. His victory meant we can be forgiven and our relationship with God restored. When that happens, the warm sunlight of the gospel makes shame disappear like the morning dew.

It should also be noted that shame is one of the world system's strongest tools of control to make people submit. Jesus did not obey the religious establishment, and in the process took all of the disgrace the system could throw at him. When He stayed on the Cross and did not come down, however, the defeat of humiliation was assured, as expressed in His resurrection on the third day. Yes, Jesus clearly defeated shame as a weapon in the arsenal of the devil.

This also set the stage for the apostles to develop the Lord's doctrine of suffering and disgrace as tools to change the hearts of evil men. When a believer is disgraced, it gives him opportunity to use the humiliation as a spiritual weapon and turn the tables, putting his accusers on trial. This Christian model works when the suffering is borne in the love of Jesus, modeled so beautifully at Calvary.

This also explains the gospel message of martyrdom. Christian martyrdom occurs when the power of the state decides to *take* the life of Jesus' followers in the effort to silence the witness of believers. The martyr actually trumps the civil authority, however, by lovingly *giving* his life. This is done with the goal to witness Christ's love to Jesus' enemies. Christian martyrdom says, "Like my Lord, I love you enough to die showing you His love."

When evil men watch innocent people die with Jesus' love in their hearts for their oppressors, it begins to tear them up in their consciences and brings reevaluation. The result shows Christ's love, revealed fully at the cross, is powerful to transform the hearts of one's tormentors. The change does not always come overnight, but church history demonstrates that it always comes. The story of John Hus (1370–1415), who died singing the gospel while burning at the stake, is but one example among a numberless multitude of witnesses in the pages of salvation history.

Christian suffering was a primary theme of the Apostle Peter's first epistle. "Pure gold put in the fire comes out of it proved pure," Peter wrote. "Genuine faith put through this suffering comes out proved genuine. When Jesus wraps this all up, it's your faith, not your gold, that God will have on display as evidence of his victory" (I Pet. 1:7 MSG).

## 24. How We Overcome Shame.

Peter also wrote:

> This is the kind of life you've been invited into, the kind of life Christ lived. He suffered everything that came his way so you would know that it could be done, and also know how to do it, step-by-step. He never did one thing wrong, not once said anything amiss. They called him every name in the book and he said nothing back. He suffered in silence, content to let God set things right. He used his servant body to carry our sins to the Cross so we could be rid of sin, free to live the right way. His wounds became your healing. You were lost sheep with no idea who you were or where you were going. Now you're named and kept for good by the Shepherd of your souls (I Pet. 2:21-25 MSG).

The difference is huge when Christian martyrdom is compared to terrorists. Christian martyrs freely give their own lives in the name of Jesus with no desire to take the life of anyone else. Suicide bombers take their own lives (suicide) while trying to spread terror by deliberately killing innocent men, women and children, and terrorists try to save their own lives while maiming and killing innocent bystanders, including children.

**Please ask yourself: how strong is the fear of shame in your life? Anxiety about embarrassment has stopped many people cold in their tracks from doing the will of God (Romans 1:16).**
**Have you accepted *your shame* was nailed to the cross with Jesus?**

John 5 has to be one of the most important discourses in the ministry of Jesus. It clearly focuses the issues and lays out the parameters of the struggle that made the cross inevitable. It is all about the choice to believe. Jesus was the rejected Son of God long before the nails were pounded into His hands and feet at Calvary. Golgotha was only the final episode; the climactic culmination of the rejection Jesus lived with every day. In fact, He was the Lamb of God slain from the foundation of the world (Rev. 13:8).

## The Big Surprise

Chapter 5 frames the challenge Jesus faced in this monumental clash of wills. Jesus had the nerve to tell these Pharisees they did not believe what Moses wrote. He did it when their whole system of righteousness was underpinned by their ideas about the Law of Moses. It must have been galling to them to tell them they did not believe Moses, and it certainly helped pave the way to Calvary.

The surprise is not that Jesus won, but the arsenal with which He won—His sole weapon was the love of God. The method of Israel's religious establishment was the sword; they would kill Jesus or anyone else to preserve their system. Jesus battled them not with a sword, but with agape love, while always demonstrating the heart of a servant. In the final scene at the cross, the religious leaders joined the hardened soldiers' mockery of the Lord and added their own merciless derision. It appeared to them their method had worked. Admittedly, Jesus' "agape love model" looked very foolish at Calvary (Luke 18:32; 22:63; 23:11, 36; Matt. 27:39-44).

> **But the third day. Ah! The third day! "God has made him who had no sin to be sin for us, so that in him we might become the righteousness of God" (2 Cor. 5:21).**

John 5 begins with one of the Lord's greatest miracles, healing the man at the Pool of Bethesda in Jerusalem. He had been lame for 38 years. Jesus actually created in an instant fully developed muscles, nerves and blood vessels—everything necessary for the man to stand on the spot and walk with perfect balance. He needed no physical therapy. The miracle demonstrated more than a mere man was walking the streets of Jerusalem—God had come down to earth in Jesus Christ.

Because it happened on the Sabbath, the miracle offered an opportunity that led Jesus to open the windows of heaven to His accusers, letting them gaze into the heart of God. Sadly indeed! Their front-seat view resulted in cold rejection.

So what follows this creative miracle and God-revealing teaching?

Have you ever wished you could have spent just one day with Jesus in His ministry? If "yes," what day would you choose?

The 24 hours recorded in John 6, in which Jesus performed two of His greatest miracles and did more of His profound teaching, would be an excellent choice.

Book Two will begin with the thrilling and mind-boggling miracles of Jesus feeding the 5,000 and then walking on water on the Sea of Galilee—both in a 24-hour timespan.